Introduction to Neuropsychotherapy

This groundbreaking volume provides a theoretical overview and clinical guidelines for the application of neuropsychotherapy. It takes a multidisciplinary approach, combining neuropsychological knowledge with recent conceptualizations from neuroscience and psychotherapy, with special emphasis on the role of working alliance.

The first part of the book focuses on the historical roots of neuropsychotherapy, and a framework of interpersonal processes in neuropsychotherapy and conceptualization for clinical purposes is described. Resistance is examined from a historical perspective of conceptualization through to the present-day demands of understanding this phenomenon in the practice of neuropsychotherapy. In addition, the neuropsychology of emotions is presented through a case intervention. The latter chapters of the book are concerned with special interest interventions and psychotherapeutic working methods suited to neuropsychotherapy.

Representing a wide variety of theoretical, research-oriented, clinical neuropsychological, and psychotherapeutic expertise, this book will interest professionals in neuropsychological rehabilitation and those working with patients with cognitive, emotional, and behavioral disorders in inpatient and outpatient settings.

Ritva Laaksonen is a psychology graduate from the University of Helsinki with a postgraduate degree of Licenciate of Psychology, and a PsL specialization in clinical neuropsychology from the University of Jyväskylä. She is an official supervisor registered by the Finnish Neuropsychological Society. She has served as a clinician, administrator, educator, and researcher in public posts at the Helsinki University Hospital Department of Neurology, and has been the chief psychologist there for 13 years. She is also a state registered psychotherapist trainer.

Mervi Ranta is a psychology graduate from the University of Jyväskylä with a postgraduate degree of Licenciate of Psychology, and a PsL specialization in clinical neuropsychology from the University of Helsinki. She is a state registered psychotherapist, and she has worked as a clinician and a supervisor in a public post at the Seinäjoki Central Hospital Department of Neurology since 1986, where she is presently serving as the chief psychologist.

Introduction to Neuropsychotherapy

Guidelines for Rehabilitation of Neurological and Neuropsychiatric Patients Throughout the Lifespan

Edited by
Ritva Laaksonen and
Mervi Ranta

Psychology Press
Taylor & Francis Group
NEW YORK AND LONDON

First published 2013
by Psychology Press
711 Third Avenue, New York, NY 10017

Simultaneously published in the UK
by Psychology Press
27 Church Road, Hove, East Sussex BN3 2FA

Psychology Press is an imprint of the Taylor & Francis Group, an informa business

Library of Congress Cataloging-in-Publication Data

Introduction to neuropsychotherapy : guidelines for rehabilitation of neurological and neuropsychiatric patients throughout the lifespan / edited by Ritva Laaksonen and Mervi Ranta.
pages. cm
ISBN 978-1-84872-622-2 (hardback) — ISBN 978-1-84872-623-9 (pbk.) — ISBN (invalid) 978-0-203-07587-6 (e-book) 1. Neurobehavioral disorders—Patients—Rehabilitation. 2. Clinical neuropsychology. 3. Psychotherapy. I. Laaksonen, Ritva. II. Ranta, Mervi.
RC350.4.I58 2012
616.8914—dc23

2012032662

ISBN: 978-1-84872-622-2 (hbk)
ISBN: 978-1-84872-623-9 (pbk)
ISBN: 978-0-203-07587-6 (ebk)

Typeset in Minion
by Apex CoVantage, LLC

Contents

Contributors

EDITORS

Ritva Laaksonen
Lic. Psych. specialized clinical neuropsychologist, registered psychotherapist, advanced level trainer and supervisor, director of training programs Vandark Ltd.:The Finnish Neuropsychotherapy Institute/ KL-institute Ltd. Helsinki

Mervi Ranta
Lic.Psych. specialized clinical neuropsychologist, registered psychotherapist, art psychotherapist, chief psychologist, Psychology Service Unit, Seinäjoki Central Hospital

CHAPTER AUTHORS

Sari Haikonen
Lic. Psych. specialized clinical neuropsychologist, private practice, Helsinki

Paula Häkkinen
Lic. Psych. specialized clinical neuropsychologist, Department of Neurology, Helsinki University Hospital

Tarja Ketola
Specialized clinical neuropsychologist, Medical Center Mehiläinen, Turku

Hanna Kiiski-Mäki PhD
Specialized child neuropsychologist, developmental and educational psychologist, psychotherapist CCSF coach, Department of Psychology, Multiprofessional Teaching Clinic, University of Turku

Sanna Koskinen PhD
Specialized clinical neuropsychologist, chief psychologist, Käpylä Rehabilitation Center, Helsinki

Arja Lindell
Lic.Psych. specialized clinical neuropsychologist, registered psychotherapist, Medishare Ltd., Turku

Jukka Loukkola
Lic. Psych. specialized clinical neuropsychologist, Neural Ltd., Oulu

Liisa Paavola
Lic. Psych. specialized clinical neuropsychologist, registered psychotherapist Neural Ltd., Oulu

Nina Sajaniemi PhD
Specialized clinical neuropsychologist, adjunct professor, principal investigator, University of Helsinki, Department of Teacher Education

Jaana Sarajuuri
Lic. Psych. specialized clinical neuropsychologist, director of the INSURE Program, Käpylä Rehabilitation Center, Helsinki

Raija Ylikoski PhD
Specialized clinical neuropsychologist, Department of Neurosciences, Faculty of Medicine, University of Helsinki

Foreword

The role psychologists play in brain injury rehabilitation has greatly expanded over the last 30 to 35 years. Early medically-oriented rehabilitation focused on the basic activities of regaining strength, avoiding complications, feeding, toileting, walking, and talking. Functional independence was the goal, to the degree to which it was possible.

Everyone recognized that cognitive and personality disorders were present after significant brain injury, but their treatment was often not the focus of rehabilitation. Little was known regarding what to do for these problems. The exception to this rule was the work of Kurt Goldstein, who in turn influenced the work of Ben-Yishay and Diller. These clinicians targeted the patient's cognitive and behavioral disorders with the goal of trying to restore, or at least meaningfully compensate for, residual cognitive deficits. Also, teaching patients better ways of behaving in social interactions was clearly an area of focus, with notable successes in some patients. Yet, the patient's personal feelings, their subjective sense of loss, their confusion, and their frustrations were not specifically addressed until the need for psychotherapy for the patient (and the family) began to become formally recognized in the mid-1980s.

It is against this historical background that the importance of this edited book by Ritva Laaksonen and Mervi Ranta should be appreciated. This book emphasizes that psychological services provided to patients with brain disorders, throughout the lifespan, should include efforts at improving cognitive functioning while also attending to the patient's emotional and motivational needs. Reflecting on and integrating the insightful observations of many clinicians from several disciplines is the clear strength of this book. Insights from neurology, neuropsychology, and neuropsychological rehabilitation are interwoven with insights from psychoanalytic theory, attachment theory, cognitive and behavioral therapies, social cognitive models of psychological intervention, brain development, cognitive development, and the biology of temperamental differences in children. Collectively, this book argues, in a convincing manner, that a thorough understanding of how a brain disorder in a given patient directly or indirectly affects their pre-existing cognitive and personality functioning must guide both scientifically driven research and the provision of clinically sensitive services.

The term used by these authors to emphasize the importance of this approach to treatment is *neuropsychotherapy*. Kiiski-Mäki, in her chapter on helping children with brain disorders, makes the point that neuropsychotherapy does not refer to "using exotic methods outside the range of traditional psychotherapies. Rather, it is therapeutic work that combines methods eclectically from other fields of psychotherapy and, at the same time, modifies them according to the ABI child's [or adult's] special needs" who has suffered brain injury. Thus, the neuropsychotherapist is acutely aware of how various neuropsychological disturbances have to be kept in mind when planning psychotherapeutic interventions and when conducting those interventions.

This book will help those clinicians who attempt psychotherapy and cognitive rehabilitation with brain dysfunctional patients throughout the lifespan. It is an important addition to our understanding of how to deal with the various problems that clinicians face when doing this work.

It is refreshing to see competent clinical neuropsychologists in Finland embrace the importance of psychotherapy in their work as clinical neuropsychologists. This book adds to the long tradition of meaningful clinical contributions that have been the hallmark of the work of neuropsychologists and neuropsychiatrists from Finland over many years.

George P. Prigatano, PhD
Barrow Neurological Institute
Phoenix, Arizona

Introduction

This book was brought about by the collaboration of a group of specialized neuropsychologists sharing common interests in neuropsychological rehabilitation from a holistic perspective in brain–mind relations. We wanted to write this book in order to share our interests and expertise with colleagues and other professionals working with neurological and neuropsychiatric patients in rehabilitation settings.

Neuropsychological rehabilitation has a long tradition in Finland, starting in the 1920s to 1940s, mainly for war veterans, and the later 1960s for civilian patient groups at university hospitals. In our professional work, the frame of reference has included personality and emotional, as well as social, contexts with the goal to treat "real people in the real world," as expressed in the writings of respected pioneers, such as Dr. Leonard Diller and A.R. Luria. Dr. George Prigatano had also expanded our awareness to the needs of ABI and TBI-patients' treatment procedures, together with professor Anne-Lise Christensen's crystallized views. However, there seems to have been a misunderstanding in treatment settings for decades, with explicit concentration mostly on cognitive exercises. Some neuropsychologists have achieved holistic training for neuropsychological treatment, while others have mainly focused on treating cognition in post-illness situations.

Our main goal is to emphasize the importance of seeing and understanding the person suffering from the sequelae of illness as a whole human being, not just the neuropsychological disturbances. Recent research in the fields of neuroscience has given us a firm basis together with the "Zeit Geist" for a more integrative approach.

Our project had its impulse in a postgraduate training program in neuropsychotherapy. It had been in the air for a long period of time. However, when Dr. Barbara Uzzel came to me at the INS meeting in

Baltimore, Maryland, and asked, "Ritva, do you have any books you're working on?" that was it: Why not a book on neuropsychotherapy? We had many experienced experts in the first 3-year neuropsychotherapy training program, all trying to integrate neuropsychological rehabilitation in a multidisciplinary fashion. The idea was there. We decided to go to Tuscany, Italy, to a retreat in 2007, in order to have peace and inspiration in our collaboration of the book project. That worked out fine. We all got to know each other better, and our individual special interests were well suited to make this book of guidelines and theoretical background for clinicians interested in a more holistic and therapeutic approach in treating different neurological and neuropsychiatric groups. Three years of collaboration in a creative spirit brought this book into life.

Ritva Laaksonen and Mervi Ranta
La Poggiarella, Tuscany,
September 24, 2009

1

Neuropsychotherapeutic Approaches in the Rehabilitation Context

Ritva Laaksonen and Mervi Ranta

Introduction

Neuropsychotherapy is a form of treatment based on recent advances in the domains of neuroscience, neuropsychological rehabilitation, and models of psychotherapy. It can be considered an alliance between scientific, theoretical and clinical knowledge in these areas (Laaksonen, 2007).

The term *neuropsychotherapy* has been used in different conceptualizations. In the context of this book, we follow the contextualization indicating that neuropsychotherapy is a name for interventions, which we need for people who suffer from emotional, behavioral, or personality disorders after neurological dysfunction or syndromes. Remediation of cognitive disturbances will also be included in the treatment process. The term *neuropsychotherapy* has also been used when neuroscientific knowledge has been integrated into psychotherapy (Grawe, 2007), or neuropsychoanalysis (Kaplan-Solms & Solms, 2000).

The concept and procedures are multidisciplinary in nature. The patient groups concerned vary within different types of central nervous system (CNS) involvement. The metatheory for guideline information in the therapeutic remediation procedure needs to be multifarious and must cover several domains of knowledge to serve as a guideline for rehabilitation in practical and ecologically valid settings.

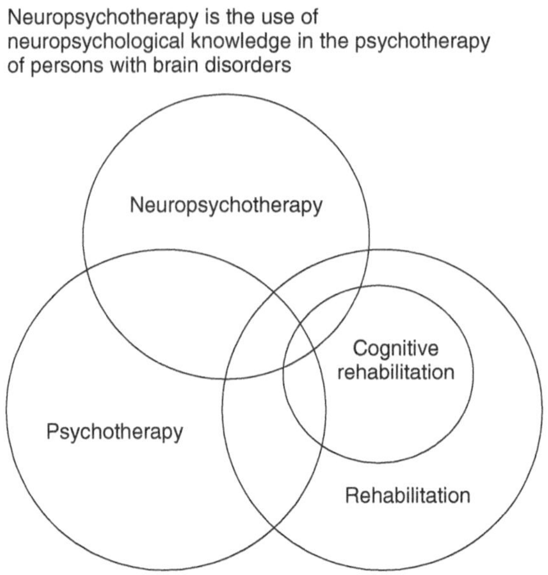

Figure 1.1 What Is Neuropsychotherapy?

Even though psychotherapy is now, according to Coetzer (2007), an approach used within several models of neurorehabilitation, a core theoretical model to guide psychotherapeutic practice is lacking. The aim of this chapter is to open a scope of applicable conceptualizations for further developments in the field of comprehensive, integrated rehabilitation procedures. Judd (1999) has conceptualized the overlap of various forms of rehabilitation of people with brain injuries. His illustration is seen in Figure 1.1.

The overlapping use of knowledge from different cases of people with brain injuries has proved necessary if suitable and efficient treatment procedures are to be designed.

Neuropsychological Rehabilitation and Psychotherapy: Historical Perspectives

Fractured minds (Ogden, 2005), shattered worlds, and grief reactions are not unfamiliar to clinical psychologists, nor to neuropsychologists. Historically, however, psychotherapy has not been considered useful in the rehabilitation of brain-dysfunctional patients

(Prigatano, 1991). It has been viewed as having little application in a brain-injured population in the past (Coetzer, 2007), despite the phenomenological necessity.

It should be kept in mind that this doesn't mean that the clinical professionals working in the field would have neglected the injured person's emotions or personality as a whole. What it means is that the writings and explicit ways of describing the interventions have often focused on remediation of cognitive functions. In the tacit level, the importance of social adjustment, individuality, and interpersonal problems have been acknowledged and worked at in real life situations by experienced professionals. There are published examples of this line of thinking, for instance, in treating cerebrovascular patients, as early as the 1970s. A historical example of treating post-stroke depression with psychological management is given by Horenstein (1970). His suggestion is a stepwise psychological approach involving structured teamwork and family participation rather than medication. Horenstein points out that depression of mood frequently accompanies isolated and multifocal cerebral vascular lesions as grief which resembles that observed after other major illness. He associates the occurrence and severity of depression also with the person's previous ability for adaptation and other premorbid factors (i.e., personality, self-esteem, intelligence, and experience). The life situation and family support are likewise important in psychosocial recovery. Since family members will also have to go through a process of grief and adaptation, it is important to include them in the comprehensive treatment procedure. Neuropsychological recognition of the deficit and appreciation of its significance in the altered state and life situation are present in depressive reactions of the patient. Knowledge of the patient's premorbid ways of reacting to illness, injury, or bereavement, as well as personality traits, may help in predicting the type and length of depression and adjustment to changes after illness. As one example of slow adjustment, Horenstein mentions premorbid obsessive–compulsive traits, which make the person apt to hostility and blaming others for his anger and disappointment in recovery (Horenstein, 1970).

In Finnish neuropsychology, the pioneer Niilo Mäki (1902–1968) treated war veterans using a holistic orientation. He was well acquainted with the work of Ahhemar Gelb and Kurt Goldstein (Laaksonen, 1987). For Niilo Maki, the whole person was important. This outlook sets more holistic goals for neuropsychologists and improves the methods of treatment interventions. Niilo Mäki's work did not have a direct continuation in civilian hospitals in Finland, but the spirit did continue (Laaksonen, 1987).

In Finnish civilian hospitals, neuropsychological rehabilitation had its roots in the late 1960s. Originally, the focus was in cognitive remediation based on the works and writings of A.R. Luria (Laaksonen, 1987). Later, quality of life was explicitly added to the goals of neuropsychological rehabilitation (Laaksonen, 1994). The core idea of Luria's tradition was that theory and methods of treatment should be continually tested. The theoretical framework included the dynamic, systemic theory of higher cortical functions in relation to localized lesions, which caused specific disturbances with different mechanisms responsible for the neuropsychological sequelae after injury. Restoration of function was to be built on careful analysis of the syndromes and constellation of disturbed functions, with distinction of primary and secondary mechanisms responsible for the disturbance. Thus, the methods of reeducation, or restoration of function, could become specific training programs aimed at reorganization of function. In some disturbed functions, direct rehearsal could also be used (Luria, 1963, 1970, 1973). Luria's theory was the source of inspiration for Finnish neuropsychologists, and continues to be so, as advances in the field build upon it.

Anne-Lise Christensen's work in Denmark has served as a model in the Luria tradition and the holistic approach, and her influence is still strong, as well. In recent writing, she points out that in qualifying the inner structure of psychological processes the method gives insight into the syndromes of difficulties of the patient. This further provides possibilities for the neuropsychologist to initiate feedback process that can be closely linked to the planning of the most effective rehabilitation of the patient's cognitive, social and behavioral way of functioning and thus create strong and valuable connection between diagnosis and treatment experiences (Christensen, 2009). Christiansen's work can function as an important guideline for psychoeducation of treatment methodology, together with updated knowledge about neuroplasticity and functioning of neural networks. The psychotherapeutic aspect must also be interwoven into a comprehensive treatment procedure. This has previously been understood by professionals in the field as a need for double training (i.e., requiring postgraduate studies in both neuropsychology and psychotherapy).

This holistic interest was also reflected in the need for studies on quality of life as early as the 1980s, even though the increased interest and the majority of studies emerged later. One of the early studies on quality of life after vascular brain injury was published by Niemi, Laaksonen, Kotila, & Waltimo (1988). The most important finding indicated that subjective tendency to get depressed was the most important variable that correlated with the deteriorated quality of life four years post-stroke. Another follow-up study with TBI-patients (Koskinen, 1998) indicated that neurobehavioral and emotional disturbances had the most significant effect on strain felt by relatives and on the quality of life of the injured 10 years post-injury. In a multicentered European study, a questionnaire (EBIQ) was created to better understand the subjective experience of cognitive, emotional, and social difficulties of brain-injured patients and their close relatives (Teasdale et al., 1997).

Depression after stroke has been of interest for many years, as we discussed earlier. The prevalence of post-stroke depression and depression of the caregivers has been studied more recently by Berg and collaborators (2001, 2003, and 2005), whose studies indicate the need for therapeutic attention. According to Berg and collaborators, about 50% of stroke patients suffer from depressive symptoms two months after the onset of stroke. The authors point out that depression has a negative effect for prognosis of recovery and quality of life. At the postacute stage, men seem to suffer from depression more often than do women. Spouses also showed marked signs of depression.

Despite individual pioneering articles and literature indicating the need for a more comprehensive approach, the research on cognitive neurorehabilitation, or reeducation to overcome the hampering neuropsychological deficits, continued to be overemphasized. This eventually led to a misunderstanding of the importance of only treating cognitive deficits with cognitive exercises.

Experiences in the practice of neuropsychological rehabilitation during the past three decades have finally allowed for the questioning of the emphasis on purely cognitive retraining in treating people with brain injuries. A welcomed critique for purely cognitive treatment has come from Sohlberg, and Mateer (2001), who state about neuropsychological rehabilitation: "The term cognitive rehabilitation was perhaps always too narrow, and focused too heavily on remediating, or compensation for decreased cognitive abilities. . . . The last 25 years have allowed a richer appreciation for the influence of contextual variables; the personal, emotional, and social impacts of brain injury; and their interactions with cognitive function. All of these factors have been incorporated to an even greater degree into treatment plans and goals" (Sohlberg and Mateer, 2001, p. 1).

Integration of Psychotherapy in the Treatment Models of TBI and ABI Patients

At the turn of the century, we have finally arrived at explicit efforts to integrate psychotherapeutic models and methods with neuropsychological rehabilitation. The term *neuropsychotherapy* has also emerged, with different conceptual connotations. The reference list directly under this term is still very short. However, the list of articles including cognitive–behavioral, or other theoretical models of psychotherapy needed in treating the brain-injured population, is much longer. In her pioneering work beginning in the 1980s, Barbara A. Wilson used the behavior therapy approach together with neuropsychological knowledge in treating brain-dysfunctional patients (Wilson & Moffat, 1984; Wilson, 1999; Wilson, Herbert, & Shiel, 2003).

One of the landmark studies penetrating the subtleties of the interpersonal process with brain-injury survivors was published by Judd and Wilson (2005). They identified the combination of educational and cognitive strategies that was most effective in addressing the challenges encountered in working with the distress of patients. The aim of therapy in their study was to help a troubled individual reduce his or her distress and enjoy greater life satisfaction through changing the patient's thoughts, feelings, and behavior. They made the argument that psychotherapy is a relational process, regardless of theoretical orientation, in which both the therapist and the client co-constitute and actively participate in the therapeutic encounter. They emphasized the quality of the therapeutic relationship as a key factor. The therapeutic alliance is the core element in this interpersonal process. In clinical practice, we can see the complex interplay between psychological and organic damage. The sequelae after brain injury can be most varying and subtle. It is of utmost importance for the therapist to understand the nature and severity of the brain damage, as well as the meaning the survivor gives to the personal experiences, postinjury identity, and the psychosocial consequences. For a successful outcome, we need to see the person as a unique human being, with deficits and strengths that challenge the therapist to engage in a mutual and sometimes lengthy arduous process of treatment collaboration. The therapeutic alliance has been a theme in a few outcome studies in neurological population. Schönberger and collaborators found correlations with the efficacy of neuropsychological rehabilitation outcomes and the therapeutic alliance, together with patient compliance with psychosocial measures like going back to work and also cognitive functioning in postacute brain injury rehabilitation (Schönberger, Humle, & Teasdale, 2006, and 2007). Scherer et al. (2007) report results of the impact of alliance on outcome in postacute brain-injury rehabilitation. According to their findings, family perception and family functioning are important determinants of therapeutic alliance for patients in PABIR (postacute brain-injury rehabilitation) programs, influencing the bonding with the program and, thus, the rehabilitation work.

The Influence of Holistic Rehabilitation Programs

Neuropsychotherapeutic aspects have also been included in the holistic rehabilitation programs for head trauma and also other patient groups in the form of psychotherapeutic sessions, even though this term has not always been used to describe those instances. These programs have influenced the concern on emotional adjustment and emotional reintegration. The development of more comprehensive neuropsychological treatment needs and procedures have also benefitted from research done on long-term outcomes of brain injury in the field of neuropsychiatry, which indicates the importance of emotional, behavioral, and psychiatric problems years after injury (Lishman, 1978). A wide variety of long-term sequelae after CNS-involvement has also been described by Cummings and Mega (2003).

The creation of holistic rehabilitation programs has also had an effect on individual treatment programs for various neurological diseases and neuropsychiatric syndromes. The Head Trauma Program of Ben-Yishay, Rattock, and Lakin (1985) and other pioneering and influential publications of holistic treatment procedures (Prigatano, Fordyce, & Zeiner, 1984; Prigatano, 1999) have served as models for many neuropsychological treatment practices. Anne-Lise

Christensen has been an arduous advocate for holistic approach in Europe, combining the Luria approach with holistic views (Christensen, Pinner, & Rosenberg, 1988). She has also suggested the importance of forming of therapeutic alliance and of emotional and social readjustment in the course of rehabilitation (Christensen & Uzzel, 1994; Christensen, 2009). These various articles have strongly inspired professionals in the field, even though the intensity of these model programs has not been possible to realize. In Finland, Sanna Koskinen, Jaana Sarajuuri, and Marja-Liisa Kaipio (Kaipio, Sarajuuri, & Koskinen, 2000) have been able to create the INSURE program according to the models of the holistic approach (see Chapter 11).

Despite the explicit emphasis on the Luria approach, quality of life has been included in the goals of Finnish neuropsychologists in most cognitive treatment endeavors in clinical settings (Laaksonen, 1994).

Neuropsychotherapy: What It Is and Can Be

The term *neuropsychotherapy* is still strange even to professionals working in neuropsychological rehabilitation. As mentioned earlier, the name has been used in two ways: (a) using neuroscience knowledge in psychotherapy, or psychoanalysis Grawe, 2007; Kaplan-Solms & Solms, 2000; and (b) using psychotherapeutic knowledge of different models and methods in treating neurological or neuropsychiatric patients with a psychotherapeutic approach, together with cognitive training exercises (Judd, 1999). The latter conceptual framework has been adopted by the authors into the neuropsychotherapeutic framework of this book. In Klaus Grawe's (2007) framework, neuropsychotherapy emphasizes the neuroscientific foundations of psychotherapy. He has proposed that psychotherapists ought to possess knowledge of the neural foundations of mental disorders. He sees neural plasticity as good news for psychotherapy: intensive utilization or stimulation and deactivation of certain areas of the brain can lead to structural changes in the brain, and neuropsychotherapy aims to change the brain by focusing on the life experiences that the brain is specialized to process and that are meaningful with regard to the needs embedded within the brain structures of each human being. In neuropsychoanalysis (Kaplan-Solms & Solms, 2000), the correlation of localized brain lesions with the results of extensive psychoanalytic exploration is studied to discern changes in deep psychology, and the neurological organization of mental functions may be determined. It is a combination of two existing methods, from Freud and Luria, proposing a general model of how the human mental apparatus might be presented in the tissues of the brain.

Our definition and outline for treatment is in accordance with the definition of Judd (1999), indicating the need of treatment also for emotional, behavioral, and personality problems of brain-injured people. Remediation of cognitive disorders is also an essential part of neuropsychotherapy. According to Judd, "neuropsychotherapy is needed when 1) the person with brain illness has significant behavioral or emotional problems resulting from illness, 2) the problems cannot be managed or improved adequately or efficiently in and by the person's setting, and 3) intervention is likely to reduce those problems" (1999, p. 9). Neuropsychotherapy is an integration of neuropsychological rehabilitation and psychotherapy, and the patient groups can come from any etiology.

Metatheory as a Guideline for Clinical Work

Theoretical framework most likely cannot be following just one theory. Diller and Gordon (1981) called for a metatheory for neuropsychological rehabilitation. This was an inspiring "invitation" to structure the neuropsychological treatment procedures in a more tailored fashion. There was an explicit suggestion for more ecological ways of working with brain-injured populations and more attention to emotional problems and their management. In addition, relevant rehabilitation programs would be needed for different etiological groups. This metatheory of rehabilitation would have theoretical basis on information of various sources: a) neurologic information, b) other medical information, c) psychometric and neuropsychological information to specify impairments, d) functional competency, e) use of time, and f) environment of the patient. Today we need some revisions on the metatheoretical aspects of rehabilitation, and this is one of the aims of this book. Coetzer (2007) has joined the ideas for the needs of theoretical foundations in psychotherapeutic work with people suffering from brain injury, mainly TBI. However, the same ideas apply to various etiological groups suffering from deficits due to CNS-disorders both in children and adults.

A wide metatheory is needed for carrying out the process-oriented neuropsychotherapy. It should include the following domains of knowledge:

1. Theory of systemic structure of brain function and the mind during the life span
2. Neuroscience correlates with clinical phenomena in different etiological groups
3. The process of crisis or grief, the emotional meanings of insult, and posttraumatic stress-reactions
4. The influences of personality predispositions and the basis for healthy attachment in the course of development
5. The interpersonal process, its ruptures, and building a good working alliance
6. The nature of neuropsychological deficits and knowledge of specific methods of cognitive retraining
7. The psychotherapeutic theory, models, and methods usable for brain-dysfunctional people
8. Understanding the environmental and family affairs and their meaning for treatment.

Theory of Systemic Structure of Brain Function and Mind

The spectacular progress of neuroscience in the 20th and 21st centuries has given us increased understanding in the brain–mind problem. However, with increasing knowledge we must stick to certain landmarks, or theoretical conceptualizations, so as not to fall into a fragmented way of thinking or working in rehabilitation. Aleksander Luria's dynamic, systemic theory of the working brain, updated with modern research findings, can give us concrete guidelines for methods and procedures in clinical practice. Luria's basic idea was that the brain works as a whole, as opposed to strict localization views. Higher mental functions are complex working constellations based on localized neural activity, even in distant areas of the brain simultaneously, each area regulating a basic mechanism or element for the function to develop and to be reorganized after injury (Luria, 1963, 1973).

For the most part, Luria's theory based on lesion data has been validated by neuroimaging studies of brain behavior relationships (Goldberg & Bougakov, 2009). Prigatano (2009) also reports on the idea of neuroimaging studies, supporting Luria's theory. The theory of functional units and neural circuits needs further qualification, however, as to the aspects of mental functioning involved in complex activity. Also hemispheric lateralization and frontal posterior structural networks can be seen in a more dynamic viewpoint and connected with novelty/familiarity, as opposed to material specialty (Goldberg & Bougakov, 2009). However, Luria's basic conceptualizations give a pragmatic framework for building up cognitive rehabilitation procedures.

In updating Luria's theory, Fuster's (2003) theoretical framework can give an extension, stating that cognitive functions do not have discrete cortical representations. Rather, cognitive functions are regulated by widely distributed and connected neural networks. The same neuronal structures can be part of various cognitive processes.

Fuster introduces the term *cognit*, which he proposes as a generic term for any representation or knowledge in the cerebral cortex. A single cognit is defined according to what parts of representations it includes and in which neural network connections it is involved. A single cognit may be part of several different cognitive processes. For example, attention and executive functions are based on several jointly working networks. They are also involved in many other mental processes (Fuster, 2003). This dynamic way of understanding the brain–mind relationship, even somewhat abstract, can be seen as fruitful knowledge for rehabilitation of cognition, emotional well-being, and behavioral alternations in terms of neuroplasticity and reorganization of disrupted neuronal connections and networks (Ergenzinger & Pons, 2000).

During the past 20 years, neuropsychology of emotion has also been described and studied in a fashion that can help clinical understanding of what happens in patients' mental processing when dealing with emotional experiences (Borod, 2000; Cummings and Mega, 2003; Damasio, 1999; Le Doux, 1999). The bonds between emotion, awareness, and patterns of behavior are also crucial in understanding and dealing with changed personality after injury. Knowledge of the amygdaloid complex and its connections with frontal hippocampal and other structures of emotion regulation and memory can give us a clue to the role of emotions in neuropsychotherapy.

Neuroscience Correlates with Clinical Phenomena in Different Etiological Groups

Knowledge of the specific consequences of different CNS disorders is necessary in differentiating between factors due to direct regulations of the brain and factors involved with primary personality and psychosocial phenomena.

The sequelae after TBI and cerebrovascular insults, for instance, do have different effects on the trainee's or patient's cognitive–emotional and behavioral properties.

Neuropsychiatric diagnosis must also be qualified as to the basic problems hidden behind the multiple, overt psychiatric symptoms (i.e., in ADHD, Asperger, and other syndromes with CNS-dysfunctions and deficiencies in mental processing).

Specific Features of Different Etiologies of Neurological Patients

- Degenerative diseases challenge accurate diagnosis and care; they are puzzling in their phenomenological forms of appearance and progressive nature of illness.
- Cerebrovascular diseases involve the most specific neuropsychological deficits handicapping everyday functioning and quality of life. Dysfunctions due to specific localizations can be qualified in more detail, and various cognitive training procedures are available in ABI. Aphasia, agnosia, and apraxias, together with milder forms of perceptual and motor disturbances, executive difficulties, and disturbances of different types of awareness, are familiar to most practitioners in neuropsychology. Cognitive training together with treatment of mood problems has been studied, but should be recognized more widely.
- In TBI-manifold, cognitive, emotional, behavioral, and somatic sequelae are to be seen and differentiated from PTSD symptoms and the "nihilism" and invalidation of the CNS injury per se. Specific disorders, as well as more diffuse symptoms, are often present. Fatigue frequently prevents the use of preserved capacity and causes additional stress unless understood and managed in daily employment. TBI patients have received increasing attention during the past decades, and proper rehabilitation programs have been developed to serve as model guidelines for treatment.
- In neuropsychiatric syndromes like Asperger, ADHD, Tourette, and other developmental disorders, diagnostics vary and are often associated with comorbidity (i.e., OCD, OCPD, schizophrenia, bipolar disorder, etc.). Treatment procedures cover both psychiatric and neuropsychological methods. Coaches to enable everyday functioning are often useful in addition to other kinds of rehabilitation.

For the clinician, initial assessment is very important. Specific disease entities require different approaches, as for cognitive training methods and/or psychotherapeutic techniques. However, as described previously in this chapter, emotional experiences with good working alliance should always be targeted as a general element in the treatment procedure. The basic knowledge of neuroscience research concerning the different diseases is abundant and can be a challenge to a neuropsychologist working with different types of etiologies. Localization aspects may have a unifying value despite the mechanism producing the disorder. What we know about frontal lesions is that orbitofrontal, dorsolateral frontal, or medial lesions will help us analyze the sequelae of TBI, ABI, or ADHD for treatment purposes, and, for instance, give us a possible way to distinguish between lack of motivation and engagement in depressive behavior, as would be the case in medial frontal SAH, or other localized lesions in that area.

Borod (2000) has described emotional changes in different disease entities as well as the domains of emotional experiences varying from perceptual sensations to emotional reactions. It is possible to differentiate between emotions themselves and the domain or element of a particular emotion, which is lacking. In clinical practice, there are patients who have "lost the ability to feel" or "experience" a certain emotion, even though the perceptions are accurate and the reaction, such as crying, may seem to indicate emotional processing.

The Process of Crisis or Grief, the Emotional Meaning of Insult, and Posttraumatic Stress-Reactions

In understanding the emotional reaction to sudden-onset extreme life events, such as acquired brain injury, posttraumatic stress disorder (PTSD) may be helpful for understanding the various aspects of patients' problems (Yeates, Gracey, & McGrath, 2008). A traumatic event is a threat to one's self as well as to one's relations to the environment.

It is realistic to say that complicating factors in the process of rehabilitation are:

- Trauma (PTSD) with various symptoms
- Stress of illness/difficulties and conflicts in personal life and family

- The grief process from initial shock through resistance and bewilderment to adaption.

PTSD was included in the third edition of the *Diagnostic and Statistical Manual of Mental Disorders* (*DSM-III*) in 1980 (American Psychiatric Association, 1980). According to Vasterling and Verfaellie (2009), PTSD is typically conceptualized as a fear-based disorder that develops following exposure to a life-threatening event, and the diagnostic symptoms of PTSD cluster into groupings that relate to reexperience of the trauma, behavioral and cognitive avoidance of reminders of the trauma, emotional symptoms, and heightened arousal. Also viewed from a neurocognitive perspective, memory and attention abnormalities belong to the clinical presentation of PTSD.

The possibility of developing PTSD after mild traumatic brain injury has been discussed. Bryant et al. (2009) studied the interplay between mild traumatic brain injury and PTSD and found the prevalence and the nature of PTSD following mild traumatic brain injury controversial because of the paradox of suffering from PTSD with impaired memory for the traumatic event. They found that patients with mild traumatic brain injury were more likely to develop PTSD than were patients with longer posttraumatic amnesia. This was associated with less severe intrusive memories at the acute assessment, indicating that PTSD may be more likely following mild traumatic brain injury, but longer posttraumatic amnesia seems to be protective against selected reexperiencing symptoms, because fear conditioning of events involving the trauma would be limited by the reduced encoding of the experience.

A cognitive model of PTSD has been developed by Ehlers and Clark (2000), integrating cognitive, behavioral, and neuroscientific knowledge about trauma. Psychological threat to self underpins the traumatic response and subsequent development and maintenance of PTSD symptoms. Coping responses, such as avoidance, worry, and rumination, are ways in which patients aim to reduce this threat. Threat is suggested to impact processes that allow integration of trauma-related representations into prior, enduring representations of self, others, and the world. In uncovering underlying traumatic meanings, personal values and expectations need to be considered. The integrations of traumatic experiences into the sufferer's prior affective and cognitive belief systems can be considered a key to adaptation.

The Influences of Personality Predispositions and the Basis for Healthy Attachment in the Course of Development

In real life therapy situations, the therapist will face an immense amount of patients with different life histories and personality types. Personality can be described in many ways. There is no single guideline as to how we should define people, as far as the concept of personality is concerned. Cognitive theory considers personality to be grounded in the coordinated operation of complex systems that have been selected or adapted to insure biological survival (Alford & Beck, 1997). Further cognitive definition of personality includes individual schematic processes, which theoretically determine the operation of major systems of psychological analyses (e.g., motivation, cognition, emotion, etc.). The cognitive perspective would emphasize characteristic patterns of a person's development, differentiation, and adaptation to social and biological environments (Alford & Beck, 1997). These patterns can be further conceptualized as specialized schema systems. The schema model has been refined by several authors. Young, Klasko, and Weishaar (2003) have built up a schema model, and Greenberg & Paivio (1997) have created a conceptual model from a constructivist cognitive framework.

Schemas have also been called *core beliefs*, which guide our cognitive, emotional, and behavioral perceptions of the world and reactions to situations from moment to moment. Cognitive or emotional schema patterns regulate well-being. Negative beliefs and biased views of the world make us vulnerable to depression (Clark, Beck, & Alford, 1999), and over- or underdeveloped belief systems may distinguish between anxiety and depressive symptoms. Cognitive distortions like catastrophizing, personalization, magnification and minimization, selective abstraction, arbitrary inference, and overgeneralization are typically seen in psychiatric states of overload of emotional reactions (Freeman, Pretzer, Fleming, & Simon, 1990). If a patient is inclined to think of himself in a distorted way in case of difficulties (i.e., "I am the worst failure in the world," or "Only bad things can happen to me"), this may create persistent resistance and noncompliance in rehabilitation. Personality disorders as classified in *DSM-III* and *DSM-IV* may form an obstacle in rehabilitation; particularly borderline, paranoid, narcissistic, and obsessive–compulsive types of personality disorders need special attention. Personality disorders have been considered long-standing inflexible patterns of perceiving, interpreting, and responding to one's environment and to oneself in a wide range of situations (Freeman et al., 1990).

How the autobiographical history can explain and give background to this kind of development may also be viewed by attachment models. According to Allen (2001), attachment is the foundation for distress regulation in clinical practice. Our task is one of pattern recognition and identifying recurring themes in interactions. The process of attachment is the basis for emotional development from the first months of life through the growing years. It may be reshaped in adulthood, if the environment is of corrective nature.

The attachment types and their influence in adulthood can be classified as follows:

1. Secure attachment
   - easy to engage, comfortable with intimacy and autonomy
2. Avoidant attachment
   - avoiding, matter-of-fact, polite, good performing/achieving behavior
3. Resistant attachment
   - protest and denial are easily provoked
4. Disorganized attachment
   - approach–avoidance pattern ("the safe heaven is alarming")

These themes recurring in adulthood can help the therapist's understanding and patience in building up the working relationship.

The Interpersonal Process, Its Ruptures, and Building a Good Working Alliance

Neuropsychological rehabilitation, or cognitive rehabilitation, as it has been also called, has traditionally placed less importance on the therapeutic relationship, until increasing interest in the past years. The same trend seems to apply to cognitive behavioral therapies (Safran & Muran, 2000). The present interest is due to the psychotherapeutic research community's consistent findings that the quality of therapeutic alliance is the most consistent predictor of treatment success. Poor outcome shows a negative interpersonal process independent of the therapeutic modality. The patient and the therapist

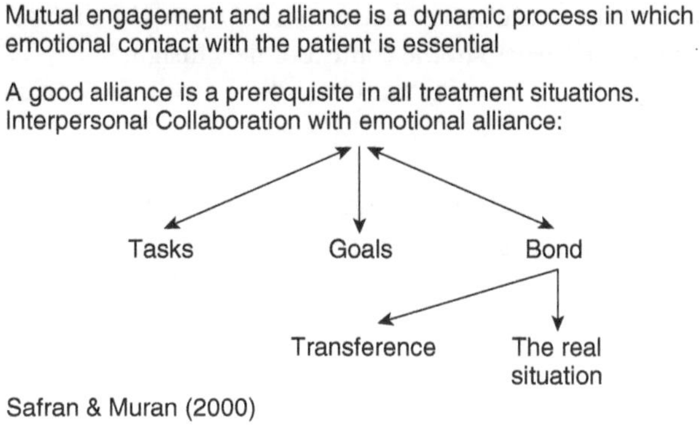

Figure 1.2 Therapeutic Alliance

are always participating in a relational configuration in psychotherapy. The same idea is true in the encounter with neuropsychological patients. Safran and Muran (2000) find relational theory to be particularly useful for organization of insights and principles from other therapeutic traditions that are relevant to the topic of therapeutic impasses and resistance (Leahy, 2001). In this book, resistance is a separate chapter, and the interpersonal process is discussed in more detail in the chapter on therapeutic methods. The concept of the working alliance, however, is to be defined in this context (see Figure 1.2).

The strength of alliance is dependent on the degree of agreement between patient and therapist about the tasks and goals of therapy and the quality of the relational bond between them. The tasks aim at cognitive, emotional, and behavioral change. Interpersonal and relational perspectives provide more scope for more technical flexibility. Trust, hope, and faith in the therapist's ability play a central role in the change process (Safran & Muran, 2000). The patient should feel respected by the therapist. When faced with resistance or noncompliance, the therapist should ally with it, not attempt to invalidate or undermine it. Ruptures are dealt more detailed in Chapters 6 and 12.

The elements of the interpersonal process in neuropsychotherapy can be summarized in the guidelines for the therapist to keep in mind:

- Emotional bond in the therapeutic alliance
- Warmth and empathy
- Sensitivity in the course of working alliance
- Validation of the trainee's ideas, emotions, and behavior; good working

collaboration, not in contradiction with the goals of change
- Support of self-worth in the context of new insight
- Identification of ruptures and resistance with understanding and flexibility.

The relational process is always a dynamic moment-to-moment procedure, no matter how structured the therapist aims to be.

According to Safran and Segal (1990), the theory process can be thought of as a series of events unfolding over time at three levels:

1. Fluctuations in the moment-to-moment state of the patient's phenomenological world.
2. Fluctuations in the moment-to-moment state of the therapeutic relationship.
3. Fluctuations in the therapist's inner experience.

This understanding gives freedom to the therapist for a relaxed and flexible collaboration with the patient.

The Nature of Neuropsychological Deficits and Knowledge of Specific Methods of Cognitive Retraining

Neuropsychotherapy should include cognitive training when it is a necessary goal. Neuropsychological disturbances are most likely best known to clinical neuropsychologists. Johnstone and Stonnington (2001) point out that, although significant strides have been made in the development of tests to assess brain function, there is still need to develop effective treatment interventions to improve specific neuropsychological impairments, and ultimately the lives of persons with brain dysfunction. Cognitive treatment methods have been a challenge even for dementia patients (Farina, Mantovani, & Fioranti, 2006). There is no disagreement that the brain regulates our mind: cognition and emotion, as well as behavior. However, to understand the functional connections, comprehensive and coherent conceptualization of the brain-based abilities and traits is needed, because those functional connections are constantly affected by both environmental and psychological factors from childhood throughout the lifespan. In Figure 1.3, the hierarchy of mental functioning aims to illustrate how impairments are interdependent. This figure has been inspired by a model described by Stuss and Benson (1986).

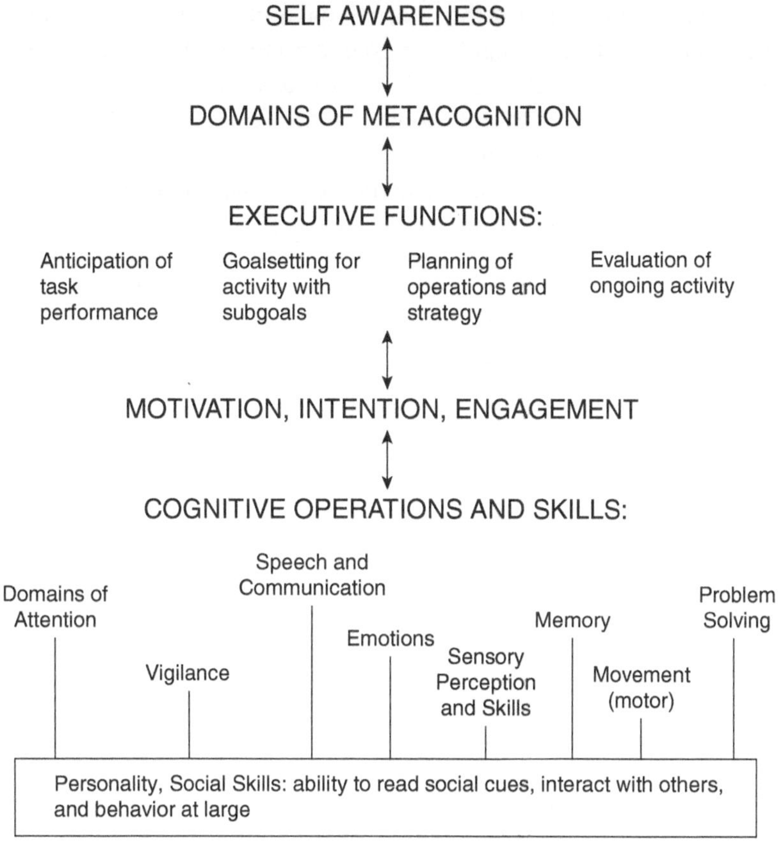

Figure 1.3 The Hierarchy of Cognitive Processing

The importance of disturbances of awareness represents a need for special attention (Fleming, Strong, & Ashton, 1996). All of these domains are structured from different elements, the study of which will give basis for cognitive reorganization of function and new learning (Powell, 1981). Cognitive exercises can be based on evidence-based methods (Cicerone et al., 2000). Another approach, such as the dynamic systemic theory approach (i.e., step-wise programs) can be used to treat a specific disorder. According to Luria's (1973) and Fuster's (2003) theories, certain elements, or mechanisms of disturbance, can affect the functional capacity in several areas. Luria's basic idea from the 1960s was syndrome analysis and reorganization of function by stepwise programs, after analyzing the mechanisms of the disturbance and understanding the preserved elements.

Luria (1973) separated three functional units: prefrontal/dorsolateral and orbitofrontal regulating goal, directed and executive functions; medial frontal/subcortical, responsible for cortical tone and vigilance; and posterior hemispheric areas, regulating most specific functional disturbances together with the other parts of the brain. The goal-directed behavior and active strategy approach of the frontal areas subserve many other functions. If the frontal type difficulties are not treated first, there is not much use of other training methods, for instance, in memory disturbances. According to Luria (1976), memory should be examined in great detail, because of its multidimensional nature.

The Psychotherapeutic Theory, Models, and Methods Useable for Brain-Dysfunctional People

Cognitive psychotherapy and the cognitive behavioral approach have frequently been used as a frame of reference in therapeutic procedures for neurological as well as neuropsychiatric patients. However, traditional forms of psychoanalytic therapies have also served their purpose in neuropsychology. Cognitive therapy approach and models in neuropsychological treatment of ABI and TBI patients are referred to in a recent publication of *The Self and Identity in Rehabilitation* by Gracey and Onsworth (2008/2009). Barbara Wilson has been an advocate of the cognitive–behavioral approach for several years (Wilson et al., 2003). Studies on psychoanalytic analysis after brain injury have been published, for instance, by Kaplan-Solms and Solms (2000). A study on the cognitive–behavioral working model with Asperger-syndrome has been published by Gaus (2007). Studies on group treatment of ADHD persons have been published by Virta and collaborators. In this study, self-reported symptoms of ADHD became less severe after a short-term cognitive–behavioral group intervention (Virta et al., 2008).

The integration of neuropsychology with psychotherapy in practical treatment situations has been needed for several years. The individual chapters in this book aim at illustrating with case examples how this integration can work in clinical practice. In cognitive therapies, the core theme is the interaction between cognition–emotion and behavior. The understanding of the human mind is based on analysis between core beliefs (or schemas), assumptions, and value systems in relation to emotional experiences and behavioral reactions

(Beck, Rush, Shaw, & Emery, 1979). The pattern of treatment is that of collaborative empiricism: interactional study of mental processing responsible for psychiatric symptoms or suffering (Freeman et al., 1990). The aim of therapeutic work is a goal-directed change to allow well-being and psychic recovery or adaption. Patients should be assisted in becoming free from brain-locking schemas, and in returning to their usual selves without the negative influences of inflexible patterns of perceiving, interpreting, and responding to their environment and to themselves. According to Alford and Beck (1997), components of cognitive theory employed in therapy with a given patient are specific to the goals or aims of the therapist, in the contextual situation. The patient's characteristics, such as personality and affective responsiveness, are crucial. Strategies for treatment of a particular case depend on the goals as derived from individual case conceptualization or case formulation. In neuropsychotherapy, there are several factors that influence the goals, and the ideal is that the aims for collaborative working are set up and agreed on by both parties. Case conceptualizations will be illustrated in the following case description and conceptualization chart. The conscious meaning of loss concerning the future plans can be partial. However, trust, faith, and hope should be among the therapeutic aspects of the acute treatment.

Case Study

Jon was a boy of 18 who had been hit by a car when he was crossing the street at a green light. The accident resulted in head trauma with clear-cut marks of contusion in the CT picture, which also revealed a local infarction in the posterior left hemisphere. Jon had memory problems, right-sided homonymous hemianopia, and ataxia, producing gait problems. When trying to get into a cafeteria, he was falsely mistaken for exhibiting drunken behavior, and was refused admittance. This strengthened his conception of a dangerous world.

The case conceptualization (Table 1.1) gives the therapist insight to Jon's shattered mind and search for help.

In the case conceptualization chart, we can see Jon's conceptions about himself and his value systems. These conceptualizations give information about preserved metacognition, as well as key goals in life to be an airline pilot. It was clear that this never would be possible. Jon was also a person with an intensive drive to exercise. Turning to religion was new in his life. Mood swings were disturbing, and the

TABLE 1.1 Cognitive–Emotional–Behavioral Conceptualization in Neuropsychotherapy (CEB)

<table>
<tr><td colspan="3">Description of/onset of brain disorder
-I was hit by a car at the age of 18.
-Everything was totally confusing and I was in the hospital for 4 weeks, and now I am in rehabilitation.</td></tr>
<tr><td colspan="3">↓</td></tr>
<tr><td colspan="3">Interpretation of what happened
-I was driven over on purpose.
-I guess I can manage after rehabilitation.
-If my plans to become an airline pilot are ruined, this is a disaster.</td></tr>
<tr><td colspan="3">↓</td></tr>
<tr><td colspan="3">Stream of thoughts
-Am I different now?
-Why do my friends not contact me any more?
-My parents worry too much.</td></tr>
<tr><td colspan="3">↓</td></tr>
<tr><td colspan="3">Life history
-I was a healthy guy with many plans for life. The goal to be a pilot like my grandfather has led me on.
-School was okay and no special problems with my parents.</td></tr>
<tr><td colspan="3">↓</td></tr>
<tr><td>How do I feel?
-My feelings change: I am really sad, or overly optimistic.
-I am lonely.</td><td>↔</td><td>What do I do?
-My gait gives me trouble, I must exercise.
-I am poor in many things.
-Do I have to kill myself?
-Does God help me?
-I spend my days painting and writing Bible verses.</td></tr>
</table>

hyperactive behavior made him vulnerable to hypomania and bipolar disorder. Suicidal thoughts reached his consciousness. The first goal was therapeutic treatment and psychoeducation. The first aid Jon needed was to come to terms with the collapse of professional goals and loss of respectful relationships. It was also important to prevent too much exercising, due to danger of fatigue and deep depression. Jon was able to carry out memory exercises to some extent. His feelings of the unjustness of fate and hopelessness for the future were subject to constructive dialogue. His vulnerability to environmental attitudes was also a focus, because suicidal thoughts were easily provoked.

Psychotherapeutic Methods for Neuropsychological Patients

The psychotherapeutic methods will be described in Chapter 12 in more detail. A summary of methods is given in this context:

- Psychoeducation (neurological/psychological information is of utmost importance for adequate metacognitive processing).
- Methods of dialogue and therapy techniques are the working tools that can be individually tailored.
- Interpersonal process: alliance, correction of process ruptures, validation, etc., are necessary for positive outcome.
- Creative methods: Narratives, poems and music, drawing/painting, role playing, empty chair, imagery, etc., are psychotherapeutic tools for different goals.

All of these methods have been used, and they appear proper for many patients.

Understanding the Environmental and Family Affairs and Their Meaning for Treatment

The families and friends of injured people will have to go through a process of grief or uncertainty. They will go through a problem of change, as well. This topic is the theme in Chapter 10: Challenge to Change in the Family Narrative, and it will be dealt with in more detail in that context.

Conclusions

To have a unified theoretical framework for neuropsychological treatment of neurological or neuropsychiatric patients is not an easy task, nor is it always necessary. However, our experiences of clinical remediation work show that it is possible with additional training. In Finland, the first three-year neuropsychotherapy training program was started for specialist clinical neuropsychologists 2005.

The training is supervised by the Finnish Neuropsychological Society, and it was begun by the initiative of the author of this article. It continued in training collaboration with Mervi Ranta until the end of 2007. This book is a result of our first training program and collaboration with experienced professionals.

What we gain from the integrated multidisciplinary approach in neuropsychological rehabilitation (i.e., neuropsychotherapy) can be briefly summarized as follows:

- Better understanding of the core problems of the patient
- More concrete basis for psychoeducation and treatment in new domains
- Continuing challenge in penetrating the fractured minds of people who never stop surprising us
- More realistic optimism for the efficacy of a multidisciplinary process
- More insight of the core role of the therapist.

The gain is aimed at a holistic and integrated relationship with the sufferers of brain injury in an efficient rehabilitation setting and mutual working alliance.

References

Alford, B.A., & Beck, A.T. (1997). *The integrative power of cognitive therapy.* New York: Guilford Press.

Allen, J.G. (2001). *Traumatic relationships and serious mental disorders* (pp. 44–77). New York: John Wiley & Sons.

American Psychiatric Association. (1980). *Diagnostic and statistical manual of mental disorders—third edition (DSM-III).* Washington, DC: Author.

Beck, A.T., Rush, A.J., Shaw, B.F., & Emery, G. (1979). *Cognitive therapy of depression.* New York: John Wiley & Sons.

Ben-Yishay, Y., Rattock, J., & Lakin, P. (1985). Neuropsychologic rehabilitation: Quest for a holistic approach. *Seminars in Neurology, 5,* 252–259.

Berg, A., Palomäki, H., Lehtihalmes, M., Lönnqvist, J., & Kaste, M. (2001). Poststroke depression in acute phase after stroke. *Cereprovascular Disease, 12,* 14–20.

Berg, A., Palomäki, H., Lehtihalmes, M., Lönnqvist, J., & Kaste, M. (2003). Poststroke depression: An 18-month follow up. *Stroke, 34,* 138–143.

Berg, A., Palomäki, H., Lehtihalmes, M., Lönnqvist, J., & Kaste, M. (2005). Poststroke depression among caregivers of stroke survivors. *Stroke, 36,* 639–643.

Borod, J.C. (2000). *The neuropsychology of emotion*. Cambridge, MA: Oxford University Press.

Bryant, R.A., Creamer, M., D'Onnell, M., Silove, D., Clark, C.R., & McFarlane, A.C. (2009). Post-traumatic amnesia and the nature of post-traumatic stress disorder after mild traumatic brain injury. *Journal of the International Neuropsychological Society, 15*, 862–867.

Cicerone, K.D., Dahlberg, C., Kalmar, K., Langenbahn, D.M., Malec, J.F., Bergquist, T.F., . . . Morse, P.A. (2000). Evidence-based cognitive rehabilitation. Recommendations for clinical practice. *Archives of Physical Medicine and Rehabilitation, 81*, 1596–1615.

Christensen, A-L. (2009). Luria's legacy in the 21st century. In A-L. Christensen, E. Goldberg, and D. Bougakov (Eds.), *Luria's legacy in the 21st century* (pp. 3–16). New York: Oxford University Press, Inc.

Christensen, A-L., & Uzzel, B. (1994). Visions for rehabilitation. In A-L Christensen & B. Uzzell (Eds.), *Brain injury and neuropsychological rehabilitation* (pp. 293–300). International perspectives. Mahwah, NJ: Lawrence Erlbaum Publishers.

Christensen, C.L., Pinner, M., & Rosenberg, N.K. (1988). Program for rehabilitation of brain damage in Denmark. In A-L. Christensen & B. Uzzel (Eds.), *Neuropsychological rehabilitation* (pp. 115–124). Boston: Kluwer Academic Publishers.

Clark, D., Beck, A.T., & Alford, B.A. (1999). *Scientific foundations of cognitive theory and therapy of depression*. New York: John Wiley & Sons.

Coetzer, R. (2007). Psychotherapy following traumatic brain injury: Integrating theory and practice. *Journal of Head Trauma Rehabilitation, 22*(1), 39–42.

Cummings, J.L., & Mega, M.S. (2003). *Neuropsychiatry and behavioral neuroscience*. New York: Oxford University Press.

Damasio, A. (1999). *The feeling of what happens. Body and emotion in the making of consciousness*. London: William Heinemann.

Diller, L., & Gordon, W. (1981). Interventions in neuropsychological rehabilitation of cognitive deficits in brain injured adults. *Journal of Consulting and Clinical Psychology, 49*, 822—834.

Ehlers, A., & Clark, M.D. (2000). A cognitive model of PTSD. *Behavioral Research and Therapy, 38*(4), 319–345.

Ergenzinger, E.R., & Pons, T.P. (2000). Growth of new connections in adult reorganizational plasticity in somatosensory system. In H.S. Levin. & J. Grafman (Eds.), *Cerebral reorganization of function after brain injury* (pp. 68–83). New York: Oxford University Press.

Farina, E., Mantovani, F., & Fioranti, R. (2006). Evaluating two group programmes of cognitive training in mild-to-moderate AD: Is there any difference between global stimulation and "cognitive"-specific one. *Aging and Mental Health, 10*(3), 211–218.

Fleming, J.M., Strong, R., & Ashton, R. (1996). Self-awareness of deficits in adults with traumatic brain injury: How to best measure the brain injury. *Brain Injury, 10*(1), 1–15.

Freeman, A., Pretzer J., Fleming, B., & Simon, K.M. (1990). *Clinical applications of cognitive therapy.* New York: Plenum Press.

Fuster, J.M. (2003). *Cortex and mind: Unifying cognition.* New York: Oxford University Press.

Gaus, V.L. (2007). *Cognitive behavioral therapy for adult Asperger syndrome.* (J.B. Persons, Series Ed.). New York: Guilford Press.

Goldberg, E., & Bougakov, D. (2009). Neuropsychology and A.R. Luria's concept of higher cortical functions in the beginning of the 3rd millennium. In A-L. Christensen, E. Goldberg, & D. Bougakov (Eds.), *Luria's legacy in the 21st century* (pp. 17–22). New York: Oxford University Press.

Gracey, F., & Onsworth, T. (2008). Editorial. *Neuropsychological Rehabilitation 18*(56), 522–526. (Reprinted 2009, in *The Self and Identity in Rehabilitation*, special issue.)

Grawe, K. (2007). *Neuropsychotherapy: How the neurosciences inform effective psychotherapy.* Mahwah, New Jersey: Lawrence Erlbaum Associate.

Greenberg, L.S., & Paivio, S.C. (1997). *Working with emotions in psychotherapy.* New York: Guilford Press.

Horenstein, S. (1970). Effects of cerebrovascular disease on personality and emotionality. Presentation 17. In A.L. Benton (Ed.), *Behavioral chance in cerebrovascular disease.* New York: Harper & Row Publishers.

Johnstone, B., & Stonnington, H.H. (2001). *Rehabilitation of neuropsychological disorders: A practical guide for rehabilitation professionals.* New York: Psychology Press, Taylor & Francis Group.

Judd, D., & Wilson, S.L. (2005). Psychotherapy with brain injury survivors: An investigation of the challenges encountered by clinicians and their modification practice. *Brain Injury, 19*, 437–449.

Judd, T. (1999). *Neuropsychotherapy and community integration: Brain illness emotions and behavior critical issues in neuropsychology.* Heidelberg, NY: Plenum Publishers.

Kaipio, M-L., Sarajuuri, J., & Koskinen, S. (2000). INSURE program and modifications in Finland. In Christensen, A-L. & Uzzel, B. (Eds.), *International handbook of neuropsychological rehabilitation* (pp. 247–258). New York: Kluwer Academic/Plenum.

Kaplan-Solms, K., & Solms, M. (2000). *Clinical studies in neuropsychoanalysis.* London: Karnac Books.

Koskinen, S. (1998). The quality of life 10 years after a very severe traumatic brain injury (TBI): The perspective of the injured and the closest relative. *Brain Injury, 12*(8), 631–648.

Laaksonen R. (1987). Neuropsychological rehabilitation in Finland. In M. J. Meier, A. L. Benton, & L. Diller (Eds.), *Neuropsychological rehabilitation* (pp. 387–395). New York: Churchill Livingstone.

Laaksonen, R. (1994). Cognitive training methods in rehabilitation of memory. In A-L. Christensen, & B. Uzzel, (Eds.), *Brain injury and neuropsychological rehabilitation* (pp. 125–133). International Perspectives. Hillsdale, NJ: Lawrence Erlbaum Publishers.

Laaksonen, R. (2007). Neuropsychotherapy as an integrated part of neuropsychological rehabilitation. *Svensk Neuropsykologi*. N.R.2-3, 8–11.

Leahy, R.L. (2001). *Overcoming resistance in cognitive therapy*. New York: Guilford Press.

Le Doux, J. (1999). *The emotional brain: The mysterious underpinnings of emotional life*. New York: Phoenix.

Lishman, W.A. (1978). *Organic psychiatry*. Oxford, UK: Blackwell Scientific Publications.

Luria, A.R. (1963). *Restoration of function after brain injury*. Oxford, UK: Pergamon Press.

Luria, A.R. (1970). *Traumatic aphasia*. New York: Mouton.

Luria, A.R. (1973). *The working brain*. London: Allen Lane the Penguin Press.

Luria, A.R. (1976). *The neuropsychology of memory*. Washington, DC: Winston & Sons, Division of Scripta Technica, Inc.

Niemi, M-L., Laaksonen, R., Kotila, M., & Waltimo, O. (1988). Quality of life 4 years after stroke. *Stroke, 9*, 1101–1107.

Ogden J.A. (2005). *Fractured minds. A Case study approach to clinical neuropsychology*. New York: Oxford University Press.

Powell, G.E. (1981). *Mechanisms or underlying the recovery of function* (pp. 1–19). In G.E. Powell (Ed.), *Brain function therapy*. London: Gover Publishing Company, Ltd.

Prigatano, G.P. (1991). Disordered mind, wounded soul: The emerging role of psychotherapy in rehabilitation after brain injury. *Journal of Head Trauma Rehabilitation, 6*(4), 1–10.

Prigatano, G.P. (1999). *Principles of neuropsychological rehabilitation*. New York: Oxford University Press.

Prigatano, G. P. (2009). Neuropsysychological foundations of human personality and Luria's legacy. In A-L. Christensen, E. Goldberg, and D. Bougakov (Eds.), *Luria's legacy in the 21st century* (pp. 62–84). New York: Oxford University Press.

Prigatano, G.P., Fordyce, D., & Zeiner, H.K. (1984). Neuropsychological rehabilitation after closed head injury in young adults. *Journal of Neurology, Neurosurgery & Psychiatry, 47*, 505–513.

Safran, J. D., & Muran, J.C. (2000). *Negotiating the therapeutic alliance. A relational treatment guide*. New York: Guilford Press.

Safran, J.D., & Segal, Z.V. (1990). *The interpersonal process in cognitive therapy*. New York: Basic Books.

Sarajuuri, J.M., Kaipio, M-L., Koskinen, S.K., Niemelä, M. R., Servo, A.R., & Vilkki, J.S. (2005). Outcome of a comprehensive neurorehabilitation program for patients with traumatic brain injury. *Archives of Psychological Rehabilitation, 86*, 2296–2302.

Scherer, M., Evans, C. C., Leberenge, J., Stouter, J., Irby, J. W., Jr., Lee, J.B., & Yablon, S.A. (2007). Therapeutic alliance in post-acute brain injury rehabilitation: Predictors of strength of alliance and impact of alliance on outcome. *Brain Injury, 21*(7), 663–672.

Schönberger, M., Humle, F., & Teasdale, T.W. (2006). The development of the therapeutic working alliance, patients' awareness and their compliance during the process of brain injury rehabilitation. *Brain Injury, 20*(4), 445–454.

Schönberger, M., Humle, F., & Teasdale, T.W. (2007). The relationship between client's cognitive functioning and the therapeutic working alliance in post-acute brain injury rehabilitation. *Brain Injury, 21*(8), 825–836.

Sohlberg, M. M. & Mateer, C. A. (2001). *Cognitive rehabilitation. An integrative neuropsychological approach.* New York: Guilford Press.

Stuss, D., & Benson, F. (1986). *The frontal lobes.* New York: Raven Press.

Teasdale, T.W., Christensen, A-L., Wilmes, K., Deloche, G., Braga, L., Stachowiak, F., . . . Leclercq, M. (1997). Subjective experience in brain injured patients and their close relatives. A European Brain Injury Questionnaire Study. *Brain Injury, 11*(8), 543–563.

Vasterling, J.J., & Verfaellie M. (2009). Posttraumatic stress disorder: A neurocognitive perspective. *Journal of the International Neuropsychological Society, 15*, 826–829.

Virta, M., Vedenpää, A., Grönroos, N., Chydenius, E., Partinen, M., Vataja, R., Kaski, M., & Iivanainen, M. (2008). Adults with ADHD benefit from cognitive behavioral oriented group rehabilitation. *Journal of Attention Disorders. 12*(3), 218–226.

Wilson, B.A. (1999). *Case studies in neuropsychological rehabilitation.* Oxford: Oxford University Press.

Wilson, B.A., Herbert, C.M., & Shiel, A. (2003). *Neuropsychological rehabilitation: A modular handbook, behavioral approaches in neuropsychological rehabilitation, optimising rehabilitation procedures.* New York: Psychology Press.

Wilson, B., & Moffat, N. (1984). *Clinical management of memory problems.* Kent, UK: Croom Helm, Ltd.

Yeates, G.N., Gracey, F., & McGrath, J.C. (2008). A biopsychological deconstruction of "personality change" following acquired brain injury. *Neuropsychological Rehabilitation 5/6*, 566–589. (Reprinted 2009, in *The Self and Identity in Rehabilitation*, special edition.)

Young, J., Klasko, J.S., &Weishaar, M.E. (2003). *Schema therapy: A practitioner's guide.* New York: Guilford Press.

2

Neuropsychological Assessment in Adults

Integrating Neuropsychological Knowledge for Treatment and Therapeutic Purposes

Raija Ylikoski

Introduction

Neuropsychological perspective serves as a bridge from neuroscience to clinical practice and treatment. It provides knowledge for understanding the underlying theories and concepts and means for the assessing functional integrity of brain-behaviour systems. Characterizing cognitive, behavioural, and emotional capabilities and deficits helps to orient the therapeutic process and focus the treatment planning.

Clinical neuropsychological assessment integrates knowledge of various sources. Research development in neurosciences and neuropsychology continuously modify the methodology used in clinical settings. Growing knowledge of neuropsychological theories and concepts helps to describe the clinical phenomena in more detail. Information on the brain-behaviour relationship is crucial in understanding the neural mechanisms of cognitive processes. Assessment methodology includes also the knowledge of neuropsychological symptoms and syndromes described in various clinical textbooks and studies. Similarly, the knowledge of the various neuropsychological symptoms or syndromes related to certain neurological, psychiatric, or developmental diagnoses guides the clinician, for example, in differential diagnoses. Neuropsychological investigation includes not only the knowledge of cognitive processes, but also integrates information of how the central nervous system develops throughout the lifespan and processes emotion. Finally, a crucial part of the assessment methodology is the interview, obtaining demographic data, and the knowledge of various clinical and psychometric tests and rating scales.

Neuropsychological findings are important in developing therapeutic plans. Rehabilitation and treatment planning requires a comprehensive understanding of the patient's life situation and clinical features. A comprehensive neuropsychological picture requires multifactorial knowledge that is integrated in a clinical investigation. Besides the clinical purposes, it may also serve as a psychoeducational treatment.

Knowledge Obtained by Neuropsychological Assessment

The design of the treatment and care of a patient is based on clinical data and recommendations of experts. Neuropsychological investigation gives background information of cognitive, behavioural, emotional, and social aspects of the patient. The assessment procedure utilizes various disciplines within the neuropsychological and neurocognitive sciences, integrating the findings and implications from diverse sources. The outcome and interpretation of neuropsychological investigation is based on the knowledge of valid cognitive processes and concepts; their brain-behaviour relationships; knowledge of clinical neuropsychological symptoms and syndromes and their relation in neurological, neuropsychiatric, or developmental diseases; knowledge of neuropsychological features in psychiatric diseases; and, finally, management of specific tests and obtaining background information (see Figure 2.1).

The knowledge concerning cognitive processes and concepts has hugely developed during the latest decades and helps the clinician to both understand and describe the cognitive and emotional features debilitated by the disease. Different concepts and processes concerning memory help to elucidate the elements that have deteriorated and that are preserved. Working memory (Baddeley, 1992), although to some degree a disputed concept, is an essential memory process, and its validity in clinical syndromes has been verified by many investigations. Executive functions are still difficult to measure, but the

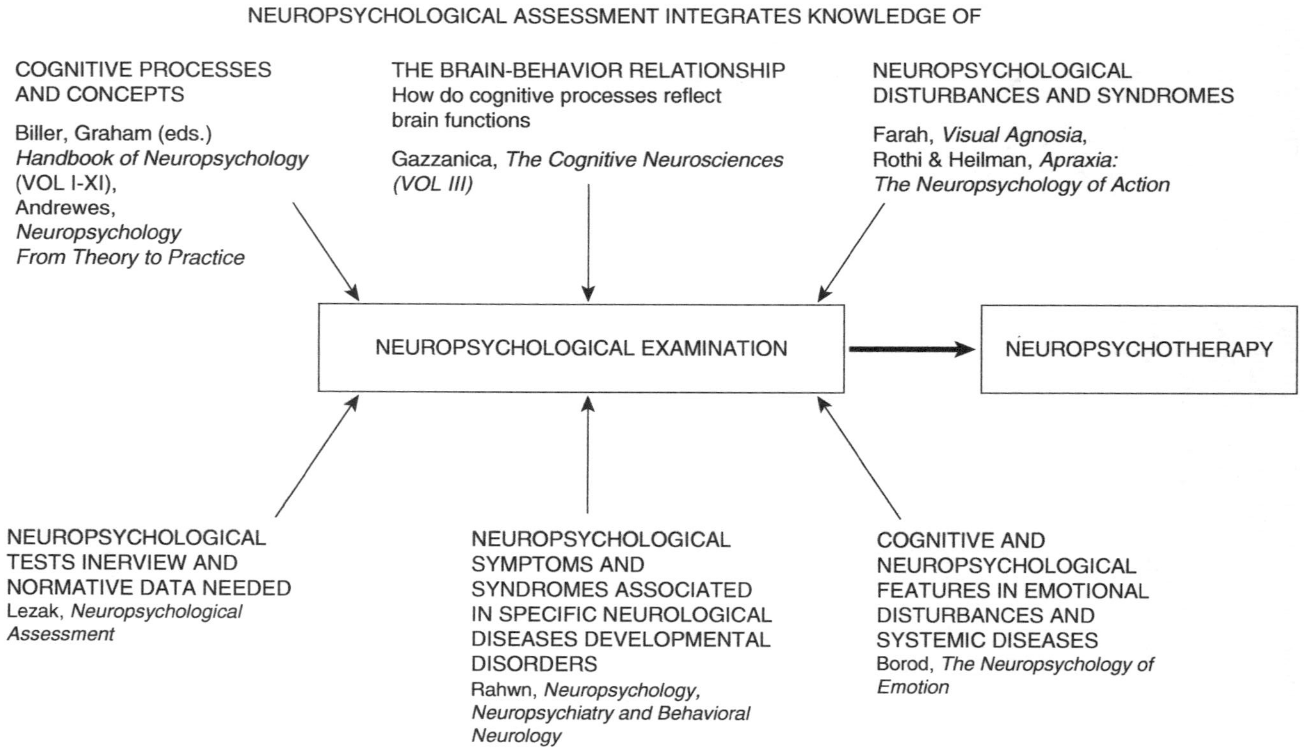
NEUROPSYCHOLOGICAL ASSESSMENT INTEGRATES KNOWLEDGE OF
COGNITIVE PROCESSES AND CONCEPTS
Biller, Graham (eds.) *Handbook of Neuropsychology* (VOL I-XI), Andrewes, *Neuropsychology From Theory to Practice*
THE BRAIN-BEHAVIOR RELATIONSHIP How do cognitive processes reflect brain functions
Gazzanica, *The Cognitive Neurosciences (VOL III)*
NEUROPSYCHOLOGICAL DISTURBANCES AND SYNDROMES
Farah, *Visual Agnosia*, Rothi & Heilman, *Apraxia: The Neuropsychology of Action*
NEUROPSYCHOLOGICAL EXAMINATION
NEUROPSYCHOTHERAPY
NEUROPSYCHOLOGICAL TESTS INERVIEW AND NORMATIVE DATA NEEDED
Lezak, *Neuropsychological Assessment*
NEUROPSYCHOLOGICAL SYMPTOMS AND SYNDROMES ASSOCIATED IN SPECIFIC NEUROLOGICAL DISEASES DEVELOPMENTAL DISORDERS
Rahwn, *Neuropsychology, Neuropsychiatry and Behavioral Neurology*
COGNITIVE AND NEUROPSYCHOLOGICAL FEATURES IN EMOTIONAL DISTURBANCES AND SYSTEMIC DISEASES
Borod, *The Neuropsychology of Emotion*

Figure 2.1

growing knowledge of the various elements and processes within the cognitive control mechanisms; planning and problem solving; initiation; flexibility; and behavioural changes gives the clinician the basic tools for describing the symptoms (Stuss & Alexander, 2000; Rabbit, 1997). Valid concepts and evidence-based knowledge of cognitive subprocesses are important tools in assessment.

The significance of a patient's symptoms and signs can be understood in the context of a functional system. The system consists of a number of parts of the brain together with their fibre connections. Damage anywhere in the system will lead to some change in the function, which the system subserves (Walsh, 1994). The nature of the change will be dependent upon which particular part of the system is damaged or the set of connections that has been disrupted, since each part contributes something characteristic to the whole. For example, the fronto-subcortical circuits of executive functions help to illuminate the concepts and clinical processes (Cummings, 1995). Attentional processes have been divided to four functional systems, each having specific circuits and connections: the arousal system, the orienting system, the perceptual attention system, and the executive attention system (Andrewes, 2001; Gazzanica, 2004). Distinct memory processes, like working memory (Linden et al., 2003) and consolidation processes (McGaugh, 2000) have been associated with specific brain functions. These are only a few examples of the vast expanding knowledge of cognitive processes and their brain-behaviour relationships. According to Fuster (2003), cognitive information is represented in wide, overlapping, and interactive neuronal networks of the cerebral cortex; any cortical neuron can be part of many networks, and, thus, of many perceptions, memories, items of experience, or items of personal knowledge. These networks can serve several cognitive functions, and cognitive functions consist of functional interactions within and between cortical networks. The expanding knowledge of the brain-behaviour relationship is a basic tool for clinical neuropsychological investigation.

Since the days of Broca and Wernicke, the clinical research data has provided many symptoms and syndromes typical for various brain lesions. Knowledge of language disturbances has developed together with the aphasia test batteries. Deficits of visual perception (Farrah, 1995), voluntary hand movements (Rothi & Heilman, 1997), and neglect have been described in detail. Neuropsychological syndrome is a unique constellation of signs and symptoms that occur together, suggesting a particular underlying process. If confronted with certain symptoms or signs, the neuropsychologist will look for the association of the other features to confirm or deny the presence of a particular syndrome. Knowledge of a variety of syndromes allows us to generate hypotheses about the nature of the disruptions of function in each individual case. Neuropsychological diagnostic symptoms and syndromes are essential tools in measuring and describing the changes caused by the disease.

Similarly, research data on the various cognitive syndromes in different disease entities is an essential component of neuropsychological assessment. Knowledge of typical cognitive features of distinct degenerative diseases, multiple sclerosis, or various stroke sites and vascular conditions guide the clinician in interpreting the symptoms and in differential diagnostics. Likewise, the knowledge of developmental syndromes affecting cognitive and emotional processes is crucial. The essential differences among neuropsychiatric syndromes often include neuropsychological features. The overview of social, emotional, and cognitive developmental disturbances within a syndrome helps to differentiate these syndromes from each other and from other diseases.

Besides obtaining knowledge of cognitive syndromes in various neurological diseases, the neuropsychological investigation also requires knowledge of cognitive features in different systemic diseases or emotional and psychiatric diseases. Differential diagnostic questions may focus the assessment procedure on analyzing known cognitive difficulties in diseases other than neurological ones. Developing neurocognitive and biological psychiatric sciences have emerged with vast amount of studies in this field. For example, memory encoding in depression has been associated with hippocampal and anterior cingulated deficits (Bremmer, Vythlingam, Vermetten, Vaccarino, & Charney, 2004). Schizophrenia patients have shown distinct neuropsychological profiles emphasizing the frontotemporal dysfunction with memory and executive function deficits (Frith, 1992). Neuropsychological knowledge of emotion processing helps to determine the behavioural changes of the disease both in neurological and psychiatric diseases (Borod, 2000).

Including all the areas of knowledge described above, the neuropsychological investigation comprises assessing cognitive functions with various tests. The most typical domains to be measured and analyzed are memory and learning, attention and processing speed, visual and visuoconstructive abilities, verbal functions, problem solving and intelligence tests, motor performance, executive functions and emotional status. Knowledge of syndromes and brain-behaviour relationships is the principal factor in determining the selection of tools. For a more detailed description of different neuropsychological tests, see Lezak (1995). Traditionally, there have been different trends in clinical neuropsychology, such as the Halsteadt Reitan comprehensive test battery, the qualitative hypothesis testing strategy (as in Goldstein, 1987; and Luria, 1973), and the process approach (Groth-Marnat, 2000). Luria's theoretical approach was directed to build up good grounds in restoration of function in brain-injured patients (Laaksonen, 1987). New technology and emerging research have combined to create several trends in clinical neuropsychology. These include computerized approaches, greater emphasis on understanding the nature of deficits, greater focus on application, organization of results around functional domains, and the development of test batteries specific to certain conditions (Groth-Marnat, 2000). A systematic method for assessing qualitative neuropsychological information, which, taken in concert with more traditional test performance data, adds sensitivity and meaning to neuropsychological assessment. The nature of the observations that will be of value, and the tests that will be applied, must rest on knowledge of the findings that are emerging from research studies. According to surveys analysing common clinical practices, flexible, hypothesis-testing approaches are becoming the dominant trend in neuropsychology (Groth-Marnat, 2000). Working hypotheses may arise from generalizations that have emerged from the research literature. As research on clinical neuropsychology grows, converging lines of evidence make the generalizations more secure and, thus, facilitate the implementation of crucial tests of the various hypotheses.

Integrating Assessment Results for Neuropsychotherapy

Neuropsychological investigation provides a synergistic and integrative picture of brain-behaviour relationships. Clinical neuropsychological assessment is the application of this knowledge to evaluate and to intervene in human behaviour as it relates to normal and abnormal functioning of the central nervous system. The perspective brought by neuropsychology serves as a bridge from neuroscience to clinical practice and treatment. Neuropsychological evaluation provides a means for explaining behavioural difficulties and characterizing cognitive, behavioural, and emotional capabilities and deficits. The outcome of the neuropsychological investigation provides a description of the impact that brain dysfunction has had on a person's cognitions, personality, emotions, interpersonal relationships, activities in daily life, vocational functioning, educational potential, and ability to enjoy life.

Rehabilitation neuropsychology integrates psychosocial and biological information from a wide variety of sources, including history, assessment procedures, behavioural observations, and medical records. Investigation for rehabilitation typically involves a careful consideration of patients' relative strengths and weaknesses, observing how these map into functioning and premorbid or demographic factors, and determining what the essential changes caused by the illness or handicap may be. Neuropsychology may contribute to the understanding of a patient's real-world potential, identification of cognitive and behavioural deficits, and discussion of their effects on the patient's ability to carry out activities of daily living (Lemsky, 2000). Neuropsychology is one element in developing a rehabilitation plan to create realistic scenarios for acute rehabilitation care and for long-term life-care planning. Baseline assessment results also provide objective data to which future behavioural and cognitive chances may be compared.

Comprehensive knowledge of the clinical features of the disease and of the patient's life situation guides treatment planning. Neuropsychological examination provides basic information of the person's cognitive, behavioural, and emotional functions, and guides the therapist in focusing the rehabilitation. In the rehabilitation context, the neuropsychological investigation may have greater emphasis on application, such as employability, responsiveness to rehabilitation, and the need for environmental support.

Therapeutic Aspects of Neuropsychological Assessment

Cognitive impairments exist in a matrix of personal, social, physical, and environmental factors that interact with one another. It is necessary to evaluate how an individual understands his or her cognitive functioning and how it affects the individual's ability to meet particular environmental demands. Comprehensive neuropsychological investigation provides valuable clinical and baseline information, and may also serve as a psychoeducational treatment. Knowledge of the underlying mechanisms in cognitive or emotional changes and their relations to brain functions may help the patient and relatives to cope with the altered situation. Education about the individual's illness or disability is also important in order to prevent excess disability, anxiety, and adjustment difficulties. The process of educating clients about illness and disability may begin with the investigation and continue later, when the feedback from neuropsychological testing is provided. The investigating neuropsychologist may also provide the patient with initial ideas of monitoring altered behaviour and of compensating for the disabilities and helping the patient to find more information about the disease. Supportive help and identification of possible psychic reactions are also crucial in the adjustment process. Especially when there is known history of premorbid psychosocial, psychological, or psychiatric difficulties, or substance abuse, it is important to assess the patient's current outlook on adjustment and functioning.

An assessment procedure can also be considered as a therapeutic intervention. The process of remediation begins with the patient's understanding of the changes in cognitive, behavioural, and emotional aspects of the disease. In addition to understanding these problems, it is important to understand patients' emotional experience of these problems. Helping patients to understand their deficits and strengths and helping to build up an altered identity can assist them in rehabilitation and adaptation (Finn & Tonsager, 1992). Information obtained from the neuropsychological investigation may also help family members to more accurately understand the disabilities caused by the disease, prevent misunderstandings, and aid in adaptation and finding appropriate services. Assessment feedback is crucial in working with alliance and therapeutic communication. Impersonal, scientific feedback may increase the chance of patients' being traumatized by the information (Finn & Tonsager, 1992). Feedback is one of the major ways to achieve therapeutic impact. Promising feedback elicits openness and cooperation and makes patients more satisfied with the assessment. Therapeutic dialogue is a major tool in giving feedback. Therapeutic assessment may decrease symptomatology, increase self-esteem, increase hope, give better compliance with treatment recommendations, and enhance alliance in therapy (Finn & Tonsager, 1992; Ackerman, Hllsenroth, Baity, & Blagys, 2000).

Neuropsychotherapy provides a bridge that connects neuropsychological rehabilitation to therapeutic processes. Neuropsychological assessment can be seen as part of neuropsychotherapy. Assessment is the beginning of the process, during which the patient is helped to meet the altered life situation and to start adaptation, coping, and developing future plans.

References

Ackerman, S.J., Hilsenroth, M.J., Baity, M.R., & Blagys, M.D. (2000). Interaction of therapeutic process and alliance during psychological assessment. *Journal of Personality Assessment, 75*, 82–109.

Andrewes, D.G. (2001). *Neuropsychology: From theory to practice*. East Sussex, UK: Psychology Press, Ltd.

Baddeley, A. (1992). Working memory. *Science, 255*, 556–559.

Borod, J.C. (2000). *The neuropsychology of emotion*. Oxford: Oxford University Press.

Bremmer, J.D., Vythlingam, M., Vermetten, E., Vaccarino, V., & Charney, D.S. (2004). Deficits in hippocampal and anterior cingulated functioning during verbal encoding in midlife major depression. *American Journal of Psychiatry, 161*, 637–645.

Cummings, J.L. (1995). Anatomic and behavioral aspects of frontal-subcortical circuits. *Annals of the New York Academy of Sciences, 769*, 1–13.

Farrah, M.J. (1995). *Visual agnosia. Disorders of object recognition and what they tell us about normal vision*. Cambridge, MA: The MIT Press.

Finn, S.E., & Tonsager, M.E. (1992). Therapeutic effects of providing MMPI-2 test feedback to college students awaiting therapy. *Psychological Assessment, 4*, 278–287.

Frith, C.D. (1992). *The cognitive neuropsychology of schizophrenia*. Hove, UK: Lawrence Erlbaum Associates.

Fuster, J.M. (2003). *Cortex and mind*. Oxford: Oxford University Press.

Gazzanica, M.S. (2004). *The cognitive neurosciences*. Cambridge, MA: The MIT Press.

Goldstein, G. (1987). Neuropsychological assessment for rehabilitation: Fixed batteries, automated systems, and non-psychometric methods. In M.J. Meier, A.L. Benton, L. Diller (Eds.), *Neuropsychological rehabilitation* (pp. 18–41). Edinburgh, UK: Churchill Livingstone.

Groth-Marnat, G. (2000). Introduction to neuropsychological assessment. In G. Groth-Marnat (Ed.), *Neuropsychological assessment in clinical practice. A guide to test interpretation and integration* (pp. 3–20). New York: John Wiley & Sons.

Laaksonen R. (1987). Neuropsychological rehabilitation in Finland. In M. J. Meier, A. L. Benton, & L. Diller (Eds.), *Neuropsychological rehabilitation* (pp. 387–395). New York: Churchill Livingstone.

Lemsky, C.M. (2000). Neuropsychological assessment and treatment planning. In G. Groth-Marnat (Ed.), *Neuropsychological assessment in clinical practice. A guide to test interpretation and integration* (pp. 535–567). New York: John Wiley & Sons.

Lezak, M.D. (1995). *Neuropsychological Assessment* (2nd ed.). New York: Oxford University Press.

Linden, D.E.J., Bittner, R.A., Muckli, L., Waltz, J.A., Kriegeskorte, N., Goebel, R., Singer, W., & Munk. M.H.J. (2003). Cortical capacity constraints for visual working memory: Dissociation of fMRI load effects in a fronto-parietal network. *Neuroimage, 20,* 1518–1530.

Luria, A.R. (1973). *The working brain. an introduction to neuropsychology.* Harmondswothr, Middlesex, England: Penguin Books Ltd.

McGaugh, J.L. (2000). Memory—a century of consolidation. *Science, 287,* 248–251.

Rabbit, P. (1997). Introduction: Methodologies and models in the study of executive function. In P. Rabbit (Ed.), *Methodology of frontal and executive functions.* East Sussex, UK: Psychological Press.

Rhawn J. (1990). *Neuropsychology, neuropsychiatry, and behavioral neurology.* New York: Plenum Press.

Rothi, L.J.G., & Heilman, K.M. (1997). *Apraxia: The neuropsychology of action.* East Sussex, UK: Psychology Press.

Stuss, D.T., & Alexander. M.P. (2000). Executive functions and the frontal lobes: A conceptual view. *Psychological Research, 63,* 289–298.

Walsh, K. (1994). *Neuropsychology, a clinical approach.* Edinburgh, UK: Churchill Livingstone.

3

Brain Development and the Everlasting Process of Self-Regulation

Implications for the Development of Perception, Attention, Language, and Memory

Nina Sajaniemi

Introduction

Resilient adaptation to environmental stressors is the most challenging mission of human life. The basic goal of adaptation is to ensure survival by maintaining physiological homeostasis under threat. This chapter deals with the developmental aspects as guidelines for understanding the individual as a whole, not just as a cluster of symptoms or neurological disorders.

Threats to well-being are manifold in daily life experience, ranging from potential danger to incidents arousing only slight discomfort. Individuals' varying vulnerability or resilience to stressful challenges is based on neural structures that regulate an organism's physiological state by executing specific actions via the musculoskeletal system, such as facial and postural expressions, and by producing chemical and neural responses aimed at the internal milieu, viscera, and neural circuits in the brain.

The autonomic nervous system connects the brain to internal organs, vessels, and sweat glands. It regulates the functions of these organ systems that are not voluntarily controlled and also monitors and regulates the somatic state, aiming to maintain homeostasis. It is the physical basis for sensing, and it forms the roots of emotions. Feelings of pleasure and discomfort are mediated through the autonomic nervous system; they are building blocs for sensations that have effects on thinking and behavior (Damasio, 1998; Schore, 2001). The autonomic nervous system consists of the sympathetic and the parasympathetic branches; specifically, the sympathetic nervous system controls the activation in response to stressful events that require high-energy mobilization of resources, and the parasympathetic activation promotes calming processes and energy restoring. The sympathetic and parasympathetic systems fluctuate normally between predominantly sympathetic or parasympathetic activation. The purpose of this fluctuation is to ensure maximum adaptation in different environments.

At the beginning of life, an infant needs comprehensive protection to maintain homeostasis and to appease negative emotions. The neurobiological systems involved in maintenance of stability through change mature and become more organized with development. Organizing, regulative strategies are learned in interaction with protective others, and they channel human development toward a more or less optimal pathway from the first days of postnatal life.

From a developmental perspective, regulation concerns interactive effects of genetic inheritance, maturational processes, and person-specific experiences, which produce individual differences in strategies for keeping oneself safe (Crittenden, 2006). Strategies can be either adaptive or maladaptive in the long term, but under immediate threat they can always be interpreted as functional behavior. However, it is important to realize that one's functional behavior might mean danger or discomfort for others. It is important to understand that observed discomfort or misbehavior is in some way adaptive for the child and should not be punished. Punishment might bring out more conflicts and cause new forms of maladaptive behaviors. Instead of punishment, it is essential to assure the child that she is physically, socially, and psychologically safe. Behavior can be resilient only when a feeling of safety is sufficiently guaranteed. Promoting resilience should be one of the most important aims in rearing children, because maximum resilience in the face of stress-evoking environmental changes throughout life can have much further-reaching consequences, both individually and socially, than any other single ability.

Stressors include not only painful experiences, but novel events as well. The majority of events are novel at the beginning of life, and an infant's arousal level is easily shifting. The development of the ability to cope adaptively with stress is directly and significantly influenced by an infant's early interaction with its primary caregiver (Schore, 2001). Timed and adequate responses to an infant's expressions indicating physiological change enhances its capacity not only to orient toward the familiar but also to approach, tolerate, and incorporate novelty. Orientation toward novelty is essential to the expansion of children's adaptive capacity to learn new information and to move towards more complexity. I argue in this paper that resilient emotion regulation is a prerequisite not only for optimal social development but also for development of motor functions, perception, language, attention, and memory. Conversely, developmental disorders and learning difficulties might be linked to maladaptive regulation strategies. When a child is extremely aroused, it is challenging for her to form accurate and organized perceptions of the environment or of the world. This will be dealt with in more detail later in this chapter.

Individual Reactivity and Temperament

Environmental events signaling threats to survival or well-being produce complex, highly orchestrated responses within the neural circuitry of the brain and peripheral neuroendochrine pathways regulating physiological functions. This integrated repertoire of responses creates an immediate, automatic shift to a state of biological and behavioral preparedness involving increasing vigilance and arousal. Individuals differ significantly in the frequency and intensity with which they experience stressful events. Boyce & Ellis (2005) have described those individual differences with a concept of biological sensitivity to context. Each individual has to calibrate his or her own genetic reaction readiness to match the environment as optimally as possible. Premises on calibration are widely different across variations in reactivity. Highly reactive individuals mount vigorous and permanent responses to stressors, have lower thresholds for anticipating threats in unfamiliar situations, and maintain greater vigilance and wariness than normative or low reactive individuals (Boyce & Ellis, 2005).

Individual biological reactivity can be interpreted in terms of temperament. Innate temperament is thought to reflect genotypic variation in a neural basis of behavior. It is manifested in differences in emotional, motor, and attentional reactivity, and self-regulation, which are relatively consistent across situations and stable over time. A growing amount of temperament studies based on factor analysis of parent-report questionnaires have reliably extracted three broad temperament factors in childhood (Rothbart & Bates, 1998). The first factor is extraversion, including activity level, sociability, impulsivity, and enjoyment of high-intensity pleasure. Second is negative affectivity, which is loaded with fear, anger or frustration, discomfort, and sadness. The third factor is effortful control, with loadings from attention focusing and shifting, inhibitory control, perceptual sensitivity, and low intensity pleasure. Brain imaging studies have provided grounds to suggest a neuroanatomical basis for individual differences in temperament (Ochsner, Bunge, Gross, & Gabriele, 2002; Rothbart, Sheese, & Posner, 2007). Higher effortful control has, for example, been associated with larger volume of orbitofrontal cortex and hippocampus in the left hemisphere. In some studies, higher negative affectivity has been linked with smaller volume of cingulate gyrys in left hemisphere (Whittle et al., 2008). Further, behavioral inhibition and anxiety has been connected with amygdalic activation (Rosen & Schulkin, 1998; Perez-Edgar et al., 2007). Although temperament is biologically based and neuroanatomical correlations can be found, it is a complicated construct, and it should be considered in the context of development. Biological givens, environmental provisions, and timing shape developmental trajectories from moment to moment during the entire life-course.

Biological reactivity is probably one of the most fundamental bases of individual differences. High reactivity predisposes an individual to behavioral inhibition and fearfulness in response to unfamiliar persons or events (Kagan, 1997; Fox, Henderson, Marshall, Nichols, & Ghera, 2005). It increases probability to withdraw from unfamiliar events, whereas approaching behavior indicates desire to engage in novel and intense activities. Approaching tendency is intertwined with fearlessness and lack of inhibition, which, in turn, increases risk-taking behavior for the sake of experiences (Zuckerman & Kuhlman, 2000). This type of child may be easily frustrated when having too many restrictions and overprotection. The overprotection might lead to invalidation of the child's natural tendencies to be active.

Overpowering stress reactivity and extremes in temperamental fearfulness/fearlessness have been conventionally viewed as maladaptive and harmful, increasing risk to mental and physical health, including both internalizing and externalizing psychopathology (Raine, Venables, & Mednick, 1997; Rothbart & Jones, 1998; Nigg, 2000; Stifter, Putnam, & Jahrom, 2008). It has also been documented in a number of studies that extremes in temperament are common in children with attention deficit, cognitive impairment, and autism (Rubin, Burgess, Dwyer, & Hastings, 2003; Bryson et al., 2007; Jarrett & Ollendick, 2008).

However, biological reactivity is as an internal scale that has to be calibrated to fit the living environment. Reactivity or any other manifestation of temperament cannot be valued as good or bad, because interaction with animate and inanimate environment determines the course of development. Extremely high or low reactivity can be associated with both risk and protective environmental influences, thus generating normal, detrimental, or improved outcomes (Boyce & Ellis, 2005).

It has been documented in several studies that highly reactive children have increased amounts of diseases and developmental disorders, but only under conditions of adversity or maltreatment. One of the most illuminating descriptions of context sensitivity comes from studies of nonhuman primates. In one of these such studies, rhesus monkeys and macaques were grouped by either high or average levels of stress reactivity and then fostered to highly skilled, nurturing mothers or to average mothers. The highly reactive infants reared by nurturing mothers had the best developmental outcomes, while the highly reactive infants with average mothers had the worst outcome. Between the extremes were infants with average reactivity, and their outcomes had only minimal variation across the two mothering conditions (Suomi, 1997).

In recent years, a growing number of studies have evidenced that gene activations are sensitive to social experiences early in development. For example, the short allele variant of the 5-HTT gene reducing serotonin transportation confers susceptibility to mood disorders such as depression and anxiety, but only when combined with adverse childhood experiences (Caspi et al., 2003). Further, another gene variant, monoamine oxidase A (MAOA), is shown to predispose to aggressive and impulsive behavior in unfavorable early rearing environments (Foley, Eavers, Wormley, & Silberg, 2004). Protective nurturing, in turn, is known to prevent the potential harmful influences of these gene variants both in humans and nonhuman primates. All of these studies direct focus to both environmental effects and the more primary biophysical properties of each infant's capacity for self-regulation.

The Roots of Regulation

The basic drive of every living organism, including human beings, is to keep itself safe and alive under any circumstances. As already mentioned, survival is buffered with the neurobiological system that is hard-wired for threat and fear-signaling stimuli. Some threats are more fundamental for survival than others; everybody needs nutrition and protection, and the ongoing lack of either of these is fatal. In every level of life it is essential to fight for food, to flee from predators, and to find shelter when needed. Preparedness to react is a deeply inbuilt animate tendency that colors the course of life from the beginning. The mobilization of the body's resources starts when emotional or physical threat destabilizes internal equilibrium. The mobilization of resources is always arousing, and is experienced as a shift toward increasing stress. When equilibrium is regained, this is experienced as a shift toward decreasing stress.

The ability of the nervous system to manage stress responses is the foundation of resilient behavior in varying situations. Inadequate regulation of high arousal during threatening or demanding events increases risk of disintegrative perceptual processes and maladaptive behavioral strategies. Stress responses in mammals are mediated by two interrelated systems: the sympathetic-adrenomedullary (SAM) and the hypothalamic-pituitary-adrenocortical (HPA) systems (Gunnar & Quevedo, 2007). The SAM system is a part of sympathetic autonomic nervous system, and its activation leads to release of adrenaline from the adrenal glands. Increases in circulating adrenaline orchestrate the flight/fight responses. The SAM facilitates the availably of energy to the body's vital organs, and is highly arousing and energy expending. The HPA system's role is to help contain, or shut down, sympathetic activation by producing glucocorticoids (GC), or cortisol in humans. Adrenaline does not cross the blood-brain barrier to a significant degree, whereas the brain is the major target of cortisol (Gunnar & Quevedo, 2007). There is a growing evidence that the inability to regulate stress responses harms brain development in various areas, including the hippocampus and prefrontal cortex, both of which are known to be fundamentally important in learning, memory, and executive functions (Gunnar & Vazques, 2006).

The cascade of events that leads to the production of cortisol by the adrenal cortex begins when environmental stressors activate the limbic brain circuits involving amygdala, hippocampus, and orbital/medial prefrontal cortex. The fast, SAM-mediated responses utilize neurons producing the corticotrophin-releasing hormone (CRH) located in the amygdala, the noradrenergic neurons located in the locus coeruleus, and other aminergic cells in the brain stem (Morilak, Barrera, & Echecarria, 2005). The locus coeruleus regulates the SAM response through its projecting NE-neurons. These pathways pass the lateral hypothalamus and activate the sympathetic preganglionic neurons, unleashing adrenaline from the adrenal medulla. The amygdala and CRH-mediated changes are also activating the HPA response to stressors. Unlike the fast SAM response, HPA-axis stimulating pathways to hypothalamic CRH-producing cells are indirect, operating through multisynaptic pathways via the bed nucleus of the stria terminals that converge on the paraventricular nuclei in the hypothalamus (Herman, Tasker, Ziegler, & Cullinan, 2002). CRH and argine vasopressin (AVP) are released by neurons of the hypothalamus. They travel to the anterior pituitary, where they stimulate the release of adrenocorticotrophic hormone (ACTH). ACTH interacts with the receptors on the cortex of the adrenal gland to stimulate the production and release of GC into circulation in the body and in the brain.

The effect of GCs depends on the receptors with which they bind. There are two GC receptors: mineralocorticoid receptor (MR) and glucocorticoid receptors (GR). In the body, GC is operating through GRs and, in the brain, through both GRs and MRs. In the brain, GC binds more easily to MR than to GS. Variations in the affinities for the receptors are critical in the regulation of both basal and stress responses of the HPA system (Gunnar & Vazquez, 2006). In the brain, MRs are 80–90% occupied when GCs are in basal range. Meanwhile, GRs are occupied at the peak of the circadian cycle or when stressors stimulate GC elevations over basal concentrations. The multiple pathways to hypothalamic CRH-producing neurons allow modulation of the strength of the HPA response in relation to the environmental stressors. A flexible nervous system is able to balance itself with a rapid neurochemical response at the right rime in order to avoid widespread disruption (LeDoux, 2003). The optimal balance of feedback circulation orchestrates the brain development toward increasing resilience.

When the stress system is chronically activated, the feedback system breaks down. Excessive and deficient quantities of cortisol cause apoptosis in the hippocampus and, therefore, a reduced number of cortisol receptors. With fewer receptors for the cortisol to bind with, the hippocampus has difficulty in turning the stress response off. The nervous system reduces the production of cortisol, and, as a consequence, the SAM system increases the production of noradrenalin. Noradrenalin maintains a high arousal level and alertness in the individual. It enhances information processing and suppresses neural activity that is irrelevant to ongoing tasks. Increased noradrenalin levels are connected with behavioral symptoms like irritability, anxiety, and reduced impulse control. These symptoms are prevailing characters in various developmental disorders, including attention deficit and learning difficulties (Teicher et al., 2003; Jarrett & Ollendick, 2008). It can be concluded that an imbalanced feedback system is especially harmful to a developing nervous system, and it may significantly increase the risk for dysfunctions in attention and learning.

The Hierarchical Brain

At the beginning of postnatal life, the brain is the most immature organ in the human being. The maturation of the human brain is much slower than in other primates, and the interplay of nature and nurture has more degrees of freedom.

The brain functions can be described from the perspective of three structural levels: the experiencing lowest level, the feeling midlevel, and the thinking highest level. All of the brain systems in every structural level are continuously interacting with each other. The brain is maturing from bottom to top, and the maturation of the lower levels induces the progression of next ones. The structure of the brain at any time is a product of interactions between genetic, epigenetic, and environmental factors. The structural maturation accelerates the development of regulative control. The structures improving regulation control are not fully matured until early adulthood years. The maturation process is deeply connected with learning capacity in every level of development. A child has to learn an accumulating number of new skills when she is adapting in an increasingly complex environment. The regulation control system channels brain development, and the process is extremely vulnerable during early childhood.

A well-designed regulation system enables an organism to match perception, motor action, and emotional responses to spatial, temporal, social, and affective dimensions of the world. When regulative system fail, it is hard to integrate perception, behavior, and emotion in relation to time and place. Early experiences in being with others lay the foundation for integrative and flexible development, while inadequate care and negative events overload the basic regulative system. When this system fails, it is hard to make a good match between behavior and environmental challenges. In such cases, the developmental course turns toward increasing risk for maladaptive strategies.

The Stone Basis of Regulation—The Brain Stem

The control of brain's regulative systems develops step by step. The most active part of the central nervous system at birth, the experiencing lowest level, is situated in the brain stem and in the core of cerebellum. The brain stem takes charge of basic regulative functions during the lifespan, and it synthesizes most of the components in the emotional system. The reactions are always immediate, fast, and unconscious. The brain stem keeps us alive by continuously scanning the environment and maintaining homeostasis in the case of possible threats. It acts also as an accumulator, loading energy to every part of the organism.

The brain stem contains the reticular activation system, which maintains an alert and aroused state when needed and which regulates basic sensory functions. Cranial nerves run along the brain stem, and they control breathing, blood circulation, digestion, calming effects, and facial expressions. Many important neurotransmitter-producing, basic orientation, and body representation nuclei are located in the brain stem.

The ability to regulate is innate in the case of vital functions like breathing or heartbeat. Brain stem structures regulate motor, sensory, and emotional states. Visual, auditory, tactile, and all the other sensory impulses pass through those areas. The brain stem gives a sense of the body in its surrounding and is the base of sensory-motor self-representation. The proprioseptive system in the brain stem provides information from the body's position in space and helps to modulate muscle tone and balance, which is fundamental in posture control and in the battle against the gravity.

Minor damages or dysfunctions in the brain stem can harm integrative and coordinated development, because the input to later-maturing brain areas is insufficient or inadequate. The possible role of brain stem dysfunction is evidenced by the fact that difficulty to regulate alertness is a known problem in attention deficits (Lecendreux, Konofal, Bouvard, Falissard, & Mouren-Siméoni, 2003; Cao et al., 2008). In addition, visuospatial impairments implicate a dysfunction to make a perfect match for body position, motor action, and perceptual goals (Dobler et al., 2001).

The Second-Order Regulation—The Dienchephalon and the Limbic System

Structures in the dienchephalon and in the limbic system take control over brain stem regulation a few weeks after birth. The dienchephalon consists of the thalamus, hypothalamus, and basal ganglia. The thalamus collects signals from the body and the sensory organs and distributes them to limbic and neocortical areas, including prefrontal cortex. The thalamus distributes impulses from the cerebellum to the basal ganglia and to the motor cortex. Thalamic pathways are deeply involved in orientation and attention, and they are fundamental in thinking, automated movements, memory, and emotions. As the thalamus collects visual, auditory, vestibular, and other sensory inputs, it is the place where coherent proprioceptive sensation appears. While the thalamus monitors the outside world, the hypothalamus monitors and regulates an organism's internal states in order to keep them in adaptive and balanced level. The hypothalamus acts as the central regulator of bodily responses to relevant environmental events.

The basal ganglia in the diencephalon organize motor skills, and they regulate the acts that are going to be executed. The basal ganglia respond with motor activity to natural rewards and threatening stimuli, and their activation causes excitement. The basal ganglia are closely connected to the prefrontal cortex and the limbic system.

While the lower structures of the brain are hard-wired to control involuntary perception and action, the limbic system mediates learning and memory. The information flow from sensory input to motor outputs is slowed down in the limbic system so that responses can be fitted more accurately to the learned aspects of situations. This slowdown amplifies the meaning of emotions in the course of development by mediating emotional states that orient attention and action to whatever is currently important. The amygdale and the hippocampus are key structures in limbic systems.

Early Interaction Modifies Regulation

At the beginning of life, an infant shows incredible readiness to join to the social world. From birth on, a child is interacting with the social environment with developing sensory capacities, especially with smell, taste, and touch (Trevarthen, 2011). Auditory stimuli are also known to be important in early development. In addition, these senses are the channels for receiving regulative protection. Some voices and rhythms are known to be more calming than the others, and a baby's arousal usually decreases when it is held gently. However, visual stimuli are supposed to have less impact on developing sensory systems and on equilibrium maintenance during first weeks of life. One significant exception among visual stimuli is an infant's striking ability to prefer faces and to imitate different facial expressions. This innate leaning toward imitation is thought to reflect the existence of a mirror-neuron system (Lepage & Theoret, 2007) that is activated in forthcoming interactive processes. The activation of the mirror-neuron system is fundamental for the development of language, social capacities, and cognition.

In spite of innate predispositions to be social, an infant is extremely vulnerable and fully at the mercy of others for protection. During the first weeks of life, most of a baby's energy is needed to adapt physiological process to match its new environment. In a new environment, a baby's arousal levels shift easily, challenging both the SAM and HPA systems. In the case of hunger, thirst, loneliness, fear, and numerous other alarming events, an infant's need for a protective other is absolute. The brain systems that mediate the equilibrium maintenance are developing rapidly in infancy, and this development is directly and significantly influenced by early interaction with protective others. Attuned and sensitive care helps an infant to balance the activation of SAM and HPA systems, providing experiences that are supposed to participate in shaping ongoing synaptic formation in developing limbic-autonomic circuits (Rinaman, Levitt, & Card, 2000).

The experience-dependent maturation of a baby's brain allows the emergence of more complex functional capacities to cope with stressors. The infant utilizes its maturing motor and developing sensory capacities to interact more vividly with the social environment. By the end of the second month, there is significant progression in the infant's social and emotional capacities. Her challenges and capabilities to organize new learning and to adapt to a rapidly changing environment are modified by interaction processes, which are continuously influencing the maturation of connections within her limbic system. It has been proposed that limbic networks are formed through ontogenic plasticity, which means natural selection of those regulative connections that match the environmental stimuli. In other words, the child learns to calibrate her biological reactivity to the context. The first two years of life are crucial for incorporating regulative skills, because limbic areas in the cortex and subcortex are rapidly growing during this time (Cicchetti & Tucker, 1994).

Limbic areas form an emotional circuit that consists of connections between cingulate gyrus, the hippocampus, the hypothalamus, and the thalamus. The circuit includes also parts of the prefrontal cortex, the brain stem, the basal ganglia, and the amygdale. The emotional circuit mediates stress-coping capacities throughout the lifetime, thus, early stress-inducing and stress-regulative events have long-lasting effects on brain development and emerging capacities.

The Importance of Gazing

Numerous brain studies have documented a developmental shift in brain functions at about eight weeks of age. At this point, a rapid metabolic change occurs in the primary visual cortex, and the importance of visual experiences in modifying synaptic connections grows. An infant turns out to be intensively interested in faces and the number of mutual gazing periods increases. It has been said that face-to face interactions are highly arousing, affect-laden events that expose infants to high levels of cognitive and social information (Feldman, 2006). During those episodes, the caregiver is synchronizing the infant's emotional states by smiling when the baby smiles and by cooling the baby down when she is overexcited.

Mutual gazing episodes are also building blocks for emerging social play, which is known to be essential for integrative development of thinking, language, and social abilities. During the gazing episodes, changes in the infant's arousal are followed by the caregiver's feedback in a sequencelike manner. This is a dialogue of visual and auditory signals in which both are matching states of emotions and adjusting their social attention, stimulation, and accelerating arousal to each other's responses (Schore, 2001). Synchronized interaction amplifies limbic emotional circuits including cingulate gyrus, which is rapidly maturing at the age of six to eight months.

Cingulate gyrus is a fundamental structure in emotional perception, and its posterior part regulates social behavior, attachment behavior, and the capacity for play. Damage to that area interrupts the drive to play and to generate mental images. Diminished or disorganized play behavior is known to be a common feature in developmental disorders like specific language disorder and attention deficits (Sajaniemi, Suhonen, & Kontu, 2008; Farrant, Maybery, & Fletcher, 2011). Ability to play is essential for developing social and cognitive skills, and decreased play behavior indicates a risk for developmental disorders (Naber et al., 2008). Paying attention to the quality of adult–child interaction might be a simple and effective way to prevent developmental disorders.

Consistent and synchronized feedback to emotional shifts has a significant effect on modification of synaptic connections in the maturing brain. The sequences of "something exciting is happening" and "excitement is decreasing" are consolidated into neural limbic circuits known as procedural, implicit memory, or body memory. An infant learns with time that arousal is not necessarily dangerous and that existence of other people can reflect safety. She finds out that negative emotions are followed by positive emotions. Processes of reexperiencing positive emotions teach the child that negativity can be endured and conquered (Schore & Schore, 2008). The repetitive nature of interactive events shape neural networks, which are reactivated in situations that have features in common with previous ones. Reactivating neural networks are, according to Stern, representation of interactions that have been generalized, or RIG. A RIG is a firing pattern that represents an average of various experiences, which is something that never happened in exactly that way and which is continuously updated on the basis of current experiences (Beebe & Lachmann, 1988). RIGs can be understood as a part of an implicit memory system that is modulating preattentive processes via value-based expectations. They are like internal working models that help to navigate in complex environments and that can create a sense of safety. If care is sufficiently consistent and synchronized, the RIGs are flooded with appropriate and coherent emotions. Internal working models like RIGs are the basis of emerging higher-order self-regulative skills. Children learn to remember that emotional shifts are a part of everyday life and that they can be dealt with.

On the other hand, if baby's arousal is frequently increased with ruptures in care, negative emotions associate with coincident events on the basis of temporal proximity. Emotional associations are strong and long lasting, because the amygdale produces fear responses independent of the cortex, or, in other words, without thinking, reasoning, or interpreting. When something in the environment is highly alarming for the baby, the other stimuli in that context are also flooding the infant's aroused brain. If the regulative other is not available, it is possible that the neural activity induced by contextual perceptions will synchronize with the state of anxiety. As a consequence, stimuli associated with negative feelings can evoke arousal even in an objectively safe environment. In such cases, development might be channeled toward increasing stress reactivity when subcortical networks are activated independently of higher cognitive functions. Sensitization for stressors amplifies tendency for chronic anxiety and panic attacks, and dampens explorative behavior, thus jeopardizing balanced development. In addition, if children are living in a disorganized and careless environment, the coherence of experiences is lost. These children might have difficulties in forming stable internal representations to facilitate the development of self-regulative skills.

Face-to face transactions also have other crucial effects on development. It has been revealed in a growing number of studies that the mirror-neuron system in the human brain has a fundamental role in social cognition, language acquisition, and mentalizing behavior. Mirror neurons belong to networks of premotor frontal executive areas, and they are activated by sensory, especially visual, stimuli associated with the intentional actions they represent. Very little is known about the mirror-neuron system in children, but some studies have suggested that some elements of the mirror-neuron system, such as imitation, are innate (Meltzoff & Decety, 2003; Rizzolatti 2004). Young infants are able to imitate oral movements, such as sticking out their tongue, when they see someone else doing the same. The neurons establish the connection between the motor cortex, sensations in the mouth, and the sight of another person's lips and tongue. Imitation studies have also documented that infants are able to distinguish between happy, sad, and surprised facial expressions (Toda & Fogel, 1993).

Recent mirror-neuron studies have shown that observation of an interesting and affect-laden act causes an especially strong activation in the premotor cortex. The activation prepares an action that is not necessarily executed. This impulse to act is not volitional; however, it indicates that the other person's behavior has been perceived. In addition, during interaction periods, the activation of the child's premotor system is recognized by the person who acts, which further influences the behavior of both.

The vast amount of data collected in recent years has highlighted that the mirror-neuron system is flexible and that experience modulates its functioning (Hari & Nishitani, 2004; Calvo-Merino, Glasier, Crezes, Passingham, & Haggart, 2005). Visually shared moments at early infancy might be essential in tuning the mirror-neuron system. When a baby smiles and the caregiver responds, the brain sets up a circuit linking the motor system that turns up the corners of the baby's mouth to the visual image of the smiling other to the positive emotional state. After a few recurrences of these episodes, the perception of a smiling face is sufficient for evoking the positive feeling. The other person's mood can thus be transferred through an unconscious motor imitation of the facial expressions, gestures, and other nonverbal signs. Seeing a friendly, angry, or fearful face can lead to activation of facial muscles and to expression of similar feeling. The activation of the mirror-neuron system is thus a prerequisite for state-sharing and empathy. It probably also has a fundamental impact on development of self-regulation, perceptual organization, and language.

Pleasant face-to-face communication enhances optimal development in various other ways as well. Seeing positive facial expressions activates the opioid system and amplifies the feeling that the current event is good and useful. Increased levels of brain opioids activate the dopamine system, which boosts stimulus seeking and interested involvement with the world. High opioid levels lead to sense of safety, and low levels in turn cause a search for care and safety. The role of social, synchronized interactions in channeling early development can hardly be ignored. Developmental dysfunctions and learning disorders should always be considered cumulative difficulties to match the behavior to environmental changes and demands.

Self-Regulation and Perceptual Organization

Curiosity is a prerequisite for explorative behavior. The world beyond the instant moment is exciting for an infant whose previous experiences are limited and who cannot anticipate what is out there. With the help of a protective other, the infant finds out that arousal is not dangerous and that it can be associated with joy or learning. The shifts in the infant's emotional state are regulated by the other in moments of shared attention in which two brains are activated at the same time in reaction to mutually shared interest. In these dyadic states, the brains are amplifying and coregulating each other's activity, and the infant's brain capacity is pushed toward new integrative skills. The importance of shared visual attention is further underlined by the fact that it promotes the growth of dopamine-induced neurons, especially in basal ganglia and prefrontal brain regions.

Optimum dopamine-induced activation is essential in initiation of movements and in feelings of involvement and excitement. The dopamine system stimulates the reward centers in the brain through the opioid system, and it is fundamental in brain development and plasticity. Disorders in the dopamine system lead to a lack of involvement, pleasure, and motivation. A growing amount of studies has shown that some developmental disorders, such as attention deficits, are linked to decreased dopamine levels and difficulties to sustain volitional motivation unless the task is highly activating. However, children with attention deficit might demonstrate remarkable concentration and motivation when they are dealing with events that they have preexperienced as extremely rewarding. It is important to take into account that unmotivated and inattentive children might have a lack of emotionally coherent interactions, and therefore have fragile connections between subcortical and cortical areas. They are unable to force themselves to keep up motivation by using "willpower," and they certainly need reconstructive experiences in being with others.

A child has to learn how to navigate efficiently toward the goal. The human brain is hard-wired for continuous and mostly unconscious cost–benefit analysis of environmental stimuli that are guiding behavior. An organism tends to avoid stimuli that are associated with unpleasant sensations or feelings and to approach stimuli that arouse positive feelings. The sensations, perceptions, and behavior in the present moment are always colored by past experiences. Fonagy et al., (1996) have pointed out that experiences are encoded by brain networks whose connections have already been shaped by the previous encounters with the world. Preexisting knowledge influences encoding and storing new memories and is essential for the organization of social, emotional, and cognitive development. When a child feels herself safe in an environment, she has the courage to seek new experiences, which are continuously changing and merging the activation of existing neural networks and thus creating potential for increasingly complex cognitive processes.

Intentional behavior develops step by step. It is controlled by two interconnected, developmentally maturing bottom-up and top-down systems. These both vertically and horizontally integrating neural networks unfold the brain from brain stem levels to posterior and anterior areas of the brain. Bottom-up control is perceptual and based on unceasing feedback information from sensory events; its goal is to define perceptions and to focus preattention toward emotionally meaningful objects.

During bottom-up processes, sensory inputs move through the lower levels of the brain toward higher, more complex levels. A sensation depends also on expectations, and prior notions affect perceptual impressions. When an event takes on particular meaning or value, the emotional experience provides increased energy and attention. Events perceived as good or bad wire the executive frontal areas that are aimed at controlling motor actions by top-down processes. Top-down processes prepare the organism to respond by either engaging in activities or withdrawing from stimuli.

Top-down processes are controlled by anticipatory feedforward (Fuster, 2003). Anticipatory feedforward enhances the efficacy of executive actions with accumulating experiences when a child is exposed to various kinds of events and objects in a rich enough environment. Fuster (2003) depicts continuously circulating perception–action cycles, which are bases of increasing complexity of information processing and of behavior. Piaget has suggested that the emerging reasoning has its foundations in early developing sensory-motor schemas, which can be understood as perception–motor cycles.

Bottom-up processes emerge from early developing brain stem structures that have limited complexity and plasticity. On the contrary, later developing neocortical areas are characterized by a high degree of complexity and plasticity. The connectivity of subcortical regions increases extensively with the development of the neocortex, thus enabling top-down processes. These networks contribute with the potential to inhibit and delay responses, which is of fundamental importance in learning and motivation. Top-down control processes are needed in all volitional behavior, and fragile connections between subcortical and neocortical areas are behind all executive breakdowns.

As the central nervous system develops, children are pushed forward toward higher levels of complexity in order to master themselves in the current environment. Experience-dependent plasticity enables children to gain information specific to the exact environment of which they are a part. This amazing plasticity opens the way to necessary adaptability to learn and develop in different environments.

Assimilation and Accommodation of Experiences

The more the child has opportunities and courage to orient toward novelty and to explore the environment, the more flexible perception–motor cycles are generated. Each new perception–motor cycle attains stability when a child assimilates events into previous experiences. Besides perceptual control, assimilation requires top-down processes with anticipatory feedforward that prepares motor reactions toward the best possible match with the goal. The accuracy and efficiency of goal-directed actions sharpens with repetition until a child has stabilized a perception–motor cycle, in other words, until a child has learned a new skill. In the process of assimilation, new and old experiences are fusing together, causing synchronization and integration of involved cycles, which promotes brain development. When perception–motor cycles are activated and synchronized in relation to environmental input, perceptual and motor neurons fire simultaneously; they are resonating.

When the neural activity caused by an outside stimulus fails to match previous patterns of perception–motor cycles without completely missing the mark, it sparks new processes. Behaviorally, it means that the child has to accommodate her actions for reaching a goal. The difference between the new and old experiences creates learning, which makes the perception–motor cycles involved in the experience stronger and more specific. They connect in growing networks within an increasingly integrated brain system.

Higher-Order Regulation and the Integrative Brain

Intentional, adaptive, and resilient behavior requires well-developed vertical and hierarchical integration of connections between the brain and the body. Optimal functioning is attained with sufficient coherence of experiences and with utilization of intuitions based on implicit memories. The maturation of cortex depends on stimulation of deeper parts of the brain, which continuously register body responses, such as changes in internal organs. The areas in the right hemisphere have better access to autonomic nervous system and body-sensing structures than do the areas in the left hemisphere. Emotional information is largely processed and regulated in the right orbitofrontal cortex during the whole lifetime. Childhood experiences act as an anchor to which all of the following experiences are attached in one way or another.

The right orbitofrontal cortex has excessive connections with underlying limbic systems, and it has dormant potential to inhibit and control intensive emotional arousal when needed. Inhibitory activation relieves the organism from the pressure to react immediately to emotional signals. It is prerequisite for the emerging ability to interpret emotional signals and to regulate emotional expressions in various social contexts. Inhibitory control is essential in motivated, goal-directed behavior.

The processes of the right hemisphere are mainly unconscious, and they enable the organism to grasp the essential emotional content of a situation. The activation of the right hemisphere marks the environment with emotional labels. Emotional labels are like glue that holds perceptions and actions together. They are the means of categorization and the bases of representations of interaction that has been generalized (RIG). The maturing sense of a coherent self, subjectivity, and ability to reflect on one's own actions are intuitive processes that are based on right-sided brain activity.

The right hemisphere matures earlier that the left, and it is dominant during the first three years of life. The different maturation rates of the hemispheres have a significant effect on child development. The processes of the right hemisphere are nonverbal, and children form representations based on spatial and temporal proximity of stimuli. The maturation of the hippocampus in cooperation with other limbic parts accelerates at the end of the first year of life, enabling the formation of explicit memories about time, place, and specific events. These memories are associated with internal body states, which are regulated in interaction with others. The early consolidation of perception–action cycles is the base of body-image and an emerging sense of self. The optimal functioning and maturation requires emotional arousal that is neither too low nor too high. Both extremes hamper strengthening and organization of neural connections, which has jeopardizing effects on development. Difficulties in maintaining coherent body-image and in controlling bodily movements in relation to space are common problems in children with developmental dysfunctions. Helping these children to master movement in space might boost integrative development.

The left hemisphere begins its growth spurt around the age of 18 months when the development of language is accelerated. Around the same time, the orbitofrontal cortex and large parts of the neocortex are rapidly maturing. With the maturing hippocampal connections, children's ability to recall events begins to develop. The connections between the right and left hemispheres are strengthening, and the child learns to label perceptions and actions with symbols. The increasing activation of the left hemisphere facilitates further interpretation and synthesizing of experienced events. The functions of the left hemisphere are fundamental in conscious reflection of behavior and in expressing feelings and thoughts through language. The explanation of experiences is delegated to the left hemisphere. In optimal development, explanations incorporate the emotional processes of the right hemisphere. The mutual cooperation of both hemispheres facilitates the integration of bodily states to perception–action cycles.

Developmental Dysfunction as a Consequence of Nonoptimal Adaptation

Developmental dysfunctions can be understood as consequences of maladaptive strategies to environment. It is important to keep in mind that the roots of maladaptive strategies are deep in an individual's developmental history. No developmental dysfunction extends in isolation, and comorbidity is rather a rule than an exception. Difficulties in adjusting to environment involve, besides emotional dysregulation, a mismatch between perception and action. This mismatch is evidenced by a number of studies revealing visuospatial difficulties in children with language impairments, attention deficits, and dysfunctions in motor coordination (Cummins, Piek, & Dyck, 2005; Dobler et al., 2005). Visuospatial abilities, as well as unconscious emotional regulation, are processed primarily in early maturating areas in the right hemisphere. Sufficient ability to regulate bodily states shapes the neurobiological environment, thus enhancing the consolidation on perception–action cycles.

A growing amount of evidence suggests the existence of a motor resonance mechanism in and between humans, which may be in the background of perception–action cycles. Motor resonance merges neuronal circuitry associated with the performance and observation of actions. The core of this neural system includes the posterior region of the inferior frontal gyrus (IFG) and the part of the inferior parietal lobule (Rizzolatti, 2004). These mirror areas are part of a complex network receiving afferents from the superior temporal sulcus (STS), where biological motion is processed, and sending efferents to the motor cortex. These anatomical and functional findings imply that visual and motor spaces are closely associated. Representations of executed and observed actions are related, and they are innately linked together, since the mere observation of a movement is shown to be sufficient to elicit activation of corresponding motor programs from very early on. This active intermodal mapping system assumes that imitation of infants is the result of a representational system that matches visual input into its proprioceptive and motor equivalent (Meltzoff & Moore, 1997).

Previous findings confirm the crucial importance of the social world in children's development. Vygotsky, a world famous pioneer of developmental psychology, was already on the right track in emphasizing co-construction in learning and development. Vygotskian tradition points out the importance and primary nature of observed intentionality in learning and development. According to Vygotsky and his followers, a child is observing the social world from the very beginning. The child is then focusing on a person who is doing something. In the moments when another person is responding to the child, the objects of observation are shared. Shared moments involve activity with intentions, and a child learns that activity is intertwined with intentions. As Vygotsky has emphasized, observation and imitation of others intentional activity is the base of all learning. These path-breaking ideas are nicely compatible with findings of mirror-neuron system and theories of neural resonance.

Another clinically and educationally significant theorem of Vygotsky is the *zone of proximal development*, or ZPD. The lower limit of ZPD refers to the level of ability reached by the child and what she can already apply independently. The upper limit refers to the level of an emerging ability that the child can accept with the assistance of a more experienced other. The ZPD captures the child's cognitive abilities that are in the process of maturing and can be accomplished only with the assistance of a more-skilled person. Acting in the ZPD is always arousing. According to Vygotsky, learning is inevitably uncomfortable at the beginning. Children's immature emotional regulation systems are challenged, and the need for an adult is magnified.

ZPD is the place where the child and adult meet. Scaffolding is a concept closely related to this; it means changing the level of support. Over the course of shared moments, a more-skilled person adjusts the amount of support to fit the child's current performance. In the other words, adults are guiding children toward performing actions or tasks that are just beyond children's current capacity. With such guidance, children can perform beyond their own capacity, and they learn. Dialogue is an important tool of this process in the zone of proximal development. In a dialogue, intentions and emotion are shared, and the unsystematic, disorganized, and spontaneous concepts of a child are met with the more systematic, logical, and rational concepts of the skilled helper.

Underscoring children's autonomy and independence in learning process can reduce possibilities to function in ZPD. The importance of a sensitive and responsive adult in learning is even more crucial when children have increased risk for developmental disabilities. Known developmental risks are preterm birth, neonatal complications, extremes in temperament, and psychosocial loads, as well as many others. Clinical experience and scientific reports have evidenced that neuropsychological dysfunctions are often associated with extremes in behavior. For example, fearful children are commonly evaluated as having visuospatial difficulties. Fearful temperament might narrow the focus of perception and action. When combined with insufficient experiences of being with protective others, development of regulative brain areas and organization of perceptions might be compromised. The cascade leads to lack of experiences and, therefore, fragile perception–action cycles. When experiences are not properly processed in the right hemispheric areas, there may be an increasing mismatch between experiences, interpretation, and verbal labeling. In such cases, development is channeled toward cumulative disadvantages.

Conclusively, children's need for adults is absolute. Psychological developments of early childhood are so important that they cannot be left to chance.

References

Beebe, B., & Lachmann, F. M. (1988). The contribution of mother-infant mutual influence to the origins of self- and object representations. *Psychoanalytic Psychology, 5*(4), 305–337.

Boyce, W.T., & Ellis, B.J. (2005). Biological sensitivity to context: I. an evolutionary–developmental theory of the origins and functions of stress reactivity. *Development and Psychopathology, 17*(2), 271.

Bryson, S.E., Zweigenbaum, L., Brian, J., Roberts, W., Szatmari, P., Rombough, V. & McDermott, C. (2007). A prospective case series of high-risk infants who developed autism. *Journal of Autism and Developmental Disorders, 37*(1), 12.

Calvo-Merino, B., Glasier, D., Crezes, J., Passingham, R., & Haggart, P. (2005). Action observation and acquired motor skills: An fMRI study with expert dancers. *Cerebral Cortex, 15*(8), 1243–1249.

Cao, Q., Zang, Y., Zhu, C., Cao, X., Sun, L., Zhou, X., & Wanga, Y. (2008). Alerting deficits in children with attention deficit/hyperactivity disorder: Event-related fMRI evidence. *Brain Research, 1219*, 159.

Caspi, A., Sudgen, K., Muffit, T., Taylor, A., Graig, I., Harrington, H., McClay, J., Mill, J., Martin, J., Braithwaite, A., & Poulton, R. (2003). Influence of life stress on depression: Moderation by a polymorphism in the 5-HTT gene. *Science, 301*(5631), 386.

Cicchetti, D., & Tucker, D. (1994). Development and self-regulatory structures of the mind. *Development and Psychopathology, 6*(4), 533.

Crittenden, P. (2006). A Dynamic-Maturational Model of Attachment. *Australian and New Zealand Journal of Family Therapy, 27*(2), 105–115.

Cummins, A., Piek, J.P., & Dyck, M.J. (2005). Motor coordination, empathy, and social behaviour in school-aged children. *Developmental Medicine & Child Neurology, 47*(7), 437–442.

Damasio, A.R. (1994). *Descartes' Error: emotion, reason, and the human brain.* New York: Putnam Publishing.

Dobler, V.B., Anker, S., Gilmore, J., Robertson, I.H., Atkinson, J., & Manly, T. (2005). Asymmetric deterioration of spatial awareness with diminishing levels of alertness in normal children and children with ADHD. *Journal of Child Psychology & Psychiatry, 46*(11), 1230–1248.

Dobler, V., Manly, T., Atkinson, J., Wilson, B.A., Ioannou, K., & Robertson, I.H. (2001). Interaction of hand use and spatial selective attention in children. *Neuropsychologia, 39*(10), 1055–1064.

Farrant, B., Maybery, M., & Fletcher, J. (2011). Socio-emotional engagement, joint attention, imitation, and conversation skill: Analysis in typical development and specific language impairment. *First Language, 31*(1), 23–46.

Feldman, R. (2006). From biological rhythms to social rhythms: Physiological precursors of mother-infant synchrony. *Developmental Psychology, 42*(1), 175.

Foley, D., Eavers, L., Wormley, B., & Silberg, J. (2004). Childhood adversity, monoamine oxidase: A genotype, and risk for conduct disorder. *Archives of General Psychiatry, 61*(7), 738.

Fonagy, P., Leigh, T., Steele, M., Steele, H., Kennedy, R., Mattoon, G., Target, M., & Gerber, A. (1996). The relation of attachment status, psychiatric classification, and response to psychotherapy. *Journal of Consulting and Clinical Psychology, 64*(1), 22–31.

Fox, N.A., Henderson, H., Marshall, P., Nichols, K., & Ghera, M. (2005). Behavioral inhibition: Linking biology and behavior within a developmental framework. *Annual Review of Psychology, 56*(1), 235.

Fuster, J. (2003). *Cortex and mind.* Oxford University Press.

Gunnar, M., & Quevedo, K. (2007). The neuro biology of stress and development. *Annual Review of Psychology, 58*(1), 145–173.

Gunnar, M., & Vazquez, D. (2006). *Stress neurobiology and developmental psychopathology.* In D. Cicchetti & D. Cohen (Eds.) *Developmental psychopathology: Developmental neuoscience* (pp. 533–577) New York: Wiley.

Hari, R., & Nishitani, N. (2004). From viewing of movement to imitation and understanding of other persons' acts: MEG studies of the human mirror-neuron system. In Kanwisher, N. & Duncan, J. (Eds.), *Functional neuroimaging of visual cognition: Attention and performance.* Oxford: Oxford University Press.

Herman, J., Tasker, J., Ziegler, D., & Cullinan, W. (2002). Local circuit regulation of paraventricular nucleus stress integration: Glutamate-GABA connections. *Pharmacology, Biochemistry and Behavior, 71*(3), 457.

Jarrett, M.A., & Ollendick, D.H. (2008). A conceptual review of the comorbidity of attention-deficit/hyperactivity disorder and anxiety:

Implications for future research and practice. *Clinical Psychology Review, 28*(7), 1266.

Kagan, J. (1997). Temperament and the reactions to unfamiliarity. *Child Development, 68*(1), 139–143.

LeDoux, J. (2003). The emotional brain, fear, and the amygdala. *Cellular and Molecular Neurobiology, 23*(4/5), 727.

Lecendreux, M., Konofal, E., Bouvard, M., Falissard, B., Mouren-Siméoni, M-C. (2003). Sleep and alertness in children with ADHD. *Journal of Child Psychology and Psychiatry, 41*(6), 803–812.

Lepage, J.F., & Theoret, H. (2007). The mirror neuron system: Grasping others' actions from birth? *Developmental Science, 10*(5), 513.

Meltzoff, A., & Decety, J. (2003). What imitation tells us about social cognition. A rapproachement between developmental psychology and cognitive neuroscience. *Philosophical Transactions of the Royal Society of London, 358*, 491–500.

Melzoff, A., & Moore, M.K. (1997). Explaining facial imitation: A theoretical model. *Early Development and Parenting, 6*, 179–192.

Morilak, D., Barrera, G., & Echecarria, A. (2005). Role of brain norepinephrine in the behavioral response to stress. *Progress in Neuro-Psychopharmacology Biological Psychiatry, 29*(8), 1214.

Naber, F., Brakermans-Kranenburg, M., IJzendoorn, M., Swinkles, S., Buitelaar, J., Dietz, C., Daalen, E., & van Engeland, H. (2008). Play behavior and attachment in toddlers with autism. *Journal of Autism and Developmental Disorders, 38*(5), 857.

Nigg, J.T. (2000). On inhibition/disinhibition in developmental psychopathology: Views from cognitive and personality psychology and a working inhibition taxonomy. *Psychological Bulletin, 126*(2), 220.

Ochsner, K.N., Bunge, S.A., Gross, J.J., & Gabriele, J.D.E. (2002). Rethinking feelings: An fMRI study of the cognitive regulation of emotion. *Journal of Cognitive Neuroscience, 14*(8), 1215.

Perez-Edgar, K., Robenson-Nay, R., Hardin, M., Poeth, K., Gryer, A., Nelson, E.,. McClure, E., …. & Ernst, M. (2007). Attention alters neural responses to evocative faces in behaviorally inhibited adolescents. *NeuroImage, 35*(4), 1538.

Raine, A., Venables, P., & Mednick, S. (1997). Low resting heart rate at age 3 years predisposes to aggression at age 11 years: Evidence from the mauritius child health project. *Journal of the American Academy of Child Adolescent Psychiatry, 36*(10), 1457.

Rinaman, L., Levitt, P., & Card, J.P. (2000). Progressive postnatal assembly of limbic-autonomic circuits revealed by central transneuronal transport of pseudorabies virus. *The Journal of Neuroscience, 20*(7), 2731.

Rizzolatti, G. (2004). A unifying view of the basis of social cognition. *Trends in Cognitive Sciences, 8*, 396–403.

Robinson, G. (2008). Genes and social behavior. *Science, 322*(5903), 896.

Rosen, J.B., & Schulkin, J. (1998). From normal fear to pathological anxiety. *Psychological Review, 105*(2), 325.

Rothbart, M.K., & Bates, J.E. (Eds.). (1998). *Temperament.* New York: John Wiley & Sons.

Rothbart, M.K., & Jones, L. (1998). Temperament, self-regulation, and education. *School Psychology Review, 27*, 479.

Rothbart, M.K., Sheese, B.E., & Posner, M.I. (2007). Executive attention and effortful control: Linking temperament, brain networks, and genes. *Child Development Perspectives, 1*(1), 2.

Rubin, K.H., Burgess, K., Dwyer, K., & Hastings, P. (2003). Predicting preschoolers' externalizing behaviors from toddler temperament, conflict, and maternal negativity. *Developmental Psychology, 39*(1), 164.

Sajaniemi, N., Suhonen, E., & Kontu, E. (2008). Verbal and non-verbal development in SLI children after early intervention. *Early Child Development and Care, 180*(4), 519–534.

Schore, A.N. (2001). Effects of a secure attachment relationship on right brain development, affect regulation, and infant mental health. *Infant Mental Health Journal, 22*(1–2), 7.

Schore, J., & Schore, A. (2008). Modern attachment theory: The central role of affect regulation in development and treatment. *Clinical Social Work Journal, 36*(1), 9–20.

Stifter, C.A., Putnam, S., & Jahrom, L. (2008). Exuberant and inhibited toddlers: Stability of temperament and risk for problem behavior. *Development and Psychopathology, 20*(2), 401.

Suomi, S.J. (1997). Early determinants of behaviour: Evidence from primate studies. *British Medical Bulletin, 53*(1), 170.

Teicher, M.H., Andersen, S.L., Polcari, A., Anderson, C.M., Navalta, C.P. & Kim, D.M.,(2003). The neurobiological consequences of early stress and childhood maltreatment. *Neuroscience and Biobehavioral Reviews, 27*(1): 33.

Toda, S., & Fogel, A. (1993). Infant response to the still-face situation at 3 and 6 months. *Developmental Psychology, 29*(3), 532–538.

Trevarthen, C. (2011). What young children give to their learning, making education work to sustain a community and its culture. *European Early Childhood Education Research Journal, 19*(2), 173–193.

Whittle, S., Yusel, M., Fornito, A., Barrett, A., Wood, S., Lubman, D., Simmons, J., Pantelis, C., & Allen, N.B. (2008). Neuroanatomical correlates of temperament in early adolescents. *Journal of the American Academy of Child Adolescent Psychiatry, 47*(6), 682.

Zuckerman, M., & Kuhlman, D. (2000). Personality and risk-taking: Common bisocial factors. *Journal of Personality, 68*(6), 999.

4

Motivational Regulation and Its Effect on Mental Processing in Neuropsychiatric Disorders

A Rehabilitation Perspective

Liisa Paavola and Jukka Loukkola

Introduction

Neuropsychiatric symptoms cause difficulties and misery in social relationships: Motivational, emotional, physiological, and cognitive balancing, as well as the equilibrium in mental self-regulation, are disturbed. The neuroanatomy of neuropsychiatry lies on the understanding of the functions of the limbic system in the brain (Heimer, Van Hoesen, Trimble, & Zahm, 2008), as well as the connections and networks to the higher cortical regions. The strict division between "the brain" and "the mind" is demanding, if not impossible, when trying to understand neuropsychiatric symptoms and their meaning in everyday life as a clinician in the neuropsychotherapeutic rehabilitation process. The key can be found when the process of motivational regulation and its losses can be expressed and analyzed in a reciprocal contact, and the therapist is able to find words, meanings, and understanding for the chaos in his patient's life.

Motivational regulation involves cognitive and emotional knowledge about the state of mind and body functions. Motivation can be defined as the potential for behaviour that is built into a system of behaviour control (Borod, 2000). Cognition is the information-handling aspect of behaviour (Lezak, 2004). Emotion is the readout of motivational potential when activated by challenging stimulus (Borod, 2000). Both the affective and motivational inputs have an important role in the registration of memories (Fuster, 2003).

In the human brain, there are several frontal-subcortical circuits (FSC), which mediate both motor activity and behaviour in humans (Baliki, Geha, Apkarian, & Chiavlo, 2008). They connect the specific areas of the frontal cortex to certain lower brain structures, which are crucial in motivational regulation. These areas are activated in both planning and execution of motor acts and in cognitive, emotional, and sensory processes (Lichter & Cummings, 2001; Tekin & Cummings, 2002). This includes emotional regulation and decision making, as well as mediating motivated attention and preparation to action. Reciprocal connections from the cortex to lower brain structures engage the somatic and autonomous reflexes that primarily evolved to ensure the survival of individuals and species (Lang & Davis, 2006). The motivational network in the brain is connected with human emotion. The same brain structures are involved in the regulation of physiological, cognitive, and emotional acts (Davidson, 2000; Adolphs, 2002; Bechara et al., 2003; Sheenan et al., 2004). The connecting brain structures may trigger behavioural responses appropriate to maintain a desired state of the cardiovascular system (Pollatos, Schandry, Auer, & Kaufmann, 2007). The meaning of this regulation will be explained.

In the regulation of motivation, an important fronto-subcortical circuit includes the anterior cingulate cortex (ACC), the structure that is critical for the interaction between cognition and emotion (Matthews et al., 2004). ACC functions during cognitive processing are closely linked to modulation of heart rate variability (HRV) and the activity of the autonomous nervous system (Kimmerly et al., 2007). The autonomic nervous system is the most important signalling system of the human body. The autonomic nervous system yields information of both physiological and psychological regulation mechanisms (Tulppo et al., 2005a, 2005b). HRV has been used as an index to predict cognitive performance in healthy adults: High HRV is associated with better performance in tasks involving executive functioning (Hansen et al., 2003, 2004). Executive functions are general-purpose control mechanisms that modulate the operation of various cognitive subprocesses and regulate the dynamics of human cognition (Miyake et al., 2000). Attention is the ability to concentrate on some events and ignore others. The term includes focused, selective, and divided attention, as well as alertness and sustained attention (Groeger, 2000; Leclercq, 2002). The three separable executive functions—inhibition of prepotent responses, mental set shifting, and updating/monitoring of working memory representations (Miyake et al., 2000; Friedman et al., 2006)—require activation of attention and memory functions. Nonexecutive attentional functions (for example, alertness) require only passive attention to the event (Hansen et al., 2004).

There is also a neural circuit that functions as a structural link between emotion, cognition, and physiological processes (Thayer & Broschott, 2005; Damasio, 1998; Devinsky et al., 1995). The knowledge about this cooperation will help us to understand normal human behaviour, as well as peculiar symptoms related to neuropsychiatric disorders, such as the consequences of TBI (van Donkelaar et al., 2006), AS, and ADD/ADHD.

When working with a patient with neuropsychiatric symptoms or disorders, it is crucial to become familiar with the ways of how he processes both cognitive and emotional information. The meaning of a wide and well-structured neuropsychological investigation in the beginning of the therapeutic work cannot be underestimated. It is a tool to organize and integrate the aims of the rehabilitation process both for the patient and for the therapist. The problems of everyday life seem to be primarily involved with the wiring and tuning of the brain toward the intentional action, not toward gaining cognitive or emotional aims or rewards. This is the basis for the dysfunctional process of motivation. The problems for seeing intentions and meanings of one's own actions are related to the dysfunction of executive skills, to the inability to reflect and use mirroring, as well as to exceptional ways to confront the feeling of arousal and messages from the physiological machinery. These phenomena appeal in clinical practice either as denial or pure self-awareness. The dysregulation of motivation, directed via the limbic forebrain and dopamine therein (Heimer et al., 2008) causes problems in the areas of planning and preparation for action.

The concept of "the limbic system," first proposed by Paul McLean (cited in Heimer et al., 2008), has broadened during the decades, and today it can be defined as an integrative brain area that has associative and reciprocal connections with subcortical and cortical brain networks (LeDoux, 1996; Damasio et al., 2000). There are many theories related to the organization and the structure of the limbic system.

When working with neuropsychiatric patients, the roles of both the basal ganglia, as well as the amygdala, are important. As clinicians, we need to know the patient's abilities to recognize emotional facial expressions, notice or separate feelings, or tune, regulate, and finish one's own movements and actions (Borod, 2000; Adolphs, 2002; Bechara, 2003). It is important to know what happens when the patient is observing another human being performing a movement or reflecting the other person's action. The mirror units (Fuster, 2003) or the mirror-neuron system (Rizzolatti & Sinigaglia, 2007; Gazzolla, Rizzolatti, Wicker, & Keyssers, 2007; Iacoboni, 2008) in the premotor–temporal cortex direct the pathways of how we connect with others and reflect the consequences of the observed processes. Neuropsychiatric patients do have problems with self-regulation, information processing, and action, as well as the regulation of attention related to neuroanatomical and functional dysregulation of brain regions responsible for these actions.

During the neuropsychotherapeutic process with the patient (Safran & Muran, 2000; Leahy, 2003; Grawe, 2007), it is essential to combine the knowledge of neurosciences and neuroanatomical findings with the therapist's clinical knowledge and communicative skills. This forms the basis for psychotherapeutic collaboration in action. In order to reach the rehabilitational goals, the clinical tools for the therapeutic alliance, setting the agendas, and working with resistance and ruptures must be negotiated.

A Case Study

A case report is presented to describe the neuropsychotherapeutic process and cooperation between a patient with a neuropsychiatric disorder and his therapist.

Background

A 31-year-old man was driving his car and collided with a moose at the speed of 100 km/hour. As a result of the accident, he suffered a skull fracture, the subluxation of the internal carotid artery, the desiccation of the right internal carotid artery with the right-sided focal paresis, and the paresis of the right nervus accessorius. The patient did not lose consciousness but experienced posttraumatic amnesia for a week. In CT scanning, a fracture of the vertebralis area was found. In MRI scannings, a hematoma near the fractured area (cerebellum in the right) was documented. Damages at the area of the right hemisphere were related to findings at the areas of brain nerves 9, 10, and 11. As a result of the injury mechanism from the car accident, the assumption was that the networks from the anterior cingulate cortex to and from the lower brain areas, as well as the frontal brain areas, were partly injured.

The three neuropsychological investigations revealed dysfunctions in word finding and inefficiency of the verbal logical memory, as well as distractibility in executive processing. Problems with visual reproductive memory and verbal–visual learning were documented. The patient also had serious types of posttraumatic pain. Two years after the accident, the disorders in verbal learning and memory functions were still obvious, and the patient was referred to neuropsychological rehabilitation.

The client is the firstborn of the siblings of his primary family. His mother died when he was 13 years old. At school, problems with motivational regulation and the fluctuation of executive skills narrowed his abilities to learn and process information according to the aspiration level. After nine years of primary education, the patient continued his studies in electronics at a vocational school. From the very beginning of his work career, he obtained a demanding and responsible status at work. Finally, he was a supervisor over 200 workers. He was offered demanding technical work abroad in the near future.

Procedure

At the beginning of the neuropsychotherapeutic rehabilitation process, the issues with verbal memory functions, as well as the physical impairment and the dysfunction of the vocal cords, were the problems. The aim for the patient himself was to be able to return to work after the physical defects were diminished. While the agenda was being set and the real problems related to verbal memory dysfunctions were being evaluated, the neuropsychological deficiencies, as recognized on the large scale, were found. When practicing the process of verbal learning, both the patient and the therapist understood the meaning of the losses of abilities in everyday life: for example, the demands of functioning in a grocery store without forgetting things and getting confused were hard. When working with computer games, or trying to draw a mental topographic map when driving a car in his hometown, the man got lost and needed guidance from his friends. Problems related to retrospective memory, as well as working memory skills, had a cumulative effect and a direct impact on executive functioning. The subjective experience of the patient was of getting lost. He described this as a grey curtain falling between his destination of awareness and the present location. He knew the destination but lost the clue of how to reach it. These deficits were documented in test behaviour when working with the Hanoi Tower Test by Cognisoft.

The patient's ability to recognize his symptoms and the severity of his injuries progressed rapidly in the beginning of the therapeutic work. As a consequence, the patient was confused with his feelings related to the future. He had the courage to look back into his past, into his life before the accident. This led to feelings of free fall, and of being broken. Technical metaphors started to gain a great role in the verbalization of the therapeutic process.

As for his memory impairments, the patient started every morning as a happy person with no feelings related to the consequences of the accident. But the motivational regulation of everyday intentions was diminished, and the patient was unable to set long-term goals for his life. The patient found similarities with his own life and the movie *Groundhog Day* (1993) by Harold Ramis, in which the main character wakes up every day into the same day. Another movie, *Memento* (2000) by Christopher Nolan, brought up feelings related to not remembering the present without making notes or other memory clues. The patient was not anxious about giving up his job ("getting out of the rat race," as he described it). Hobbies and the ability to see the continuity of life began to give him some tools for understanding the ongoing process of everyday life, despite the memory losses.

The ability to use attention in the service of working memory as a function to "look back," and attention regulation as a resource to plan the executive functions (Fuster, 2003) narrowed remarkably. The neuropsychotherapist described the ongoing situation for his patient as this:

> Because of your memory impairments, you are living in a time span where the orientation to the next step is very short. However, it is a matter of great importance to have long-term goals and dreams—aims for shorter as well as longer periods of life. In

> order to set these aims, you need tools to use and reinforce the potential for bringing up the memories from the past to the use of your working memory skills. This process, related to remembering things that have given pleasure and emotional satisfaction, will broaden the ways to set the goals for future events. These memories will form the basis for orienting to new demands and making plans that carry on in the future. The working memory skills form a bridge between the past and the present—they are like a rudder that orients and looks to the past, but that also gives the direction for becoming dreams and goals.

Problems with episodic memory functions diminished the patient's ability to encode and store verbal material and new information. In order to bring back the memories and reconstruct the past, the patient started to keep a diary. At the beginning, the process went on smoothly. Then the patient began to forget to bring along the memory stick, where he stored his writings. The therapist understood that the written texts made the patient very anxious: The patient wrote notes and afterward, while reading through them, was unable to connect the described episodes with his own memories. He got the strange feeling that the stories were from some other person's life, even though he had been the writer. From the neuroanatomic point of view, this process refers to the dysregulation of the limbic cooperative brain area in the lower brain structures—mainly, the networks of the basal ganglia and the amygdala.

During the following weeks, the patient grew anxious and felt that the verbal processing and memorizing was getting too emotional. He had difficulties in recognizing and regulating the ongoing processes of emotional information. The feeling of being broken was devastating and strongly affected the patient's abilities to handle his everyday life. As the neuropsychotherapeutic process went on, the therapist was forced to slow down the speed and look for ways to regulate the force of forgotten memories and feelings of being lost. It was an urgent time for a new agenda to be set.

The patient took part in the rehabilitation course for a month, as well as a short work trial in his previous job. Both of these processes led to a depressive period that lasted a couple of weeks.

Then the patient began to take photographs. He was talented with analyzing and editing the photos with computers, and the process helped him make a good contact with his visual-perceptual world. He began, very carefully at first, to take photos of his surroundings and themes that helped him to regulate the level of emotional loading. He found new meanings for water drops, landscapes, and other elements of nature. While working together with his therapist, he started to connect with emotionally loaded material and memories that arose when the patient was looking at his photo gallery. As the process went on, the patient began to be able to write descriptions and find words for his visual expressions. The connection between visual memory, episodic memory losses, the lost feelings, and the narrative story behind the traumatic process started to integrate. The abilities to plan, focus and, regulate the patient's actions, to have a hold on to executive functions, were also achieved within the emotional level of the rehabilitation process. The procedural memory functions, related to photo gallery pictures, good and bad days, the files of happy and sad times, maintain the bridge between emotional and cognitive descriptions of past phenomena. There are always some photos with a special meaning and greater importance, and they form a ribbon, binding past and present together. The visual pathway of information processing opened a new way to analyze the emotional messages from the ACC and the limbic structures.

Conclusions and Future Aspects?

From the clinical perspective of the process, the patient has started to restructure his life. The effects of the rehabilitation of the procedural memory skills cannot be underestimated. The patient also found tools to regulate his moods and the stages of misery and loss. The feeling of "I have life" is most rewarding for both the patient and the neuropsychotherapist.

The future is still open. Four and a half years after the accident, the patient retired from his work. The photographs still work as a part of limbic cooperation areas in the brain—naming and giving meanings to life after the accident, as well as finding the ways to express anxiety and depression. The abilities for emotional bonding have awakened. The tools that form the rudder when both working memory modalities and the retrospective memory functions are narrowed have shown to be useful. The therapist's work as a mirroring person has reflected back the patient's intentions and therapeutic wishes in a reciprocal way. The process has revealed the importance of "hard" neuroanatomic data, neuroscientific knowledge, and neuropsychological findings, as well as the usefulness of neuropsychotherapeutic tools in the rehabilitation process. Both the therapist's and the patient's self-awareness has been a key to proceed toward the mutual goals. Also, the cooperation of the writers of this article—one as a clinician in the neuropsychological investigation, the other as a neuropsychotherapist, has been a mirroring process for both.

The main agenda for the neuropsychotherapeutic work was to create a rudder for the patient's needs. By taking photographs and analyzing this data, the patient was able to save and encode the episodic material from his life, as well as to let feelings arise into a conscious level. This process helps him to create a vision for the future and to make plans. He was able to have long-term dreams and goals and also to fulfill them. The feelings of total boredom started to diminish, and the patient learned to use his emotions as a bridge between old and new memories. After a period of having no past or future, the patient awakened to the reality of the ongoing process of time regardless of his memory losses. The ability for emotional tuning and bonding brought with it a broadened capability for experiencing and sharing empathy.

References

Adolphs, R. (2002). Recognizing emotion from facial expressions: Psychological and neurological mechanisms. *Behavioral and Cognitive Neuroscience Reviews, 1*, 21–62.

Baliki, M.N., Geha, P.Y., Apkarian, A.V., & Chiavlo, D.R. (2008). Beyond feeling: Chronic pain hurts the brain, disrupting the default-mode network dynamics. *The Journal of Neuroscience, 28*(6), 1398–1403.

Bechara, A., Damasio, H. & Damasio, A.R (2003). Role of the amygdala in decision-making. *Annals of the New York Academy of Science, 985*, 356–369.

Borod, J. C. (Ed.). (2000). *The neuropsychology of emotion*. New York: Oxford University Press.

Damasio, A. R. (1998). Emotion in the perspective of an integrated nervous system. *Brain Research Reviews, 26*, 83–86.

Damasio, A. R., Grabowski, T. J., Bechara, A., Damasio, H., Ponto, L. L., Parvizi, J., Hichwa, R.D. (2000). Subcortical and cortical brain activity during the feeling of self-generated emotions. *Nature Neuroscience, 3*(10), 1049–1056.

Davidson, R. J. (2000). Emotion, plasticity, context and regulation: Perspectives from affective neuroscience. *Psychological Bulletin, 126*, 890–909.

Devinsky, O. (1995). Contributions of anterior cingulate cortex to behaviour. *Brain, 118*, 279–306.

Friedman, N. P., Miyake, A., Corley, R. P., Young, S. E., Defries, J. C. & Hewitt, J. K.(2006). Not all executive functions are related to intelligence. *Psychological Science, 17*(2), 172–179.

Fuster, J.M. (2003). *Cortex and mind. Unifying cognition*. New York: Oxford University Press.

Gazzolla, V., Rizzolatti, G., Wicker, B., & Keyssers, C. (2007). The anthropomorphic brain: The mirror neuron system responds to human and robotic actions. *Neuroimage 35*(4), 1674–1684.

Grawe, K. (2007). *Neuropsychotherapy: How the neurosciences inform effective psychotherapy*. USA: Mahwah, NJ: Lawrence Erlbaum Associates.

Groeger, J. A. (2000). *Understanding driving. Applying cognitive psychology to a complex everyday task*. East Sussex, UK: Psychology Press, Ltd.

Hansen, A. L., Johnsen, B. H. & Thayer, J. F. (2003). Vagal influence on working memory and attention. *International Journal of Psychophysiology, 48*, 263–274.

Hansen, A. L., Johnsen, B. H., Sollers, J. J., Stenvik, K. & Thayer, J. F. (2004). Heart rate variability and its relation to prefrontal cognitive function: The effects of training and detraining. *European Journal of Applied Physiology, 93*(3), 263–272.

Heimer, L., Van Hoesen, G., Trimble, M., & Zahm, D. (2008). *Anatomy of neuropsychiatry. The new anatomy of the basal forebrain and its implications for neuropsychiatric illnesses*. Burlington, VT: Elsevier.

Iacoboni, M. (2008). *Mirroring people*. New York: Farrar, Straus & Giroux.

Kimmerly, D-S., Wong, S.W., Salzer, D., Menon, R. & Shoemaker, K. (2007). Forebrain regions associated with post-exercise differences in autonomic and cardiovascular function during baroreceptor unloading. *American Journal of Physiology. Heart and Circulatory Physiology, 293*(1), 299–306.

Lang, P. J., & Davis, M. (2006). Emotion, motivation and the brain: Reflex foundations in animal and human research. *Progress in Brain Research, 156*, 3–29.

Leahy, R.L. (2003). *Cognitive therapy techniques: A practitioner's guide*. New York: Guilford Press.

Leclercq, M. (2002). Theoretical aspects of the main components and functions of attention. In Lecrercq, M., & Zimmermann, P. (Eds.) *Applied neuropsychology of attention* (pp. 4–41). London: Psychology Press.

LeDoux, J. (1996). *The emotional brain: The mysterious underpinnings of emotional life*. London: Simon & Schuster.

Lezak, M. D. (2004). *Neuropsychological assessment.* New York: Oxford University Press.

Lichter, D. G., & Cummings, J. L. (Eds.). (2001). *Frontal-subcortical circuits in psychiatric and neurological disorders.* New York: Guilford Press.

Matthews, S. C., Paulus, M. P., Simmons, A. N., Nelsen, R. A. & Dimsdale, J. E. (2004). Functional subdivisions within anterior cingulate cortex and their relationship to autonomous nervous system function. *NeuroImage, 22*(3), 1151–1156.

Miyake, A., Friedman, N.P., Emerson, M.J., Witzki, A.H., Howerter, A., & Wager, T.D. (2000). The unity and diversity of executive functions and their contributions to complex "frontal lobe" tasks: A latent variable analysis. *Cognitive Psychology, 41*, 49–100.

Pollatos, O., Schandry, R., Auer, D.P., & Kaufmann, C. (2007). Brain structures mediating cardiovascular arousal and interoceptive awareness. *Brain Research, 1141*(13), 178–187.

Rizzolatti, G., & Sinigaglia,. (2007). Mirror neurons and motor intentionality. *Functional Neurology, 22*(4), 205–210.

Safran, J. D., & Muran, J. C. (2000). *Negotiating the therapeutic alliance: A relational treatment guide.* New York: Guilford.

Sheehan, T.P., Chambers, R.A., & Russell, D.S. (2004). Regulation of affect by the lateral septum: Implications for neuropsychiatry. *Brain Research Review, 46*, 71–117.

Tekin, S., & Cummings, J. L. (2002). Frontal-subcortical neuronal circuits and clinical neuropsychiatry. *Journal of Psychosomatic Research, 53*(2), 647–654.

Thayer, J.F., & Broschott, J.F. (2005). Psychosomatics and psychopathology: Looking up and down from the brain. *Psychoneuroendocrinology, 30*(10), 1050–1058.

Tulppo, M. P., Kiviniemi, A. M., Kallio, M., Hautala, A., Pietarila, P., Seppänen, T., Mäkikallio, T., & Huikuri, H. (2005b). Physiological background of the loss of fractal heart rate dynamics. *Circulation, 19*(112), 314–319.

Tulppo, M. P., Shoemaker, K., Tutungi, E., Kimmerly, D.S., Gelb, A., Hughson, R.L., Mäkikallio, T., & Huikuri, H. (2005a). Feedback effects of circulating norepinephrine on sympathetic outflow among healthy subjects. *American Journal of Physiology, 288*, H710–H715.

Van Donkelaar, P., Osternig, L. & Chou, L.S. (2006). Attentional and biomechanical deficits interact after mild traumatic brain injury. *Exercise and Sport Sciences Reviews, 34*(2), 77–82.

5

Effects of Brain Injury on Emotional Reactions in a Therapeutic Process

Arja Lindell

Introduction

In addition to cognitive problems, brain injury also often causes patients to suffer from different problems with emotional processing. Emotional processing and regulation help in defining where, when and how emotions are expressed. This may happen consciously or automatically. In the context of rehabilitation, problems in emotional processing have received less attention than difficulties in memory, attention, language, and perception. Although changes in the ability to express and perceive emotions have been clinically recognized for a long time, the ways in which the symptoms have been understood and reacted to have varied greatly at different times. Patients themselves might have described their emotions as disorganized or mixed up. Emotions and their neural background have been the object of growing interest in neuroscience research (Borod & Madigan, 2000). Some emotional processes are now better known, such as the origin of the fear reaction (LeDoux, 2002), but studies into the neural basis of emotional reactions have only just begun (Leppänen, 2006). Working out the emotional changes with a patient suffering from brain trauma is often the task of a neuropsychologist or psychotherapist. The special problems that neurological patients face pose challenges to therapy work and to the application of current methods.

Tedd Judd (1999) defines three main factors that affect the emotional state, behavior, and personality of a patient with brain injury: (a) The basic personality of the patient; (b) The patient's psychological reaction to illness and its consequences; (c) The organic changes in cognition, emotions, and behavior directly linked to the injury.

According to Judd, the first two factors can be understood through traditional psychological theories and can be dealt with in terms of either traditional or modified psychotherapy. However, to work with organic emotional changes, a neuropsychotherapeutic approach is needed. In neuropsychotherapy, not only can the different practices of psychotherapy be applied, but also the approaches of neurological rehabilitation, such as retraining, compensation, and adaptation. Recognizing organic symptoms and taking them into consideration in therapeutic work is essential—for example, fatigue or troubles with taking initiative can be direct organic consequences, instead of being caused by another mental illness, such as depression. It is also essential to alter therapy so that it fits the patient by using ways to work around cognitive difficulties. Furthermore, the therapist must orient to the patient's altered ability to respond. Challenges to psychotherapeutic work brought about by brain lesions have also been explored by Judd and Wilson (2005) and Laaksonen (2007, 2008).

While the losses caused by illness or disability can trigger strong emotional crisis reactions, the primary focus of this chapter is to examine changes in emotional processing and regulation produced by brain injury and to consider their significance for therapy among adult neurological patients. My aim is to demonstrate—through practical examples—disturbances in emotional processing among neurological patients as I have encountered them and the ways in which my patients have taught me about them by sharing their experiences. Finally, I will present a case description in which I explore cognitive symptoms, and issues regarding behavior and emotional monitoring, as well as troubles with autobiographical emotional memories.

Emotions, Memories, and the Brain

Emotions as Multilevel Processes

Despite the emphasis placed on intelligence in modern society, we would not have come this far as a species without the cooperation of intelligence and emotions. The adaptive significance of emotions, and especially emotional reactions, has been emphasized in numerous studies and theories (Borod & Madigan, 2000; Damasio, 2003; Leppänen, 2006). Emotional reactions offer meaningful insight into ourselves and our relationships with the world around us. They guide our attentiveness, and are connected to memory, decision making, and interpretation. They inform us about the inner conditions of our bodies as well the meanings of outer elements and circumstances, and they inform others about our intentions and well-being. They also guide behavior and arrange both thought and action (Greenberg & Paivio, 1997). When talking about emotions in everyday terms, we come to mean the whole spectrum of emotional processing. However, in theoretical models dealing with emotions, divisions are created concerning the different phases of emotional processes—some of which take place unconsciously. When studying emotions, the episodic nature of the experience is often emphasized. An emotional episode lasts for a certain period of time, after which it abates and finally disappears; it is not a permanent state of mind or mood. In everyday terms, we often speak of an emotional outbreak that we know to subside at some point.

There is no specific way to define emotions. In studies concerning this topic, some emphasize the body's correlates in their emotional concepts, while others stress the moods created by the connections of the body's correlates to the brain. On a physical level, we can distinguish "affects," by which we mean the body's different biological (automatic, physiological, motivational, and neural) correlates to a stimulus (Buck, 2000; Greenberg & Paivio, 1997; Karila, 2008). They are unconscious and always present. An experiential and a more conscious side associated with "affects" can be called "feelings" and "desires." One can always assess how hungry, thirsty, irritated, happy, or content he is or if he has "a lump in his throat" (Buck, 2000; Karila, 2008, p. 530). The level at which a consciously experienced sensation connects with cognition has been defined in many ways. Greenberg (1997) calls this level "emotion," Damasio (2003) "feelings." In emotions, according to Greenberg & Paivio different sensations such as fear, anger, or grief—which are in relation to efforts and facial expressions that guide actions—are combined experientially with a mutual judgment of the situation and self. Damasio (2003) sees "emotions" as the process's externally visual, physiological occurrences and calls the mind's inner functions "feelings." As a brain researcher, he places more weight on the neural connections of emotional processes.

When we react to emotionally significant stimuli (inner or outer), our brains send messages that alter the inner states of our bodies. To the outsider, this alternation can be seen in changes in behavior, facial expressions, posture, or tone of voice. According to Damasio, these changes are registered in areas of the brain that sense the body, forming in a way a map referring to the parts and state of the body. These neural maps are viewed as the basis for sensing feelings. In other words, feelings are connected to neural maps of the body's condition. Along with this perception of the body states, "there is the perception of thoughts with themes consonant with emotion, and a perception of a certain mode of thinking," (Damasio, 2003, p. 85). According to Damasio, outer occurrences are transmitted to our minds through bodily states, but he also states that, in order for a feeling to occur, the brain can activate an inner neural map of the body's state different from the true body state; for example, when we are in a situation of danger, we often do not notice pain. Despite the differences, both Damasio, Greenberg and Paivio view feelings and emotions as multileveled processes that function in a synchronized fashion. In this chapter, feelings and emotions are not conceptually differentiated, but by them I mainly imply, along the lines of Greenberg & Paivio a conscious experience that includes both an inner and an outer side.

Emotional Categories and Dimensions

A rather common way to classify feelings or emotions is to divide them into categories of basic or primary emotions, and complex or secondary emotions (Damasio, 2001, 2003). Primary emotions include—among others—fear, anger, grief, joy, disgust, and surprise (Damasio, 2003; Sherer, 2000). It is thought that primary emotions are fixed systems distinct from each other, and that they are tied to their own stimuli, physiological reactions, and expressive and behavioral ensembles, such as the escape-approach and characteristic facial expressions (Sherer, 2000). Secondary emotions, on the other hand, are more complicated entities, which can be formed after primary emotions and can be reactions to these (Greenberg & Paivio, 1997); for example, anger may arise as reaction to depression, or shame as reaction to fear. Moreover, secondary emotions can be more social, such as sympathy, embarrassment, jealousy, envy, and thankfulness (Damasio, 2003). Damasio (2001) has proposed that trauma to the limbic system of the brain can cause disturbance to processing of primary emotions, whereas trauma to the frontal lobe will disrupt processing of secondary emotions.

Another basis for examining emotions is dimensional. According to dimensional emotional models, emotions are not separate, but can be distinguished by basic dimensions, such as valence (positive–negative, pleasant–unpleasant), activation/arousal (calm–excited), and the direction of motor activity (approach–avoid; Sherer, 2000).

Conscious and Unconscious Processing of Emotions

Processing of emotional information can take place consciously or unconsciously. Studies into fear conditioning and emotional processing of facial expressions have produced information about this (LeDoux, 2002; Nummenmaa, 2006). Concerning the brain, especially important is the amygdala, which in the presence of a threatening stimulus receives information both rapidly and slowly into its input area (the lateral nucleus). When an emotional stimulus, such as to a snake-resembling stick, reaches the thalamus, it is rapidly directed from there as an incomplete representation of the stimulus to the amygdale (the rapid route). The amygdala also receives a more complete and further processed representation of the stimulus via a slower route, through the brain's cortical areas (LeDoux, 2002; Nummenmaa, 2006). On a behavioral level, we are first alarmed when we encounter the "snake," but are then relaxed as the realization "it is, in fact, a stick" sets in. Slower processing enables emotionally based reflection and decision making (Greenberg, 1997). The information may also move on from the amygdala to the cortex after the emotional content has been recognized. Emotional reactions can be fine-tuned and modulated through the cortical routes (Nummenmaa, 2006).

Emotion Regulation

Emotional experiences activate many areas of the brain, both cortical and subcortical; however, the strongest connections can be found in the frontal areas and the upper structures of the brain stem (Kober, Feldman Barrett, Joseph, Bliss-Moreau, Lindquist, &

Wager, 2008). It is thought that in the monitoring of emotional processes, the younger cortical structures monitor and, through reciprocal connections, take part in the functions of earlier inner structures (Borod & Madigan, 2000). Connections from the prefrontal cortex to the inner structures, such as the amygdala, have been proven to be highly inhibitory (Nummenmaa, 2006). The amygdala appears to be the most studied of subcortical structures, and its role in the processing of emotional stimuli has been established as exceedingly vast. In their 2005 study, Phelps and LeDoux state that the amygdala participates in implicit emotional learning and memory, facilitates and enhances attention and perception of emotional stimuli, and is linked to social behavior (such as recognition of facial expressions and observing social interaction). In addition to playing a part in triggering fear and anger emotions (Phelps & LeDoux, 2005), the amygdala activates when one sees expressions of grief and loathing (Leppänen, 2006). Patients with a damaged amygdala have been observed to miss healthy fear reactions (Phelps & LeDoux, 2005). The role of other subcortical structures in processing emotions is less known and many studies have been conducted on animals.

Emotions and Memory

Essential structures in the processing of emotional memories are the systems of the temporal lobe and the frontal lobe, especially the amygdala, the hippocampus, and the right frontal area (Ochsner & Schacter, 2000). The amygdala has an important role in the modulation of emotional memories; through its vast connections, it strengthens the storage of memories in the hippocampus and other areas important for memory (Phelps & LeDoux, 2005). A trauma to the amygdala has been recognized to weaken delayed retention for emotional stimuli (Phelps & LeDoux, 2005). The hippocampus apparently helps in finding memory traces and supports the recollection experience (Ochsner & Schacter, 2000). Associated with memory recollection is also the so-called "similarity assumption," which in practice means that similarities between emotional states in times of memory encoding are helpful for memory retrieval (LeDoux, 2002). The right frontal lobe has been proven in many studies to have an important function in producing efficient memory retrieval strategies (Ochsner & Schacter, 2000).

Different means to remembering past events—such as the associative and strategic—have also been linked to different parts of the brain (Schacter, 1997). The associative is an automatic reminder process that takes place, such as when you hear your favorite song and instantly remember where you first heard it. Associative recollection is dependent upon the hippocampus. Strategic remembering, on the other hand, depends on the prefrontal cortex, especially the right frontal lobe, and it happens when, for example, you try to bring to your mind what you did last Saturday. While reminiscing, you search for clues that will eventually trigger a part of associative memory.

Trauma to the hippocampus will result in serious difficulties to store postinjury memories, but earlier autobiographical memories may be spared. In case the strategic recollection system is damaged, but the automatic, associative search process stays unharmed, it should be fairly easy to remember the past, but only if the right clues needed for association are there (Schacter, 1997). The ability to bring back to mind memories of one's own person is fundamental for the perceived continuity of self.

Memory has also an important role to play in preserving one's self-image and identity. A central mechanism in the forming and preserving of self and who we are is the storage of implicit and explicit memories of life experiences (LeDoux, 2002). Implicit systems store features of ourselves, which we use constantly, but are not necessarily aware of, such as characteristic ways of speaking, walking, or thinking—learned skills. Explicit memories are time- and place-connected and can be consciously recollected (LeDoux, 2002). Awareness of self and self-image entails that we can bring back to mind, from long-term memory, an understanding of who we are. Brain injury can disturb this ability.

According to Conway and Rubin (1993), the memories of ourselves that we recollect exist on three levels. The first level contains information about longer, "lifetime periods," such as the lower secondary school times or a possible year spent abroad. The second level contains memories of shorter time periods, or "general events" (for example, holiday trips, sporting events, or your first summer job). Finally, the third level consists of single, specific moments or "event specific knowledge." Here are stored memories of events that only lasted for some hours, minutes, or just seconds. The different levels create a basis for an autobiographical memory, and the memories of longer "lifetime periods" form a backbone for the whole structure of narrative memory.

Emotional Changes Caused by Cerebral Trauma

Among persons with brain injury, we may meet people who have disturbances in the collaboration between emotions and cognition, resulting in confusion in themselves and often also in those around them. Brain trauma can change the ability to *express, observe, or experience emotions.*

Tedd Judd (1999) has given an inclusive report concerning problems in organic emotional processing, with suggestions for therapeutic work. Here, I shall deal with the issue mainly grounded on Judd's work. I will not scrutinize specifically each and every possible differential diagnostic neurological or psychiatric condition in which similar symptoms have been observed—for those seeking further information on the issue, I recommend the original work.

Deterioration in Abilities to Express and/or Understand Emotions

It has been well established that damage to certain areas of the brain will result in difficulties in expressing one's emotional state, either verbally or with gestures or facial expressions. Studies concerning lesions to the left and right hemispheres have been able to prove that, although patients suffering from damage to the left hemisphere often experience aphasia, their ability to express emotions through, for example, tone of voice, can be better than those with damage to the right hemisphere (Heilman, Blonder, Bowers, & Crucian, 2000). Damage to the anterior parts of the right hemisphere, especially, can result in minimal facial mimicry, impaired expressiveness, and monotonous voice. Although the patient might seem euphoric or indifferent, their inner emotional experience may or may not be wholly different—the patient may speak of depression even if it is not conveyed through any other form of expression. Depression is more consistent with the appearance of patients with lesions to the left hemisphere, and they seem to experience depression more often than those suffering from damage to the right hemisphere (Robinson & Manes, 2000). Disturbances in emotional expression are often discovered in sufferers from damage to right frontal areas, especially the inferior, posterior, lateral area, and in lesions to subcortical or peripheral structures, which results in dysarthria (Judd, 1999).

Patients with decreased verbal understanding (especially those suffering from damage to the left hemisphere) have been known to understand tones of voice or prosody and facial expressions that correlate emotions (Heilman et al., 2000). Those with lesions to the right hemisphere may, despite good speech recognition, suffer from a weakened ability to understand or observe nonverbal emotional messages, such as gestures, facial expressions, or prosody. They may take jokes very literally or factually and have a weak sense of empathy. The deterioration in understanding emotional communication is often to do with damage to the right temporal and parietal areas (Heilman et al., 2000). Some patients have difficulties with expressing emotions, others with understanding them, and for some the problems are more wide ranging.

An example. A man who suffered serious brain damage seven years ago, and who still has damage and trauma-inflicted difficulties with emotional regulation. His facial expressions are still subdued, although the situation has improved somewhat. (P=patient, T=Therapist).

P: Like a friend of mine said recently … I'm still, that I'm still really serious … before the accident I used to be all smiles.
T: And …
P: Nowadays he [the friend], when he hasn't seen me for years, he, like, looks at me so that I don't notice, and thinks "he's always so serious."
T: Even to this day?
P: Yeah.
T: Still?
P: [Nods] There's no smile on my face… . I hear I used to smile all the time in the past… . The smile just won't come back anymore… . I've tried smiling in front of the mirror in the mornings; it just won't come… .
T: Right.
P: Even if there's starting to be some smiles inside of me, it's just gone from the face.

It is important to keep in mind that a person lacking initiative due to organic reasons may give out a similar appearance as a person with weak emotional expressiveness. Disinhibition or emotional lability due to brain lesion may appear as if the patient did not understand other peoples' emotions (Judd, 1999). Problems with cognitive control, such as excessive talkativeness or stimulus boundness, may also appear as indifference, although the inner experience might be adequate. For many, this brings about practical problems, such as being misunderstood or relationships becoming strained.

An example. A patient suffering from serious damage to the inferior part of the left frontal lobe has a critically ill relative. The relative's illness has affected the patient emotionally, but in the therapy session, he always returns to talking about the first unrelated thing that comes to mind, moving from one familiar topic to another. Only when the patient is asked directly about the issue and his experience of the relative's illness may he remember what he meant to say about it or what he thinks about the issue.

Involuntary Crying or Laughing, Automatic Swearing

Some patients may show excessive crying or laughing, usually called pathological, reflexive, or automatic crying or laughing. Despite the different names, the essential feature of the condition is that the patient may break out crying or laughing, with this action having very little or nothing to do with the patient's actual emotional state (Cummings & Mega, 2003). The patient may laugh, having nothing to laugh about, or cry, having nothing to be sad about. Even if the reaction corresponds with the experienced emotion, it is often overemphasized in relation to the stimulus created by the experience. Often, these reflexes are brought about by the slightest hint on a topic, and at times there seems to be no reason for them whatsoever. Expressions of crying and laughing are episodic and stereotypical reactions, the duration and magnitude over which the patient has no control. After the outburst passes, the patient may continue the conversation from where he or she left it. For some, reflexive crying is more prominent, for others reflexive laughter, and for some crying may change to laughing in an instant, or vice versa.

An example. A 21-year-old female who suffered from brain injury in a traffic accident a year ago.

T: Tell me about this crying [The patient is teary eyed.]
P: It comes when we, like, just talk, or if someone just asks about it, it'll start ... so the crying just comes.
T: It just comes.
P: Yeah, even if I don't, like, necessarily want it, it'll just, like ... start.... I will just get tears in my eyes.
T: Do you start to feel really sad at the same time?
P: I don't know.... No.
T: No...
P: I think so ... but you just get kind of ... mad ... you, like, get down....
T: So do you get nervous about the crying?
P: I think so, yeah, because you also become a little embarrassed.
T: Oh yeah... ?
P: So I guess you get kind of anxious, like, "I'm gonna start sobbing again!!" but I feel like I shouldn't.
T: How do those around you react to it?
P: They don't ... well, they know I'm sensitive.
T: You have been in the past?
P: Yes.
T: So what do you do when you realize you're going to start crying again?
P: Try to swallow, wipe away the tears, and explain that I'm, like, sensitive.
T: Do you ever tell them that this is caused by the accident?
P: No, I don't usually, it depends on the situation so much... . Like yesterday when I was at the surgeon's, I started again, when I just asked why my operating surgeon wasn't there to take care of me.
T: Would you tell a little about the laughter ... ? Does it come more easily?
P: Well, it comes more easily. I start to, like ... it goes a bit overboard like ... hahaha!
T: It gets exaggerated, or ... ?
P: Yeah ... so in some situations you think, like, "OH! I didn't need to laugh like that!"

The patient from the example has suffered the trauma recently and is still learning to live with its consequences, including the automatic crying. Crying causes her to have secondary emotions of irritation, but it also confuses her and makes her partly sad (going around to a primary emotion). Her foremost wish for therapeutic work is to get rid of the excessive crying.

Reflexive crying and laughing may occur due to a number of neurological conditions, such as MS (multiple sclerosis), ALS (amyotrophic lateral sclerosis), Parkinson's and Alzheimer's diseases, brain tumors, and strokes, as well as after brain damage (Judd, 1999;

Tateno, Jorge, & Robinson, 2004). The neural pathways through which the cortical regions of the brain control the lower laughter and crying reflex centers have been noted to be damaged (Heilman et al., 2000). Cortical damage itself is not necessary. It has been put forward that reflexive crying would be accentuated in vast damages to the left hemisphere, whereas reflexive laughter would be brought about by damage to the right hemisphere (Sackeim, Greenberg, Weiman, Gur, Hungerbuhler, & Geschwind, 1982). Automatic swearing may occur along with severe aphasia, and it is involuntary, unlike normal swearing. Due to a severe aphasic disorder, swear words may be the only words the patient can produce, even if he does not intend to swear. A brain damage patient with problems in cognitive control may also swear more than in the past. Here, however, swearing has more to do with actual situations than in the above cases (Judd, 1999).

Difficulties with Emotional Reactivity, Subdued, Labile, and Excessive Reactions

For some patients, brain damage may cause emotional reactions to dull when compared to pretraumatic situations. Patients may report feeling emotions of, for example, joy, sorrow, and anger, but that the experiences have weakened or subdued, and they may occur less frequently, if at all (Judd, 1999). Patients may also know what kind of emotions a certain experience would have brought about in them before, but not experience those emotions after the injury. The emotions might also now be triggered only by very strong stimuli. This may render patients seemingly indifferent, even robotlike. Furthermore, they are not as excitable as they might have been pretrauma/illness. Decreased emotional reactivity may occur alongside periods of heightened emotional sensitivity. Here, between longer periods of indifference, the patient may portray sudden outbursts of emotion. The inner experience of emotion must be differentiated from the difficulty in outer emotional expression. On the cerebral level, subdued emotions have been shown to occur due to damages in the dorsolateral frontal cortex, basal ganglia, and limbic area, especially in cases of Parkinson's and Alzheimer's diseases (Judd, 1999).

An example. Discussing experiencing emotions after the trauma with a male who suffered severe frontal lobe damage four years ago.

T: Has anyone ever mentioned anything in line with ... that you might be missing the ability to empathize?
P: I try to be pretty empathetic.... I can't always internalize the issue, but I still try to be so that .... I don't like to be indifferent, because I never was that way.
T: Has this [brain damage] changed that?
P: Yeah, I'm more indifferent; it has done that, but I still try to be....

In many neurological conditions, it is common for emotional reactions to become more labile. Emotions are experienced as stronger than before and are easily exaggerated, when compared to the stimuli that brought them about. Some patients ashamedly explain how, after the injury, they have become more sensitive, as they now cannot watch the news or a movie without becoming anxious or starting to cry. Emotional lability may be confused with reflexive crying or laughing, but it differs in emotional content and intensity. Emotional lability occurs especially in orbitofrontal lesions and in lesions of the limbic system, diffuse damage, and degenerative illnesses.

An example. A man suffering from severe cerebral damage still has oversensitivity, although the situation has improved since the years directly after the injury. Discussing rehabilitation seven years after the injury:

T: How do you personally feel—did the injury affect your emotional experiences or regulation in any way?
P: Yeah, it had an effect.... It kind of created distance; I cry easily—all I need is to watch some sad program on the TV, and I'll get tears in my eyes.
T: Did that happen before the injury?
P: No! I never used to cry, except maybe sometimes as a small child.
T: Well... ? How do you feel about crying?
P: It's really weird. I feel ashamed, can't say to anyone, like, hide my head and be like "there's something wrong with my glasses" ... or stuff like that ... so no one would pay attention to the crying. I was, like, embarrassed!
T: Embarrassed?
P: It was weird, something I couldn't comprehend.
T: And?
P: It can still come out, in any situation.

The emotional experience can also stay "turned on." In clinical experience, many patients, especially those suffering from damage to the frontal lobe, describe it as emotions getting "stuck."

An example. A young man with multiple contusions in the brain. It has been five years since the accident.

P: It's strange, like it ... in a way I already have feelings, like I can't get over an assignment ... so in a way, like, those feelings get stuck.... It's usually the bad ones.
T: And...
P: Like, I can't get over failing something; now it's really exciting because I've done something positive ... so in a way I've got this good feeling on all the time ... that I've done ... I've done something good to someone else ... so a kind of truly good feeling
T: Yes, what day was it when you... ?
P: Yesterday.
T: ... Yesterday you mowed the lawn [helping his parents].

There can be a number of reasons for reactions such as irritability and impulsive anger after brain injury. However, it is important for a clinician to be aware of the organic irritability and anger reactions. Irritability is common in diffuse brain lesions, such as in traumatic lesions, encephalitis, and dementia. Being easily irritated often has to do with overloading, tiredness, and confusion. Some patients, on the other hand, have a tendency for impulsive anger and agitation. Excessive stimulation, exhaustion, or a straining task may provoke anger or agitation. Negative feelings to slight irritation to rage can be seen as a continuum. Judd (1999) emphasizes that impulsive anger is seldom purely neurological or psychological. This holds true for many patient groups. Impulsive anger occurs easily in frontal (especially orbitofrontal) lesions when the controlling prefrontal, inhibitory connections to inner areas of emotional processing are disrupted. Injury to frontal regions of the temporal lobes, the structures of the hypothalamus and thalamus, may also result in aggressiveness in people (Judd, 1999).

An example. Discussing emotions in relation to a preliminary evaluation of rehabilitation with a man who suffered from injury to the frontal lobe four years ago.

P: I get irritated by small things more easily. Like yesterday I had to read some insurance papers, stuff about pension-insurance. I just simply can't stand to read that stuff. But now I read them this morning, when it was quiet and she [his wife] was out.

T: Hm ...
P: There was no other noise.
T: So you're irritated and so on, but do you.... Do you ever get proper fits of rage?
P: I don't get those anymore.... At first I got all kinds of fits ... and it didn't ... like the wife didn't even know what it was and we would argue. I've gotten over that now.
T: Hm...
P: I've learnt.
T: Describe the bursts of anger to me a little. What were they like and how did you personally feel about them?
P: At work I would, for example, get mixed up about even simple things, and the machines, the machines.... Even though I had, I had built some of the machines from start to finish myself, I would get messed up on using them ... straightforward things, it should be just like riding a bike, simple ... and then when I had to design some new casts or fix something, and I've lost my tools, and I'm freaking out, and so, then I would throw a tool or break something, and it would make it better for a while ... like throw a screwdriver through the wall, so that it's definitely not safe to be in the same room with me! I would scream mindlessly and throw that tool. . . .

This type of behavior is also not understood by friends or peer groups, unless clarified with the others at work or in the home environment.

Means to Endure Encounters

Disturbances in emotional expression or experience brought about by a neurological injury, depending on its severity, call for intervention either directly or mediated into the surroundings. Disturbances may also cause secondary anxiety and shame, along with other visible or invisible neurological deficiencies. The means to encounter and treat disruptions should be tailored case-specifically. However, common for all is the necessity of informing patients and their families about the symptoms caused by injury and the nature of those symptoms. Explaining the matter on a single occasion or handing out an informative leaflet is seldom enough, but psychoeducation is needed continuously along the way. Coming to terms with the symptoms and processing the emotions they create take time. Additionally, how well the patient recognizes the symptoms affects the advancement of treatment.

In cases of *problems with understanding emotions*, family members can be advised to express their own feelings to the injured relative, and not to expect that something such as tone of voice will be enough to convey their emotions. A patient, whose problems of understanding deals with the difficulty of perceiving emotional expression, may in turn be guided to pay more attention to the ways in which others express emotions and may think to ask how others are doing (Judd, 1999). As exercises, forms of emotional expression can be studied in therapy via videos, TV programs, and other means, either individually or in group therapy. If the issues are in relation to *expressing emotion*, and not so much with understanding, it is fundamental to get to know the existing emotion. If the patient's nonverbal communication skills are weak, but he has awareness of the symptoms, he can be taught how to compensate communication with verbal expression. In turn, those around the patient are to be guided to pay attention to the patient's message, even if it does not correlate with his gestures. We can also strive to strengthen nonverbal communication where the understanding of emotional communication has remained intact. Along with psychoeducation, rehabilitative methods may also be considered to aid patients in coming to terms with their symptoms and acknowledging them (Judd, 1999). An expressionless or monotonously speaking patient's facial expressions or voice may be difficult to modify to be more vibrant. However, the patient can learn to acknowledge the deficit in his communication and to compensate for it. Giving feedback requires a safe working relationship and the forming of particular feedback to fit the patient's situation.

In cases of *excessive talkativeness*, we can attempt to enforce the patient's inner methods of monitoring and controlling his actions if he has the capacity for it. Often, external feedback is necessary, at least in the beginning. When a patient begins to talk excessively, he often misses external messages. The patient and his relatives can be directed in ways to communicate to the injured and in which situations they should stop the excessive talking. In *reflexive crying and laughing*, we can attempt to inquire of the patient, when he is relaxed, how he wishes to deal with the issue (i.e., do we continue with the topic, try not to pay attention, leave him alone for a while, etc.?).

Patients suffering from severe reflex crying often wish that no attention be paid to them. Those suffering from milder symptoms may wish for a sign of empathy, such as a light touch. Some can learn to control the symptoms by moving their attention or line of vision elsewhere for a moment. Therapist and patient together can think of ways for the patient to communicate his or her symptoms (e.g., showing a card; Judd, 1999). In nonvoluntary expressions of emotion, the guidance of relatives is essential. If the patient suffers from reflexive laughter, the people around him should know not to laugh with him. In cases of *automatic swearing*, the primary methods are guidance of relatives, making the reason behind the patient's behavior known in social situations, cue cards that explain the symptom, and, finally, humor. In difficult cases, Judd proposes the use of more behavioral methods. If *emotional expression has subdued*, it is important for relatives to learn how not to take it personally. We can attempt to stimulate emotional reactions with objects and things the patient has liked in the past (such as, photographs, movies, places, experiences, etc.). In instances of *over sensitive reactions*, it is important to stay calm and empathetic, without joining the emotional outburst and making it stronger. When it has been clearly established that lability is an organic, not a psychological, reaction to illness, it is good to make this obvious to relatives. Specific analysis of the symptom situation can clarify both the provoking and the relieving factors (for example, exhaustion, pain, hunger, etc.). At times it is good to avoid situations in which reactions are heightened, especially at the beginning. It can be investigated as to whether shifting attention, moving away from the situation, or external hints have any effect. If lability is permanent and disturbing, some traditional methods of cognitive therapy can be used if they help with the symptom or with getting used to it. *In anger and fits of rage*, psychoeducation should also be used, along with guidance and investigating what the provoking actors are. It is essential to avoid overstimulation, learn strategies of self-control, and, if needed, create a safe environment. It is important to explain peacefully to an easily angered person what is in fact is happening, as many outbursts are due to confusion or overloading. Brain damage can weaken the skill to adapt to rapidly changing situations, and many patients do not like "surprises." Judd proposes the use of cue cards (i.e., risk situations, anticipating signs, etc.), role playing, and, if needed, behavioral methods. As a control method for episodes of aggressive outbursts, a therapist can try to move away, direct the patient's attention elsewhere, and reorient the patient to the situation.

Reflections

The methods to encounter problems with emotional regulations are manifold and differ on multiple levels, depending on the symptom's intensity and the patient's acceptance of the symptom. The methods range from external to internal control, supporting personal acceptance of symptoms, and psychoeducation to specific psychotherapeutic techniques. With the use of psychotherapeutic methods, especially with a cognitive approach, it is possible to help patients to make sense of the emotional experience and of their own behavior, supporting self-monitoring and symbolizing the experience, as long as we acknowledge the changes in patients' abilities to receive and control information. In some cases, the awakening or strengthening of emotional expression is justified; in others it is not. Greenberg & Paivio (1997), for example, does not recommend the reinforcement of emotions in patients with inadequate regulation skills or clearly impaired cognitive abilities, nor those depicting psychotic behavior or suffering from severe borderline personality disorders. Additionally, it is important to keep in consideration that emotions can get "stuck" easily in organic emotional problems. Even though problems with emotional regulation caused by brain damage need special attention, the greater purpose of therapy should naturally be to support the patient's adjustment to identity changes and limits set by the injury. After brain injury, the patient often has to redefine his sense of "self," as previously established modes of behavior do not necessarily function any longer. The symptoms of injury or illness can hit deep into one's understanding of self and identity. Individuals will strive to maintain the sense of continuity of self, although they might notice that their own actions and ways of thinking are not quite as they used to be. The construction of a new sense of self takes time, experiences, and insight. Due to cognitive deficits, learning and reintegration take longer. There are ways to support the integration process, such as narrative methods and suggesting the creation of self portraits, by helping to interpret and name occurrences and experiences, and by encouraging the patient to join peer-support groups. Not all patients require formal therapy, but most need at least some guidance and aid (Judd, 9 (1999)).

A Case Description—Emotional Monitoring, Memory, and the Self

Following is a description of a neuropsychotherapeutic rehabilitation case, in which psychological rehabilitation has been combined with psychotherapy. The case in question is a 22-year-old female, who I will call TM. Six years after an operation on her brain tumor, TM began to regain the ability to recall childhood memories. She had severe symptoms in the frontal lobe, which made controlling emotions and behavior difficult and interfered with memory and concentration. The rehabilitation process has now lasted for six years.

Background Information

At the time of entering rehabilitation, TM was a 17-year-old student, who had undergone an operation on a tumor 2cm in diameter in her right frontal lobe. In a neuropsychological test carried out at the hospital, the following findings were made typical for frontal region damages: slight difficulties in executive functions, a tendency to repeat or mix up memories, mild problems with finding words, problems with inhibiting stimuli, slowness, a tendency to make mistakes, and a slightly narrow auditory attention span.

The estimate was, however, that the entire magnitude of the symptoms might not be revealed in a structured testing situation. TM later complained about problems with her memory, getting things mixed up, having trouble with concentration, and irritability. Doing her homework was taking up more time than in the past, and in exams she ran out of time. TM had also noticed that she could only remember things that had happened during the year before her operation, and that she had no recollection of the time before that. TM was studying for a dual degree at a vocational institute.

The Course of the Rehabilitation Process: Challenges in Behavior and Everyday Life Caused by Damage to the Frontal Lobe

In the beginning, it became apparent that studying for two degrees simultaneously was too much. TM was tired and suffered often from severe migraines, but she was not yet ready to give up on her plans for higher secondary education. It would take a year for her to let go of her hopes for a dual degree. Her relatives explained how she studied actively but did not succeed as she had in the past. They also felt a change in TM's personality. The following came up when interviewing the relatives:

> TM had been nice and gentle in the past, but now she would swear and say aloud things she did not mean to. At first she would even comment on strangers in public. Her prudence in social situations had deteriorated. She would say inappropriate things or the wrong things in the wrong places. She would talk to outsiders about private affairs without discretion.

TM had also noticed the change in her behavior and felt strange about it. Her own priority was to get through her education. She was studying for a profession she had dreamed of since childhood—she felt as if she had to succeed. Psychologically, TM was also having problems with her self-esteem and was experiencing anxiety about her illness. To the outsider, she gave an impression of herself as diligent and energetic, and she had not cried for years. At times, she would become disturbed by getting her thoughts mixed up and experiencing déjà vu.

During the rehabilitation process, TM would concentrate on succeeding at school and learning to recognize and cope with her new self. She explained that in the past, she had been quiet and had been picked on, but now she would talk straight back to people—she did not have many friends at school. Feedback from teachers clearly depicted the problems TM was having due to the brain lesion:

> "... is a determined student, but cannot handle the same amount of work as the other students in her class. She often needs instructions to be repeated and at times is unable to bring to mind a familiar word, but needs clues to remember it. In practical work situations she cannot time her actions like the others and when she is exhausted she can be sharp tempered."

Decreased productivity is typical in patients with frontal lobe injuries, and TM needed clear guidelines and structures in her studies and everyday life, for her own thoughts might get mixed up or stuck during work processes. Without clear structures and guides given from teachers, the text TM produced would be just a flow of thoughts that was off the topic, repetitive, and could end abruptly. Written guides and learning to ask for instructions made it easier for her to cope at school, and writing things down helped her keep things organized, as otherwise she would forget easily. Written work that focused on a clear topic and structure began to improve. The school cooperated in her rehabilitation. Her ability to use different compensation methods for memory deficiency and techniques to calm herself down improved steadily (for example, methods such as task lists, memory alarms, relaxation, etc.). The incidents of thoughts getting stuck or being repeated, being too frank with words, and déjà vu experiences reduced gradually, but these symptoms have not disappeared entirely. TM graduated with a vocational degree in three years, with a partly adjusted syllabus. Being able to finish one degree and get a profession she always had wanted was a great achievement for TM, and strengthened confidence in herself. She sometimes expressed the wish to study for another degree, but she also knew it would be hard.

Challenges with Self-Esteem, Self-Image, and Orientation

As TM's control over herself began to improve, she felt an increasing need to contemplate her self, self-esteem, and illness on top of her previous goals in rehabilitation, such as recognizing her symptoms, learning to control her speech and behavior, coping with studies and everyday life, and recognizing the factors that exposed her to outbreaks.

Together with her occupational therapist, TM began to build a "Me-folder," in which she collected things about herself, her aspirations, and her abilities. Her childhood memories were still gone. She did not remember anything about her time in lower secondary school, her own confirmation party, or many other events of the past. Principal knowledge of where she had lived, which schools she had gone to, what type of childhood she had had, and some states of mind (such as having been bullied) were there, but the ability to bring back memories of important events in her life was gone. She could describe important people, or a pet she had as a child, and she knew that she had been on a journey, but nothing more specific. Stories or pictures of herself did not raise any memories. Having these missing memories was difficult for TM. This is what she wrote about herself after graduation:

> "I have gone through a rough time, for five years I've known that I have a brain tumor, which can't be operated on, so I don't know

> what I think about the future but I remain trustful.... So it just feels like I'm moving forward in my life. I would like to get my life back when it comes to memories. I would like to know about my childhood and about myself, not so that someone has to open up my memory with key words. That's not life, I wish to be as I was before, although I don't regret not being a wuss—today I can hold my ground."

When it came to expressing herself emotionally, TM gradually turned more sensitive and she would cry more easily. The first fits of crying lasted for nearly an hour. She also had obvious trouble with her feelings. Before, it had been characteristic for her to repress her feelings. She did not always seem to be in contact with her feelings or would attempt to disregard them. ("I will put those difficult emotions away.") TM would also ask too much from herself, going overboard and not noticing her body's signs of exhaustion. She began to display physical symptoms in her stomach, heart, and joints, and there was an increase in panic attack–like fits, even after graduation, as she had to struggle with job training and internships. After her secondary courses were over, her headaches subsided, but still returned in new stressful situations. She was diagnosed with fibromyalgia, and as she explained it herself, her "body would break down." An experience of getting stuck in an elevator increased the force of her panic attacks, and she was more and more distressed by her annual MRIs. She began to stay away from elevators and the risk for avoidance behavior grew.

Toward Emotional Work and Emotional Memories

In rehabilitation, it was necessary for TM to stop and explore her inner experiences. Relaxation exercises (of the progressive, later "mindfulness" type) were intensified, and ways to name and express emotions were explored. In the beginning, so-called "emotional pictures" as well as photographs, taken by TM were utilized. TM was fond of photography, and, when feeling restless, she would set out to take pictures, as she found it relaxing. She liked to photograph nature and social events she had attended. Furthermore, she enjoyed editing the pictures. However, in the long run, photography was not a sufficient route to expressing her own emotions. The rehabilitation work was extended to include pictures and texts found in magazines, which TM would gather and build into different collages. A division of labor was agreed upon with her occupational therapist. During occupational therapy, TM would concentrate on her physical well-being, increasing physical activity and relaxing. She would also photograph nature with her therapist. TM got easily concerned about other people's problems and would get stuck on problems or issues that did not necessarily involve her. When she began to worry about something, she could not draw a line between her own and other people's worries, and needed help in pointing it out. Situational analysis, cognitive analysis of thoughts and emotions, and writing them down, as well as testing out her own beliefs, helped in structuring. According to TM's experience, free-writing did not aid her in clarifying thoughts and emotions; she needed clues and guidance.

Learning to relax and carrying out exposing practices helped quickly with the avoidance behavior. During support work for her emotional expression, the use of readymade emotional cards helped TM to communicate her feelings more multidimensionally than she could otherwise. Photography helped her record important occasions, and pictures of nature would soothe her. However, explaining her feelings through pictures and captions from magazines turned to be out more personal and efficient. In collages, TM would gradually collect things that gave her energy and joy, but also things she found difficult. She found the collages to give form, pictures, and words to her state of mind. The words were found among short lines of text, and, as a side effect, childhood memories began to slowly come to mind.

An example. Arriving at reception, TM was thrilled by a memory experience; she had remembered something about her childhood a few days earlier.

TM: We had a family gathering last autumn and my cousin E was there. It's been probably like 10 years since I last saw her. So we talked about things we had done in the past, but, I couldn't grasp any of it! Now yesterday when we [TM and her occupational therapist] were watching, or listening, to the relaxing music it popped in to my mind, E talking about that stuff, and I got all these feelings and the laughter and jokes and such!! They were there, there.... Hey, this is what E was talking about!!! All those relaxing forest sounds [on the tape] ... I started thinking, like, this is feeling somehow familiar, and then I instantly thought of P, and then I thought P and E?? Wait, yes! This is the thing I've been thinking about for so long, which E talked about, and now suddenly came to my mind .... That music kind of resembled what had happened to us back then.

T: What happened back then? What was the environment?

TM: A forest … we were doing something, like … I can't remember if we were playing or something, but we were cooking sausages and just being like cousins are. Ten years from that I couldn't remember it, but NOW! On Monday I remembered everything E had talked about [laughs]; this is so strange, but somehow that relaxing music brings back those memories. It's like this one time I went swimming with J at our summer cottage, we barbequed sausages, and chatted—I even remember the things we talked about. I can't remember them now, but that music opened them up, what were we talking about [thinks]? It must have been about boys again, but I can't find it now, but it brought back the scents, tastes, and laughter, and everything!

TM: It's the same when looking at photographs nowadays, like this was the occasion… [talks about memories].

T: [Astonished] So you're looking at old photo albums?

TM: Yeah, I found this old album in the cellar when cleaning; it brought back all kinds of memories. Like this picture is taken at that time and then I write it down so I can remember. Even from the field trip I recalled all these strange memories I thought I'd never remember…. During this past week I've remembered all these things I thought were gone forever.

TM: I got these clips and looking at the photos there was more; it's like some chest opened up in here [points to her head]…. Maybe it started when I saw my brother and we talked about everything we've done as kids, like mischief [laughs] and stuff… .

T: Earlier, when making the collage, you said you got the same feeling?

TM: It also brought back those memories…. Those photos also had a meaning, that's what it is! I was, like, wait a minute! In that one picture I'm 6 years old, and I didn't want to go there or do something, and I just asked my mother if that was the case, and she said, "Oh! You remember? How in the world?" It feels so good to find these things I thought I'd lost forever.

A month later, old photographs were looked at again in therapy. The ability to bring back memories had remained.

T: How old are you in this one?

TM: That has to be elementary school, 5th or 6th grade. It's a family gathering. I recall some parts; it was nice.

TM: I'm 4 or 5 in this one; I'm getting some small memories… .

T: It is normal not to remember everything about one's childhood; a certain amnesia belongs in childhood, and you might just get flashes of memories.

TM: But now that I look at these I get .... It's nice to remember things from when I was 5 to 12, but after that I get these black holes. But at least I got back some of that childhood; I was so sad when I couldn't remember a thing about it.

T: Exactly.

TM: But still I have nothing from my confirmation or that. . . .

T: Yes.

TM: But first I'd just like to get that childhood to open up. . . .

T: Yes, to get an understanding of what it was like. . . .

TM: Yes, so it would be that I just look at something and be like, "Oh yeah, this is that occasion! And wait, here we were with my grandparents!" And then I got such a good feeling, that I REMEMBER, YES! [laughs]

It was also difficult for TM to bring back in mind things that happened after the operation, but clues and writing down, when she recalled something, helped.

TM: Then there's our trip to the Canary Islands. . . . This is the only picture left from there.

T: This was in the 2000s, with your mother two years ago?

TM: Yeah, with Mom and Dad. But still I don't have many, well, I just remember having fun and liking it a lot.

T: Is your hotel in the picture?

TM: I think that's me in the picture taken at the hotel. . . .

TM: There's also the problem that I can't remember what happened three weeks ago, but luckily I have a calendar to solve that problem. . . .

T: So the calendar helps to open those memories?

TM: [nods]

TM: When I get to write it down, it stays in my memory... [talks about photos]

T: ... So looking at these ...

TM: Something just popped into mind, so I just wrote it down, like who is in it. . . . I got these flashbacks basically of scents and feelings and the irritation and hm. . . . That kind of things, like, "No, that's what that is, what was I thinking!" hahaha. . . .

Memories are still feeble and when viewing photos again, things can get mixed up, partly due to the reencoding process of memories. After over a year had passed, this is how TM described reviving memories:

TM: I still only remember, like, confirmation parties and these short flashes. From photos I can recognize where I am, but I don't get the whole story. . . .

T: And ...
TM: It starts to slowly get back to me, and then gets mixed up again.... .
T: Right ...
TM: And when I finally get the whole thing, I start to talk about something else and they get, like ... like those déjà vu type things; they get all messed up.
T: You mean the stories, times, and places?
TM: Yes. I get these short .... But I can remember! That's what I'm really happy about! Even if they do get mixed up, I'm just so happy to remember some of the childhood things, like trips to Ostrobothnia with grandparents!

Reflections

Experiences of recollecting childhood episodes and emotions have been invigorating for TM. She feels like she knows herself and who she is better. In TM's case, it can be stated that the role of memory, and especially consciously accessible autobiographical memories, is essential for the construction and maintenance of self and identity (LeDoux, 2002). TM's emotional memories are at times fragmentary and linked to different senses. They highlight the situations in positive and negative connotations. Nevertheless, the "backbone" of her autobiographical memory gained support and tone from the recalled event-specific knowledge and episodes (Conway & Rubin, 1993).

Associative memory recollection systems appear to function in reminiscence situations as activated by nonverbal stimuli. The atmosphere created by relaxing music and the visual material began to support memory in general, but they also revived emotional memories, in line with the experiential similarity (LeDoux, 2002). Similarities in emotional states in times of memory encoding and rehabilitation sessions would have eased the access to memories. Strategic reminiscing is still poor, and the damage to the right frontal lobe is still causing memories to mix up—a tendency of which TM is well aware. TM's memory problems are in accordance with what has been put forward in academic literature; the right frontal lobe has an important role in the formation of strategic memory recollection processes (Ochsner & Schacter, 2000). According to Schacter (1997), without the support of the frontal lobe, the memory system of the temporal lobe is left waiting for proper clues. A memory is not born according to a simple stimulus-response model, but is dependent on the combined effect of multiple factors. The temporal lobes and posterior regions of the brain, which store information about memories (engrams), have strong collaborative connections. The stimulus itself affects what we remember and how the memory is structured. Schacter has compared it to the reconstruction of a dinosaur skeleton out of individual bones. Why did the automatic associative memory receiving system start to function now, five or six years after TM's operation, and not earlier? It is possible that with time, the connections strengthened and invigorated. Rehabilitation work that focused on emotions might also have played a part. Additionally, TM's family went through a crisis episode, with which she needed support, during her rehabilitation. Could the emotionally tough situation during her rehabilitation have promoted the easier access to emotional memories?

At the end of TM's rehabilitation process, her capabilities were depicted as follows: She could function well in a relaxed situation, when allowed to work at her own pace and to use memory support. She would, however, be easily exhausted. In regard to impulsiveness, she had become more foresighted and could control her anger better. Physical aggressiveness had not surfaced in years.

Regarding cognitive monitoring of emotions and behavior, TM has learned quite well to compensate her behavior with "inner" speech, and she has learned to forecast difficult situations (she stays away from them or "psyches herself up"). She has learned to apologize. She did not always see her frankness as a bad thing, but was at times bothered by her lack of sensitivity and thoughtlessness. Hence, difficulties with cognitive control brought about by the damage still exist, although compensation skills have improved. For memory and structuring problems—caused by the frontal damage—TM still has to compensate with being systematic and making schedules. This is necessary for her, but might appear as stiffness or inflexibility to others.

Three phases can be distinguished from the rehabilitation process. *The first phase* emphasized neuropsychological rehabilitation, controlling impulsiveness, cognitive control, increasing regulation, and creating a therapeutic relationship. *The second phase* placed the emphasis on psychotherapy, as problems with emotions and adaptation were gradually charted with emotional terms. Essential to this phase was utilizing Greenberg's and Paivio's model to guide TM's attention toward inner experiences and to support her understanding of being able to affect her emotional experience (Karila, 2008; Greenberg and Paivio, 1997). *In the third phase*, due to receiving emotional memories, TM's life history and sense of self were strengthened.

Conclusion

For years, scientists and clinicians have attempted to answer the question, "Concerning a patient of brain lesion, what are the content and process of psychotherapy?" In their research questionnaire, Judd and Wilson (2005) collected the experiences of 21 psychologists working and creating alliances with patients with brain injuries. As central challenges, the psychologists brought up the deterioration of memory functions, the lack of acknowledging symptoms, and overall cognitive stiffness or inflexible thinking. In some cases, the symptoms were found to slow down or prevent the formation of a therapeutic alliance. The most efficient tools in facing the symptoms were found to be combinations of different educational, psychosocial, and cognitive work strategies. Under the title of neuropsychotherapy, T. Judd (1999) has put forward similar thoughts, to which I have referred in this paper. Neuropsychotherapy is the use of neuropsychological knowledge in the psychiatric therapy of a patient suffering from brain damage. It is needed especially when the patient experiences problems with emotional or behavioral monitoring, problems which are not treatable within the framework of ordinary rehabilitation, and when it is estimated that an intervention will help the situation (Judd, 1999).

References

Borod, J., & Madigan, N.K. (2000). Neuropsychology of emotion and emotional disorders: An overview and research directions. In J.C. Borod (Ed.), *The neuropsychology of emotion* (pp. 3–28). New York: Oxford University Press.

Buck, R.W. (2000). The epistemology of reason and affect. In J.C. Borod (Ed.), *The neuropsychology of emotion* (pp. 31–55). New York: Oxford University Press.

Conway, M.A., & Rubin, D.C. (1993). The structure of autobiographical memory. In A. F. Collins, S. E. Gathercole, M. A. Conway, and P. E. Morris (Eds.), *Theories of memory*. Hillsdale, NJ: Erlbaum.

Cummings, J.L., & Mega, M.S. (2003). *Neuropsychiatry and behavioral neuroscience*. New York: Oxford University Press.

Damasio, A.R. (2001). *Descartesin virhe*. Helsinki: Terra Cognita.

Damasio, A.R. (2003). *Spinozaa etsimässä. Ilo, suru ja tuntevat aivot*. Helsinki: Terra Cognita.

Greenberg, L.S., & Paivio, S.C. (1997). *Working with emotions in psychotherapy*. New York: Guilford Press.

Heilman, K.M., Blonder, L.X., Bowers, D., & Crucian, G.P. (2000). Neurological disorders and emotional dysfunction. In J.C. Borod (Ed.), *The Neuropsychology of emotion* (pp. 367–412). New York: Oxford University Press.

Judd, D., & Wilson, L. (2005). Psychotherapy with brain injury survivors: An investigation of the challenges encountered by clinicians and their modifications to therapeutic practice. *Brain Injury, 19*(6), 437–449.

Judd, T. (1999). *Neuropsychotherapy and community integration. Brain illness, emotions, and behavior*. New York: Kluwer Academic/Plenum Publishers.

Karila, R. (2008). Tunnepainotteinen kognitiivinen psykoterapia. In S. Kähkönen, I. Karila ja, and N. Holmberg (Eds.), *Kognitiivinen psykoterapia* (pp. 528–544). Helsinki: Duodecim.

Kober, H., Feldman Barrett, L., Joseph, J., Bliss-Moreau, E., Lindquist, K., & Wager, T.D. (2008). Functional grouping and cortical-subcortical interactions in emotion: A meta-analysis of neuroimaging studies. *Neuroimage, 42*, 998–1031.

Laaksonen, R. (2007). Johdanto neuropsykoterapiaan. In M. Lindeman, L. Hokkanen ja, and R-L. Punamäki (Eds.), *Hermoverkot, mielenterveys ja psykoterapia*. Helsinki: Psykologien Kustannus Oy.

Laaksonen, R. (2008). Aivot ja kuntoutuminen. Suomen Taideterapiayhdistys Ry:n jäsenjulkaisu: Teemana taideterapia neurologisten potilaiden kuntoutuksessa.

LeDoux, J. (2002). *Synaptinen itse. Miten aivot tekevät minusta minut*. Helsinki: Terra Cognita.

Leppänen, J.M. (2006). Emootiokategoriat ja niiden tutkiminen. In H. Hämäläinen, M. Laine ja, and A. Revonsuo (Eds.), *Aivot ja mieli* (pp. 311–317). Kognitiivisen neurotieteen tutkimuskeskus: Turun yliopisto.

Nummenmaa, L. (2006). Kognitio ja emootio. In H. Hämäläinen, M. Laine ja, and A. Revonsuo (Eds.), Aivot ja mieli (pp. 301–310). Kognitiivisen neurotieteen tutkimuskeskus: Turun yliopisto.

Ochsner, K.N., & Schacter, D.L. (2000). A social cognitive neuroscience approach to emotion and memory. In J.C. Borod (Ed.), *The neuropsychology of emotion* (pp. 163–193). New York: Oxford University Press.

Phelps, E. A, & LeDoux, J. E. (2005). Contributions of the amygdala to emotion processing: From animal models to human behavior. [Review]. *Neuron, 48*, 175–187.

Robinson, R. G., & Manes, F. (2000). Elation, mania, and mood disorders: Evidence from neurological disease. In J. C. Borod (Ed.), *The neuropsychology of emotion* (pp. 239–268). New York: Oxford University Press.

Sackeim, H. A., Greenberg, M. S., Weiman, A. L., Gur, R. C., Hungerbuhler, J. P., & Geschwind, N. (1982). Hemispheric asymmetry in the expression of positive and negative emotions. *Archives of Neurology, 39*(4), 210–218.

Schacter, D. L. (1997). *Sökandet efter minnet*. Jönköping: Brain Books AB.

Sherer, K. R. (2000). Psychological models of emotion. In J. C. Borod (Ed.), *The neuropsychology of emotion* (pp. 137–162). New York: Oxford University Press.

Tateno, A. T., Jorge, R. E., & Robinson, R. G. (2004). Pathological laughing and crying following traumatic brain injury. The *Journal of Neuropsychiatry and Clinical Neurosciences, 16*, 4.

6

Resistance in Treating Neurological Patients

Paula Häkkinen

Introduction

A psychotherapeutic process faces many challenges. There can be difficulties in the working alliance and ruptures may emerge. One important process factor is resistance. Ruptures may stem from resistance. Psychotherapy with brain-injured patients can largely be regarded as helping them to improve their levels of awareness, acceptance, and realism (Klonoff, 1997), but psychotherapy can be particularly challenging because of the combination of cognitive, emotional, behavioural, and communicative impairments. Judd and Wilson (2005) have listed main challenges that affect the forming of a working alliance with brain-injured patients: lack of insight, impaired memory, inflexible thinking, poor attention, language difficulties, disinhibited behaviour, and emotional lability. These neuropsychological deficits can also be deemed important in resistance.

From the traditional viewpoint, resistance in patients with central neural system deficits is not necessarily the same kind of resistance that occurs when dealing with psychotherapeutic patients. Some reasons for resistance can be associated with neuropsychological deficits. There are some commonly considered features of resistance, such as not coming to sessions or coming too late, but when the patient with memory problems is concerned, the reason for not coming to the session may be resistance or simply forgetting the session time. There are some groups of patients who often seem to exhibit quite a strong resistance, such as patients with neglect syndrome and brain-injury patients with impaired self-awareness. It is important to analyze whether there is resistance and what kind of resistance it is.

Five main dimensions can be identified in the conceptualization of resistance dealing with neurological patients: (a) those elements which are present in the therapeutic process; (b) personality dispositions; (c) social relationships; (d) psychological reactions after the onset of illness; and (e) neuropsychological syndromes.

The concept of resistance is considered in this chapter in an eclectic way, and a summaries of the following theories of resistance will be presented: psychoanalytic theory (Freud, 1926), cognitive model (Ellis, 1985), and the integrated social–cognitive model (Leahy, 2003). The elements in the therapeutic process, such as transference, countertransference, and therapeutic alliance, are presented briefly, as are personality dispositions. Psychological reactions after the onset of illness may include, for example, anger, depression, anxiety, and post-traumatic stress disorder. The effects of neuropsychological deficits, such as impaired self-awareness, impaired memory, inflexible thinking, poor attention, language difficulties, impaired emotional awareness, and emotional lability, will also be discussed.

Neuropsychological rehabilitation requires integrated knowledge about the brain-behaviour relationship, the nature of neurological illness, cognitive processes, and neuropsychological syndromes. However, this is not enough; the neuropsychologist should also be aware of psychological and therapeutic elements, which are present in a confidential relationship. The concept of resistance must be modified when dealing with neurological patients to fit the issues of real-life interactions.

The Concept of Resistance

Resistance is a clinical manifestation of the individual's needs to defend himself against impulses, memories, and feelings, which would provoke anxiousness, pain, or threat when coming into consciousness (Fromm-Reichmann, 1967). The patient, who has sought professional help, opposes the process in a variety of ways, which may ruin the objective to change (Moore & Fine, 1990). Because pathogenic conflicts arouse painful feelings, the patient tries to keep them out of consciousness. The methods he uses to keep mental content from his awareness are called defences. When manifested in the treatment either as subtle or as overt oppositional behaviour, these defences are called resistances (Pulver, 1995). According to psychoanalytic theory, resistance can manifest in "attitudes, verbalizations, and actions that prevent awareness of a perception, idea, memory, feeling, or a complex of such elements that might establish a connection with earlier experiences or contribute insight into the nature of unconscious conflicts" (Moore & Fine, 1990, p. 168). Leahy (2003), on the other hand, is speaking about resistance in cognitive therapy. He defines resistance "as anything in the patient's behaviour, thinking, affective response, and interpersonal style that interferes with the ability of that patient to utilize the treatment and to acquire the ability to handle problems outside of the therapy and after therapy has been terminated" (Leahy, 2003, p. 11).

The phenomenology of resistance can be manifold; some forms are obvious, some harder to see. Resistance may appear as the patient's unwillingness to talk about issues of importance in therapy (Fromm-Reichmann, 1967). Other behavioural features of concern are not coming to sessions, coming too late, not paying for treatment, devaluing the therapist or the treatment, or finishing treatment too soon (Leahy, 2003). Quite obvious resistance is silence and selective inattention or misinterpretation to suggestions offered by the therapist (Fromm-Reichmann, 1967; Sandler, Dare, & Holder, 1992). Less obtrusive resistance remains hidden. It may show itself as the patient's doubting whether the therapist is the right person with whom to work. The patient can report seeing the justification of the interpretive suggestion intellectually, but cannot follow it up emotionally. Resistance can be recognized in lack of improvement, even though therapeutic work appears to be proceeding overly well (Fromm-Reichmann, 1967). Resistance can also show itself as overcompliance: The patient agrees with everything that the therapist says. Somatic symptomatology can be resistance. The patient may have a headache, stomachache, or general pain as excuse to prevent the patient from collaboration and participation in rehabilitation.

The Theoretical Framework of Resistance

A few examples of theoretical angles will be reviewed: psychoanalytic theory (Freud, 1926), cognitive therapy (Ellis, 1985), and integrated social–cognitive model (Leahy, 2003).

Psychoanalytic Theory

Resistance is a crucial concept in psychoanalytic theory. Freud (1926) has distinguished five forms of resistance: repression-resistance, transference-resistance, resistance deriving the gain from illness, id-resistance, and superego-resistance. These sources of resistance outlined by Freud remain central in the theory of psychoanalytic orientation today, although the list may be expanded upon (Sandler, Dare, & Holder, 1992), with sources such as resistance arising from inappropriate procedures, resistance depending on social relationships, resistance prompted by the danger of cure and the loss of the therapist, resistance due to the threat of the therapeutic work to the patient's self-esteem, resistance to giving up of past adaptive solutions (Sandler, Dare, & Holder, 1992), character resistance (Reich, 1933), and narcissistic resistance (McLaughlin, 1995).

Cognitive Therapy Conceptualization of Resistance

In cognitive therapy, according to Ellis (1985), resistance is caused by dysfunctional thinking. Beck has conceptualized maladaptive schemas (Beck, 1970; Beck, et al., 1990), which can also be viewed as a reason for resistance and will be dealt with more extensively in the section on personality dispositions.

According to Ellis (1985), resistance is caused by dysfunctional thinking, and there are irrational beliefs behind dysfunctional thinking. In his pioneering work, Ellis (1985) offers the following reasons for resistance: fear of discomfort, fear of shame, feelings of hopelessness, desire for self-punishment, fear of change, reactance and rebelliousness, receiving secondary gains, and patients' hidden agendas. The first mentioned, resistance created by fear of discomfort, is resistance stemming from a low frustration tolerance. This is called also discomfort anxiety. Ellis uses cognitive, emotive, and behavioural techniques of overcoming resistance in his rational emotive therapy, or RET (later known as REBT).

Multidimensional Model of Resistance

Leahy's (2003) categorization is an integrated social–cognitive model in which there is a classification of separate models of resistance.

Dimensions of resistance in his model include: validation resistance, self-consistency, schematic resistance, moral resistance, victim resistance, depressive resistance, and self-handicapping. Leahy has also made guidelines for treatments of resistance. These dimensions are described here briefly.

Validation resistance: Patient demands for understanding, empathy, and care from the therapist to the detriment of effective problem solving or rational perspective.

Self-consistency: People are motivated to maintain consistency in their thoughts, emotions, and self-concept, and they seek information that verifies their self-concept and which is familiar to them. Thoughts against these expectations are easily met with resistance.

Schematic resistance: Schemas seem to originate quite early in human development and, that is why schemas are quite regressive, and resistance can emerge. Patients often feel schemas protect them from further loss. The goal in therapy cannot be complete elimination of schemas, because removal of defensive maneuvers may result in resistance toward the therapeutic relationship.

Moral resistance: Many patients resist change if they believe there are moral or ethical issues involved.

Victim resistance: Some resistant patients believe that they deserve to suffer and resist problem solving and considering their own role in the problem. The therapist's role may center on validating the patient's suffering and being careful not to invalidate the injury and normalize his response.

Depressive resistance: The goal of the depressive mode is to avoid further loss. "Do not expect too much, and you will not to be disappointed." The depressed utilize a strategy that minimizes change. These strategies lead to resistance to change, resulting in maintenance of the depression.

Self-Handicapping: Self-handicapping focuses on avoiding direct evaluation of one's ability or self.

Leahy (2003) has also examined several aspects of procedural resistance in cognitive behavioural therapy. Problems in therapy can take the form of problems in agenda setting, collaborative set, homework compliance, lack of continuity of appointments, abusive or seductive behaviour, splitting the transference with other therapists, and premature termination. Leahy's model could be seen as appropriate when dealing with neurological patients, but it must be modified and the special issues of patients with neuropsychological deficits taken into account, which is out of the scope of Leahy's reference. For example, there is a possibility that the traumatic brain-injury patient (TBI) has experienced violence, and as such the victim role is different. In cognitive therapy, it is expected that the patient set the agenda. With the patient who has executive problems, it is more often the therapist who is setting the agenda. Active problem solving can also be difficult for the neurological patient. It is common that the patient in neuropsychological rehabilitation has not carried out the patient's homework. In cognitive therapy, it is expected to be the patient's own responsibility, but as Judd (1999) describes, in the continuum of responsibility between nursing staff and the patient recovering from sudden brain illness, personal responsibility recovers progressively; similarly, the share of responsibility between the patient and therapist depends on the nature of the brain damage and severity of neuropsychological syndrome. When the patient has severe neuropsychological deficits, the patient has the minority of the responsibility and the therapist has more, but when the patient is capable of taking more responsibility, the therapist's responsibility subsequently lessens.

A crucial difference in neuropsychological treatment is that the therapist has more responsibility than the patient in the collaboration process. However, also with neurological patients, there is need for mutual collaboration. This means the validation of feelings and needs, homework compliance, ability to give feedback to each other, and recommendations for change. These elements may reduce resistance and improve the patient's ability to work with problem-solving orientation.

Resistance has been traditionally understood as any aspect of the patient's activity (either intrapersonal or interpersonal) that obstructs the therapeutic process, but nowadays it is understood more as the conceptualizing of a two-person perspective (Safran & Muran, 2000). Safran and Muran divide theoretical framework of resistance into three categories: intrapsychic, characterological, and relational resistance. According to Ellis (1985) and Leahy (2003), dimensions of resistance can be seen as intrapsychic resistance, but also as interpsychic or relational resistance, as they both discuss also countertransference, which is dealt with in more detail in the next section on the psychotherapeutic process.

Psychotherapeutic Process

In this chapter, resistance is presented in the context of the therapist–patient relationship. Elements, such as transference,countertransference, and working alliance, are present in the therapeutic process. Freud considered it necessary to study the therapist–patient relationship and transference. According to Freud, all our relationships are patterned by our early relationships with the significant others in our environment in infancy and childhood (Fromm-Reichmann, 1967). Unresolved difficulties in interpersonal relationships with significant others in the patient's early life are transferred into the therapist–patient relationship (Fromm-Reichmann, 1967). The patient may reexperience repressed feelings and experiences and develop transferences from past figures to the therapist. The patient's new feelings about the therapist may be felt as threatening, and this may cause the most intense resistance (Sandler, Dare, & Holder, 1992). The pioneers of psychoanalysts considered transference–resistance as being the most powerful obstacle in the path of psychoanalytic treatment.

Countertransference means that the therapist's feelings and attitudes towards a patient are derived from earlier situations in the therapist's life, or it can be narrowly defined as a specific reaction to the patient's transference. Both Ellis (1985) and Leahy (2003) deal with countertransference. Ellis (1985) speaks of resistance sparked by the therapist's relationship problems. Ellis's rational emotive therapy, or RET, specializes in helping the therapist to look at his own countertransference problems by encouraging him to discover and to dispute the irrational beliefs that lie behind therapist's prejudices.

Although it is important to study transference (Fromm-Reichmann, 1967; Ellis, 1985), the actual experience arising in the ongoing situation between therapist and patient must be studied as well (Fromm-Reichmann, 1967). Resistance can emerge from problems of the working alliance. It is important to validate the patient and negotiate the therapeutic alliance. Ruptures may create resistance, but on the other hand, the negotiation and understanding may solve the problems and make the process even more efficient. Safran and Muran (2000) deal with resistance in terms of therapeutic alliance and ruptures in it. They have also made guidelines for working with resistance. Interpersonal process and therapeutic alliance are elaborated in Chapter 12 by Laaksonen and Ranta.

According to Bordin (1979), a working alliance includes agreement on goals, an assignment of tasks or series of tasks, and the development of a bond. Resistance can emerge if the therapist's and the patient's goals are different. The therapist's goal can be that the patient better understand limits because of cognitive disturbances, and the patient's goal may be to recover to the same level as before illness. Patients with impaired self-awareness can have difficulty to setting their own goals or personally valued outcomes (Ownsworth & Clare, 2006). Neurological patients may have difficulties understanding tasks or following them, and tasks may need to be modified in order to be suitable for patients with cognitive deficits. If the bond is not strong enough and of the right kind, resistance can emerge. A good working alliance is the basis of successful rehabilitative work. The patient's experience of a good emotional bond with the therapist has proved to be related to positive awareness ratings (Schönberger, Humle, & Teasdale, 2006a).

Personality Dispositions

The interpersonal process in psychotherapeutic settings naturally depends on previous experiences in a patient's autobiographical history. Problems arising in working alliance can be explained with the attachment model. Particularly it is great difference in security for the person who has undergone disorganized attachment and may be unstable in personal reactions and opposing attitudes toward different types of interactions (Allen, 2001). On the other hand, for a patient with secured attachment, the interpersonal process can be smooth and collaborative. That is why autobiographical family relations have to be studied and understood.

It has been suggested that cognitive, affective, and motivational processes are determined by the idiosyncratic structures, or schemas, that constitute the basic element of personality (Beck 1970; Beck et al., 1990; Alford & Beck 1997). In cognitive therapies, the methods aimed at emotional balance have been named compensatory strategies, which can be constructive or maladaptive. Therapists should be careful not to shatter the compensatory strategies too soon when the patient still has poor understanding of what has happened. Clark, Beck, and Alford (1999) have linked resistance in working alliance to two personality types: sosiotropic and personality with highly developed autonomy. The patients who easily resist and drop out of therapy are those with overautonomy (Clark et al., 1999). Individuals with a personality disorder tend to show certain patterns of behaviour that are overdeveloped, and other patterns that are underdeveloped, (e.g., passive-aggressive personality disorder uses resistance as overdeveloped strategy; Beck, et al., 1990). Resistance can be greater and different depending on different personality types.

In schema theory (Young, Klosko, & Weishaar, 2003), the contents may involve schemas, which interfere with the choice of therapeutic methods as well as with therapeutic interactions to an extreme. Young et al. (2003) have defined early maladaptive schemas, which influence people's human relationships in adulthood. When confronting patients' schemas, resistance is also dealt with (Leahy, 2003). It is important to find out the core schema or core belief.

One patient didn't come to session because of pain. When her thinking schemas were analyzed, it was found as a core belief that she thought she was a valuable person only if she was perfect. This case of a 49-year-old woman illustrates the power of cognitive schemas in treatment resistance. After CVA, the patient's main complaint was continuous headache, which prevented her from participating in various therapies. The neurological deficits were right hemiparesis and dyphasic disturbances with limited ability to express herself. When the dilemma of noncompliance in therapy was brought into the open, it was possible to understand the patient as well as to proceed in the therapies. The patient had a very fixed value schema of self-worth: The only way it was worthwhile to participate in rehabilitation was to be sure that she would make a total recovery; otherwise she would not be a worthwhile person. So it was not the headache that was the source of resistance, but the patient's mind and concept of self-worth.

Patients with preexisting psychosocial problems are especially vulnerable to negative reactions, including prolonged emotional distress (Mateer, Sira, & O'Connell, 2005). Prigatano, Fordyce, Zeiner, Roueche, Pepping, and Wood (1986) have used following classification of personality disorders in traumatic brain injury: Some disturbances can be considered reactionary in nature; others are neuropsychologically based; and still others are characterological or premorbid in nature. Klonoff and Lage (1991) propose that individuals with the history of narcissistic problems that predate acquired brain injury show special problems with accepting and coping with the effects of the brain injury. Narcissistic and borderline personalities of schema modes have been described by Young et al. (2003). Patients with characterological disturbance usually lack psychological flexibility, and they have often difficulty forming a therapeutic alliance (Young et al., 2003). For persons who have strict opinions, it is difficult to accept other opinions than their own, and the change is difficult to achieve. Young's schema therapy has been proved to help patients with personality disorders.

Resistance Depending on Social Relationships

Resistance may emerge from social relationships: family relationships, changes in social role, and work situations, or it can be dependent on age. Young people can have much difficulty accepting a brain injury and may feel themselves different or worse than others. The social framework of teenagers and young adults poses a great challenge from a therapeutic standpoint—how to help the patient cope with the healthy young persons he will be intimate with in his future life.

Family Relationships

Patients with traumatic brain injury are usually young, and their residual handicaps and mental changes place a great emotional, social, and financial burden on their families, as well as a strong demand on rehabilitation services (Gainotti, 1993). The patient's family can experience significant distress and may resist accepting the patient's neurobehavioural deficits; according to McLaughlin and Carey (1993), this is called adversarial alliance, which is often established between the family and the staff. Families evaluated to have been highly stressed were also perceived to experience more conflict with the rehabilitation team; family stress was related to poorer adjustment to the patient's disability; and greater family/team conflict correlated with lower cognitive and physical functioning at admission, longer length of stay, younger patient age, and lower programme satisfaction (McLaughlin & Carey, 1993). It is important to develop a therapeutic relationship between family and the team in brain injury rehabilitation. Family members may need psychological consultation in coping with a brain-injured relative. As the families become better educated about the complexity of the problems of a brain-injured relative, they become more realistic and hopefully manage the patient more effectively. Several avenues have been identified for working effectively with family members (Prigatano & Klonoff, 1988). These activities are extremely important, since psychotherapy with brain-injured patients will be ineffective if there is not an equally ongoing work relationship with family members (Prigatano & Klonoff, 1988).

Workplace Relationships

The social resistance encountered by the patient at the workplace is probably more difficult, if the attitudes at the workplace are intolerant and colleagues are suspicious of the performance of a handicapped person. A typical procedure to reduce this kind of social resistance is to hold a common meeting where representatives of nursing staff, workplace, and the patient discuss the practical aspects of work, estimate possible difficulties, and agree on measures of how to facilitate employment. A follow-up period is necessary and if problems arise due to underperformance of the patient, it may be worth consideration to help the patient accept a position with different work status.

Psychological Reactions

Psychological reactions after the onset of illness are manifold and vary in nature and severity. The spectrum is wide, but the most frequent reactions we see are anger, depression, anxiety (Judd, 1999; Prigatano et al., 1986), and reactions due to posttraumatic stress disorder (Judd, 1999). There are also reactions due to the psychosocial stress after the onset of illness, which occur in physical health, mood, and behaviour. It is clear that aggravated reactions due to grief usually manifest themselves in the same type of emotional and behavioural problems. Psychosocial distress after the onset of illness or following acquired brain injury may last for a long period, and can be difficult for the patient to deal with.

The onset of illness is a very emotive occurrence, and psychological reactions after it can be manifold. Patients who have experienced a brain injury, have faced not only a traumatic event, but also personal loss, and the coping strategies employed by acquired brain-injury patients prior to their injury may no longer be available to them (Mateer et al., 2005). Emotional consequences of brain injury are significant (Mateer et al., 2005). On the other hand, emotional processing per se may be changed due to central nervous system dysfunctions. Judd (1999) enumerates the following symptoms: grief reactions, denial, depression, anxiety, perplexity and embarrassment, frustration, catastrophic reactions, and posttraumatic stress disorder (PTSD).

The therapist is faced in these types of situations with different types of options regarding how to meet the challenge of the therapeutic process. The therapist must validate the patient's strong and important feelings. At least three global categories of affective expression in therapy can be identified; they are primary emotions, secondary emotions, and instrumental emotions (Greenberg & Safran, 1987). Primary emotions are anger, sadness, and fear. It is only primary emotions that aid adaptive problem solving and integrated functioning (Greenberg & Safran, 1987). Secondary reactive emotions are expressed in response to a more primary emotion or cognition. Instrumental emotions are emotional behaviour patterns that people have learned to use to influence others. Primary sadness is often a very core feeling. People who are afraid of their own tears are often difficult to work with therapeutically because they are holding back. In order to experience primary emotions in therapy, the patient needs to attend to, recognize, and stay focused on certain internal cues (Greenberg & Safran, 1987). Many individuals with acquired brain injury, as well as other neurological patients, suffer from depression (Mateer et al., 2005). Post-stroke depression is common (Berg 2001, 2003; Pohjasvaara, Leppävuori, Siira, Vataja, Kaste, & Erkinjuntti, 1998; Palomäki, Lehtihalmes, Lönnqvist, & Kaste, 2001). It is also possible that the patient has a tendency to depression. Then the depression may take the form of resistance.

One patient had a stroke (infarct on left media-area), resulting in speech difficulties and mild neuropsychological deficits. She repeatedly cancelled the appointments. She has had earlier depression and because of the premorbid causes she couldn't engage herself to neuropsychological rehabilitation. Here, depression manifests itself as passivity, fear of engagement, and fear of rejection.

The patient can have feelings of frustration or despair. After stroke, generalized anxiety disorder may be seen (Leppävuori, Pohjasvaara, Vataja, Kaste, & Erkinjuntti, 2003). Anger is often seen in brain-injury patients (Demark & Gemeinhardt, 2002). Anger can manifest itself, for example, as criticism.

A patient was badly been abused and suffered severe brain injury (multiple contusions), and neurosurgical operations were needed (decompression craniotomy, subdural hematoma evacuation, shunt placement). He had speech difficulties and neuropsychological problems: amnesia, difficulties in concentration and executive functions, and impaired awareness. He was verbally angry with the staff: He said that the staff was inferior and even the hospital was in bad condition. At that stage he wasn't able to handle the sorrow and anger he surely felt with those men whose had abused him.

To be taken ill can be so threatening for some patients that they don't want to come to the rehabilitation, because every appointment reminds them of the illness.

Neuropsychological Deficits

The cognitive, behavioural and emotional changes due to central nervous system dysfunctions form a central target for cognitive remediation, but on the other hand, they can be easily confused with psychological reactions.

Psychotherapy with brain-injured patients can be particularly challenging because of the combination of cognitive, emotional, behavioural, and communicative impairments. Judd and Wilson (2005) have listed the main challenges that affect the forming of a working alliance with brain-injured patients: lack of insight, impaired memory, inflexible thinking, poor attention, language difficulties, disinhibited behaviour, and emotional lability. These neuropsychological deficits can also be identified as important in resistance. Memory, cognitive, and language deficits affect patients' comprehension and verbal expression, making communication difficult (Klonoff, 1997). Carberry and Burd (1986) identify some important obstacles to the psychotherapeutic process to be, for example, a tendency to ramble verbally, decreased verbal attention and concentration, rigidity of thought processes, memory deficits, deficit in empathic response, and deficits in abstract thinking.

One of the most important neuropsychological factors behind resistance is impaired self-awareness and metacognition. It is very possible that the patient is not collaborative if he is not aware of his deficits. Problems in awareness may contribute to significant resistance for participating in rehabilitation (Prigatano et al., 1986). Impaired self-awareness has been linked to poor therapeutic compliance (Prigatano, 2005), and according Schönberger et al. (2006a), awareness is predictive of a patient's compliance. On the other hand, brain-injured patients who are aware of their deficits tend to have better treatment performance (Lam, McMahon, & Priddy, 1998).

The issue of impaired self-awareness is of utmost importance with many patients (Prigatano & Schacter, 1991; Prigatano, 1999, 2005). Anosognosia is usually seen in patients with cerebrovascular lesions in right hemisphere (Starkstein, Fedoroff, Price, Leiguarda, & Robinson, 1992; Pedersen, Nakayma, Raaschou, & Olsen, 1996; Orfei et al., 2007), and it is commonly associated with visual neglect in the early stages of the condition (Robertson & Halligan, 1999).

For conceptualizing lack of awareness after brain injury, Langer and Padrone (1992) have proposed a tripartite model, with components including information, implication, and integration. The first source of "not knowing" may be not having the information; in the second level, the patient is not able to glean the full implications; and the third source of "not knowing" is denial. Accurate assessment of the sources of limitations is essential to effective treatment: Just as treating a neuropsychological deficit as resistance is counterproductive and ineffectual, so is the converse—treating denial as a neurologically based unawareness (Langer & Padrone, 1992). Denial can protect the patient from facing the reality prematurely. Pushing a patient prematurely to know what he can't tolerate emotionally may be destructive to the psyche (Langer & Padrone, 1992).

The patient can use different methods of coping. Some methods reflect premorbid coping strategies that are nondefensive in nature, and some are defensive, like denial (Prigatano, 1999). When the patient is engaging psychological denial, he frequently demonstrates a resistance when he is shown his difficulties (Prigatano, 1992).

According to Prigatano (1999), when a patient has a complete syndrome of impaired self-awareness, the therapist may try to establish a therapeutic alliance by working to reduce patient's frustration by entering their phenomenological field and by appropriate management of the environment. At that time, the patient exhibits little, if any, resistance (Prigatano, 1999). Resistance or denial can emerge when the patient's awareness is partial (Prigatano, 1999, 2005). In the first place the therapist must negotiate the therapeutic alliance, validate, and try to help the patient to be aware of his deficits. The therapist guides patient slowly toward recognition of how the patient's higher cortical functions have been affected (Prigatano, 1991, 1999).

Cognitive deficits can place limits to psychotherapy, and there are many neuropsychological deficits that must be taken into account. Language difficulties may bring problems for mutual understanding of the patient's intended speech, and limited language capacity must be taken into account in therapy methods. The patient can have troubles in sustaining concentration and remembering issues that have been dealt with in sessions, thinking can be inflexible, reasoning tends to be quite concrete, the ability to generalize is often impaired, and insight tends to be poor (Bennet & Raymond, 1997). Traumatic brain-injury patients often have poor insight into various brain-related impairments and often show poor social judgement and reduced verbal control of behaviour. The patient may have trouble concentrating on the therapy session or following the agenda because of executive dysfunction, concentration problems or emotional lability, irritability, and impulsiveness. Impaired social comprehension can make the patient misinterpret what the therapist says. Because of disorders in judgement and perception, the patient may misinterpret actions or intentions of others (Prigatano et al., 1986).

The patient can also become confused on being presented with multiple bits of information at one time (Prigatano et al., 1986). There can be organic emotional changes: Perception of emotions and expression of emotions can be changed and patients' emotional awareness can be disturbed. All these dysfunctions can interrupt the flow of the therapeutic session.

The main cognitive deficit must be determined in order to help the patient, for example, by offering memory aids, psychoeducation, and support. According to Judd and Wilson (2005), good strategies include providing accurate information, setting a structure, encouraging patient's self-evaluation and reflection about deficits, and providing support and hope.

Therapy with brain-injured adults needs to be more direct, structured, and innovative (Carberry & Burd, 1986). The therapist should take a more active and more responsible role (Bennet & Raymond, 1997), and, according to Prigatano and Klonoff (1988), the therapist may take a more direct, gently confrontative approach. Judd and Wilson (2005) have listed therapeutic strategies used to address challenges in forming a working alliance with brain-injury survivors: education and information about brain injury (TBI) and its effects, memory aids, involvement of the patient's significant others, and behavioural management programmes.

The concept of resistance must be modified when dealing with neurological patients: What is traditionally seen as resistance is not necessarily the same kind of resistance, but the reasons for resistance can be different and are associated with neuropsychological deficits.

There are only few studies of resistance in neuropsychological rehabilitation research literature. However, there is evidence that good alliance (Schönberger et al., 2006a, 2006b) has a strong effect on rehabilitation efficiency. In addition, the term noncompliance can be used when dealing with resistance. For example, Schönberger et al. (2006a, 2006b) have studied working alliance and patient compliance in brain-injury rehabilitation.

It is important to make a comprehensive neuropsychological examination of neuropsychological syndromes and also to take into account the patient's personality, coping strategies, and defensive mechanisms. Failure to understand an important resistance may lead to impasse (Pulver, 1995). It is important to take into account the psychodynamic factors in neuropsychological rehabilitation or in neuropsychotherapy and to examine the therapeutic elements in order to be able to carry out a successful neuropsychological and therapeutic procedure as an integration of the described domains of knowledge, and to understand their meaning as a necessary basis for metaconceptualization by the therapist.

References

Alford, B.A., & Beck, A.T. (1997). *The integrative power of cognitive therapy.* New York: Guilford Press.

Allen, J.G. (2001). *Traumatic relationships and serious mental disorders.* New York: John Wiley & Sons.

Beck, A.T. (1970). *Depression: Causes and treatment.* Philadelphia: University of Pennsylvania Press.

Beck, A.T., Freeman, A., Beck, J., Davis, D.D., Fleming, B., Meyer, J., Padesky, C. … Trexler, L. (1990). *Cognitive therapy of personality disorders.* New York: Guilford Press.

Bennett, T. L., & Raymond, M. J. (1997). Emotional consequences and psychotherapy for individuals with mild brain injury. *Applied Neuropsychology, 4*(1), 55–61.

Berg, A., Palomäki, H., Lehtihalmes, M., Lönnqvist, J., & Kaste, M. (2001). Poststroke depression in acute phase after stroke. *Cerebrovascular Diseases, 12*, 14–20.

Berg, A., Palomäki, H., Lehtihalmes, M., Lönnqvist, J., & Kaste, M. (2003). Poststroke depression. *Stroke, 34*, 138–143.

Bordin, E.S. (1979). The generalizability of the psychoanalytic concept of the working alliance. *Psychotherapy: Theory, Research and Practice, 16*, 252–260.

Carberry, H., & Burd, B. (1986). Individual psychotherapy with the brain injured adult. *Cognitive Rehabilitation, 4*, 22–24.

Clark, D., Beck, A. T., & Alford, B. A. (1999). *Scientific foundations of cognitive theory and therapy of depression*. New York: John Wiley & Sons, Inc.

Demark, J., & Gemeinhardt, M. (2002). Anger and its management for survivors of acquired brain injury. *Brain Injury, 20*, 91–108.

Ellis, A. (1985). *Overcoming resistance: Rational-emotive therapy with difficult clients*. New York: Springer Publishing Company.

Freud, S. (1959). Inhibitions, symptoms and anxiety. In J. Strachey (Ed. and Trans.), *The standard edition of the complete psychological works of Sigmund Freud, Vol. 20*. London: Hogarth Press. (Original work published in 1926)

Fromm-Reichmann, F. (1967). *Principles of intensive psychotherapy*. Chicago: University of Chicago Press.

Gainotti, G. (1993). Emotional and psychosocial problems after brain injury. *Neuropsychological Rehabilitation, 3*(3), 259–277.

Greenberg, L. S., & Safran, J. D. (1987). *Emotion in psychotherapy*. New York: Guildford Press.

Judd, D., & Wilson, S. L. (2005). Psychotherapy with brain injury survivors. An investigation of the challenges encountered by clinicians and their modifications to therapeutic practice. *Brain Injury, 19*(6), 437–449.

Judd, T. (1999). *Neuropsychotherapy and community integration. Brain illness, emotions and behaviour*. New York: Kluwer Academic/Plenum Publishers.

Klonoff, P. S. (1997). Individual and group psychotherapy in milieu-oriented neurorehabilitation. *Applied Neuropsychology, 4*(2), 107–118.

Klonoff, P. S., & Lage, G. A. (1991). Narcissistic injury in patients with traumatic brain injury. *Journal of Head Trauma Rehabilitation, 6*(4), 11–21.

Lam, C. S., McMahon, B. T., & Priddy, D. A. (1998). Deficit awareness and treatment performance among traumatic head injury adults. *Brain Injury, 2*, 235–242.

Langer, K. G., & Padrone, F. J. (1992). Psychotherapeutic treatment of awareness in acute rehabilitation of traumatic bran injury. *Neuropsychological Rehabilitation, 2*, 59–70.

Leahy, R. L. (2003). *Overcoming resistance in cognitive therapy*. New York: Guildford Press.

Leppävuori, A., Pohjasvaara, T., Vataja, R., Kaste, M., & Erkinjuntti, T. (2003). Generalized anxiety disorders three to four months after ischemic stroke. *Cerebrovascular Diseases, 16*, 257–264.

Mateer, C. A., Sira, C. S., & O'Connell, M. E. (2005). Putting humpty dumpty together again. *Journal of Head Trauma Rehabilitation, 20*(1), 62–75.

McLaughlin, A. M., & Carey, J. L. (1993). The adversarial alliance: Developing therapeutic relationships between families and the team in brain injury rehabilitation. *Brain Injury, 7*(1), 45–51.

McLaughlin, J.T. (1995). Resistance. In B.E. Moore & B.D. Fine (Eds.), *Psychoanalysis. The major concepts.* Chelsea: Book Crafters.

Moore, B.E., & Fine, B.D. (Eds.). (1990). *Psychoanalytic terms and concepts.* New Haven: Yale University Press.

Orfei, M.D., Robinson, R.G., Prigatano, G.P., Starkstein, S., Rüsch, N., Bria, P., Caltagirone, C., & Spalletta, G. (2007). Anosognosia for hemilegia after stroke is a multifaceted phenomenon: A systematic review of the literature. *Brain, 130,* 3075–3090.

Ownsworth, T., & Clare, L. (2006). The association between awareness deficits and rehabilitation outcome following acquired brain injury. *Clinical Psychology Review, 26,* 783–795.

Pedersen, P. M., Nakayma, H., Raaschou, H.O., & Olsen, T.S. (1996). Frequency, determinants, and consequences of anosognosia in acute stroke. *Neurorehabilitation and Neural Repair, 4,* 243–250.

Pohjasvaara, T., Leppävuori, A., Siira, I., Vataja, R., Kaste, M., & Erkinjuntti, T. (1998). Frequency and clinical determinants of poststroke depression. *Stroke, 29,* 2311–2317.

Pohjasvaara, T., Vataja, R., Leppävuori, A., Kaste, M., & Erkinjuntti, T. (2001). Depression is an independent predictor of poor long-term functional outcome post-stroke. *European Journal of Neurology, 8,* 315–319.

Prigatano, G.P. (1991). Disordered mind, wounded soul: The emerging role of psychotherapy in rehabilitation after brain injury. *Journal of Head Trauma Rehabilitation,* 6(4), 1–10.

Prigatano, P.G. (1992). Personality disturbances associated with traumatic brain injury. *Journal of Consulting and Clinical Psychology, 60*(3), 360–368.

Prigatano, G.P. (1999). *Principles of neuropsychological rehabilitation.* New York: Oxford University Press.

Prigatano, G.P. (2005). Disturbances of self-awareness and rehabilitation of patients with traumatic brain injury. A 20-year perspective. *Journal of Head Trauma Rehabilitation, 20,* 19–29.

Prigatano, G.P., Fordyce, D.J., Zeiner, H.K., Roueche, J.R., Pepping, M., & Wood, B.C. (1986). Neuropsychological rehabilitation after brain injury. Baltimore: The Johns Hopkins University Press.

Prigatano, G.P., & Klonoff, P.S. (1988). Psychotherapy and neuropsychological assessment after brain injury. *Journal of Head Trauma Rehabilitation, 1,* 45–56.

Prigatano, G.P., & Schacter, D.L. (1991). *Awareness of deficit after brain injury. Clinical and theoretical issues.* New York: Oxford University Press.

Pulver, S.E. (1995). The psychoanalysis process and mechanism of therapeutic change. In B.E. Moore & B.D. Fine (Eds.), *Psychoanalysis. The major concepts.* New Haven: Yale University Press.

Reich, W. (1933). *Charakteranalyse.* Wien: Manzsche Buchdruckerei.

Robertson, I.H., & Halligan, P.W. (1999). *Spatial neglect. A clinical handbook for diagnosis and treatment.* East Sussex, UK: Psychology Press.
Safran, J.D., & Muran, J.C. (2000). *Negotiating the therapeutic alliance. A relational treatment guide.* New York: Guildford Press.
Sandler, J., Dare C., & Holder, A. (1992). *The patient and the analyst: The basis of the psychoanalytic process.* London: Karnac Books.
Schönberger, M., Humle, F., & Teasdale, T.W. (2006a). The development of the therapeutic working alliance, patients' awareness and their compliance during the process of brain injury rehabilitation. *Brain Injury, 20,* 445–454.
Schönberger, M., Humle, F., Zeeman, P., & Teasdale, T.W. (2006b). Working alliance and patient compliance in brain injury rehabilitation and their relation to psychosocial outcome. *Neuropsychological Rehabilitation, 16,* 298–314.
Starkstein, S.E., Fedoroff, P., Price, T.R., Leiguarda, R., & Robinson, R.G. (1992). Anosognosia in patients with cerebrovascular lesion. A study of causative factors. *Stroke, 23,* 1446–1453.
Young, J.E., Klosko, J.S., & Weishaar, M.E. (2003). *Schema therapy.* New York: Guilford Press.

7

Process-Oriented Neuropsychological Outpatient Rehabilitation

Practical Examples of Various Etiological Groups at the Post-Acute Stages

Arja Lindell and Tarja Ketola

Introduction

Neuropsychological outpatient rehabilitation is a part in the path of rehabilitation for many neurological patients, at least for those with acquired brain injuries. The distribution of services and funding vary from country to country. In Finland these services are mostly available in the larger cities and take place in private practices or clinics with outpatient services. The services are provided by trained clinical neuropsychologists. Costs are in most cases covered by the local communities (national health care), national health insurance or private insurances, and in some cases even by the social welfare system—rarely by the patients themselves. Periodically patients can participate in inpatient rehabilitation programs administered by rehabilitation centers.

In clinical practice, outpatient neuropsychological rehabilitation interventions vary in length and intensity depending on the patient's needs and available rehabilitation resources. The process often starts after discharge from the hospital and aims to continue to the point where the patient has reached a new balance of life, hopefully with improved sense of control over his or her own life, and the ability to enjoy life.

The duration and intensities of the individual rehabilitation processes depend on many factors: the neurological and neuropsychological findings of the patient, motivation, personality, etiology of the neurological state, family situation, living conditions, general economic situation, and so on, but they also depend on the therapist and on his or her competence and therapeutic orientation. The attained level of awareness of the neuropsychological symptoms and other changes caused by the neurological illness also determine many of the therapeutic means and goals.

In the early days of neuropsychological rehabilitation, much emphasis was laid on retraining cognitive functions (Laaksonen, 2007). However, this view has nowadays been proven to be too narrow, at least in the clinical rehabilitation context. During the last decades, the personal, social, and emotional impacts of brain injury have been better acknowledged and incorporated into treatment plans in cognitive rehabilitation (Sohlberg & Mateer, 2001). In brain-injury rehabilitation, holistic treatment programs have been developed, and their effectiveness is well known (see Chapter 11, by Koskinen and Sarajuuri). Lately, the treatment of organic emotional and behavioral changes has been brought forth as a distinct form of neuropsychological rehabilitation, in other words neuropsychotherapy (Judd, 1999).

The growing reintegration among the fields of neurology and psychiatry, as well as the emerging interest in emotional brain-behavior relationships in neurosciences, has supported the move to broader perspectives in rehabilitation. In outpatient rehabilitation, the concrete needs of our patients and families direct us to work from a holistic perspective on the basis of the patient's cognitive, emotional, and social situation. Cognitive or emotional dysfunction, as well as family perspective and the patient's intrapsychic goals, should be considered and targeted in neuropsychotherapy.

In outpatient rehabilitation, patients seldom have multidisciplinary teams to support them. Instead they may have one or more therapists working with them. Still, the whole patient and his life situation have to be considered. Working without the support of a multidisciplinary team is of course more stressful for a therapist, and adequate counseling is recommended.

On the other hand, we know that in official or community settings where the patient can receive various multidisciplinary interventions, it is not self-evident or guaranteed that the total approach is holistic or client centered. Too often interventions and decision making are widely scattered within the health care system, and the views on rehabilitation vary strongly across and within different disciplines. The therapists and doctors working as a team or alone in private practice are, according to our view, best guided by a process-oriented view of rehabilitation. When viewing the patient's rehabilitation as a path and a process, the client and his needs guide the intensities and timing of different therapies, not vice versa. The fact that the patient is the subject rather than the object of rehabilitation is still easily forgotten in clinical practice and decision making. It is important to remember that the empowerment of the patient's feeling of agency should be strengthened, instead of emphasizing his dependency and feelings of inadequacy. In outpatient rehabilitation there may also, despite well-meaning care, sometimes be errors in timing and in the amount of offered help—sometimes too much assistance offered in the beginning of the recovery process and too little in the end. Viewing rehabilitation as a path can guide different therapists to form a more dynamic perspective view of the client's situation, despite different therapeutic interventions and theoretical standpoints. Brain-injury literature and research has in the last decades repeatedly demonstrated that brain-injured patients often need long-lasting support from acute to latter stages of functional and psychological recovery. In order for an effective and client-centered rehabilitation process to take place, there must of course be a rehabilitation plan and possibilities for the therapists to be networking around the patient.

Clinical Practice in Outpatient Rehabilitation

The Beginning: Getting Started

The patient has usually undergone an extensive neuropsychological assessment at the hospital, or at another referring organization when entering outpatient rehabilitation. For rehabilitation purposes further assessment is still often needed (Judd, 1999). The effects of the brain dysfunction on the patient's daily life and the view of other informants must be further explored. The therapist also needs to know about the preinjury personality of the patient, such as what he or she has enjoyed most, what has made him or her happy, what he or she has liked to do, and what his or her likes or dislikes have been. This can be obtained by means of interviews, behavioral observations, cognitive tasks and tests, personality assessment, and assessment of the patient's environment. Also, we need to become familiar with the patient's immediate field of experience, however scattered and confused that may be. From this we can get material with which to work during the therapy process.

In the beginning of the process the patient is often in a crisis or more or less unaware about what the consequences of his illness or injury really are. There are frequently questions such as "Why has this happened?" or "What's wrong with me?" and questions about long-term recovery that cannot be fully answered. Most patients are also not used to attending therapy, or having appointments with psychologists. They are afraid of being labeled as mentally ill or incompetent. In the beginning we sometimes also have to normalize the concept of neuropsychology. The joint task of the patient and the therapist is to learn, step by step, what the brain injury has done to the patient's living skills and sense of well-being.

In Finland patients are usually referred for 20–40 visits per year in the more intensive phase of the rehabilitation. The amount of visits may decrease parallel to diminished needs. Usually the sessions are individual but as often as possible and needed, family members participate as well. How often and how many family members or close others take part in the process varies significantly, but seldom do we work solely with the patient. Sometimes it can take a long time before the patient allows anyone else to know what has happened. During that time, we have to collaborate with the emphasis on awareness and good working alliance.

Outpatient rehabilitation is an excellent way to support and coach the patient to get by in everyday life. The challenges of everyday life are usually quite complicated, and the patient should not be forced to deal with too-complicated things without sufficient help. The difficulty in outpatient rehabilitation is to provide optimal challenges, even when the patient is at home. For some patients, everyday functional activities are no longer a problem. For them the therapeutic challenges may be handling their finances, trying to work or study, or developing an interesting leisure time activity.

Goal Setting

In neuropsychological rehabilitation, the initial formulation of the patient's problems and strengths is made from a wide range of perspectives: from physical to cognitive to emotional to social (Sohlberg & Mater, 2001). During the subacute rehabilitation phase after injury or illness, the patient's main focus of interest often lies in cognitive functioning and motility, (i.e., on what he or she is able to do—walk, talk, get dressed, remember, read, write—and on what is lost). Eventually, after the discharge from hospital or rehabilitation clinics, patients face the multiple demands of daily living at home. At this stage, usually both emotional support and further information about the injury is needed. Along with the stages of recovery, the patient's needs change, and problems, strengths, and goals need to be reformulated. Goal setting is done in collaboration with the patient and sometimes also with members of his or her family.

The first goals of the patient and of the therapist can in some cases be quite different. The patient may set as his goal to be going back to his old job or recovering completely, while the therapist sees the goal as helping the patient to build some awareness or understanding of his situation and to allow himself to start working on his recovery (i.e., admitting his need for help). These latter types of goals, usually set in the beginning, are often "the therapist's goals." Despite different perspectives on the patient's situation, joint goals or working themes should be formulated. For example, a patient with poor insight may still accept a working theme of "finding out what the brain injury has done to my cognition, memory, temper, strength... ." Later, the patient may himself express goals like self-acceptance, to better learn about the reactions of other people, to understand their feelings, how to show caring, etc. Most patients start to work with their rehabilitation despite lack of insight and eventually a good working alliance can be built. Still, there are cases where this does not succeed. But recovery is a long process, and the patient can gain from a second try in the future.

In the beginning, members of the patient's family often tolerate even terrible behavior just because the injured person did survive, but as time goes by, their tolerance gets shorter, and they expect more normal behavior. It is difficult for family members to understand why the person with TBI does not "learn" or "want" to do things in the normal way, though they have often informed the patient of how he should behave. Not only in the beginning, but also later in the recovery process, it is essential that members of the family get adequate information and guidance.

Example of rehabilitation process.

M was a 21-year-old student who had acquired a severe head injury after falling from approximately 10 meters. Brain scans showed multiple brain contusions bilaterally, but especially frontally and in the right hemisphere. A neuropsychological examination at the hospital showed problems in executive and memory functions, problem solving, and specific problems in visuospatial functions, in which the patient had formerly been gifted. After his injury, the patient had had to move back home with his parents. He was referred to neuropsychological rehabilitation 7 months after his injury. While attending rehabilitation, he complained about memory problems and concentration difficulties. His mood was generally good, and he easily overestimated his performance, but he was also somewhat concerned about his cognitive abilities and wanted to do cognitive training. He wanted eagerly to see and to have it be confirmed that he was improving. His parents reported forgetfulness, occasionally repeating himself, increased talking and commenting, changing subjects while talking, irritability, difficulties in time management, losing track in new situations, needing help in remembering and organizing daily activities, and tiredness in the evenings. His insight in these changes was partially lacking. He also fatigued very easily after the injury.

In the first phase of the rehabilitation process, treatment goals were awareness training, introducing the use of a calendar/memory aid, structuring of daily programs, and psychological support, including reassurance and education about brain injury and its recovery processes, both for the patient and for his parents. Independence in daily living and mobility were his primary focus. One of his main goals was moving out of his parents' house. However, at this early stage, that was not yet a realistic goal.

During the first year of rehabilitation, much improvement happened in these primary and mostly functionally oriented goals. Eventually the goals of treatment had to be reevaluated. In this second phase, much focus was laid on improving working endurance, capacity to concentrate, and retraining of other cognitive skills. Along with these, M had to learn to consider his fatigue and learn to cope with his reflex laughing. He slept poorly, and he had to take rests during the day. Before his injury, he had considered himself quite good in social and verbal skills, grasping jokes and situations quickly, sometimes putting himself somewhat above others. Still, prior to his accident, he had suffered from anxiety and sought psychological help. He was very disturbed by his present loose way of commenting on things after the injury, and he started to withdraw from new social contacts. Prior to his injury, he had been very good in mathematics and visuospatial skills. Now these capacities had strongly decreased. Despite an intensive wish to improve, these abilities were only partly recovered. His losses were great, and his sense of himself was vague.

With verbal skills now being his strengths, he began to concentrate on improving his reading and ability to learn. Eventually he attended an academic course, which he found interesting, but he could not maintain his concentration or make notes during lecture. In a written assignment as a part of the course, he needed much help in structuring. He got a good grade for the assignment, which helped him to value himself more. It had an enormous impact on his self-confidence.

His awareness of emotions had been poor before, and after the injury, there was a flatness in emotional expressions with periodical outbursts. M was first glad that he no longer had any symptoms of anxiety. But with recovery, even the anxiety came back, along with nightmares. A reformulation of problems and goals once again took place. He was now, about 2 years after his injury, more prepared to focus on the emotional problems of the brain injury and on his own personality.

In the last phase, the therapeutic goals included learning to relax, being more able to recognize and name emotions, learning more ways to cope with outspokenness and cognitive deficits, being able to grieve losses, building a new sense of self, and finding meaningful life contents.

M was slowly, during the next 2 years, better able to name his feelings and manage his anxiety, and he dared to try out new activities. The reflex laughing diminished eventually, and he also learned to better control his talkativeness. Eventually, admitting to himself the brain injury, he became able to talk about it with others. He tried out some small worklike activities, but the enduring fatigue and vigilance problems prevented him from returning to any kind of work. He eventually moved to his own apartment and improved from partial independence to being able to handle his finances and daily tasks by himself. He has a family he can ask for guidance and help if needed.

How to Proceed

How therapy is done is often eclectic. Our task as neuropsychologists or neuropsychotherapists is to guide the patient on the way to rehabilitation by teaching him or her to understand what the changes are and how they affect the ability to do what he or she wants to or is used to doing, as well as by supporting constructive feelings and helping the patient to overcome the unconstructive ones.

It can be compared to concocting a suitable cocktail of psychoeducation, training, therapeutic interventions, and communication designed individually for each patient. The more therapeutic skills the neuropsychotherapists has in his or her repertoire, the larger the quantity of clients he or she can help.

The work can be carried out by having individual sessions or using outpatient groups. Also, within "adaptation training" (see page135) courses, many of these concepts can be applied.

Individual Sessions

In the beginning of rehabilitation, the contents of individual sessions more emphasis is placed on evaluating the situation, analyzing the symptoms, and trying to get a picture of the life history of the patient. We need to recognize the strengths and interests of our patients to make the most of rehabilitation. Individual sessions include the guiding of spouse or other members of family, as well as any additional significant others, whenever possible.

Rehabilitation Groups

Often it is more effective to work with a group of people with the same handicap. This method is more effective if it is possible to select the participants carefully to get a group that is homogeneous enough. Groups meet usually 6–20 times and carry out a program that is planned according to their needs. Work with the groups is often done together with another therapist, speech therapist, occupational therapist, or other.

Adaptation Training

In Finland, we have a long history of rehabilitation courses we refer to as "adaptation training." The training model originates from the 1960s and was at that time done within handicap associations. The idea was in the beginning to combine peer support, psychoeducation, and the benefits of group process in rehabilitation by taking those persons with some handicap, their partners or spouses, and professionals for a week or two to be together at a resort, far from normal surroundings. The psychoeducation was conducted in practical situations by doing different things together and simultaneously giving the information needed. Participants were shown that they could still live a full life with their handicaps. This is a very effective, stimulating, and innovating way of participating in rehabilitation, and it gives good results in a short period of time. In adaptation training, peer support happens under the guidance of professionals in order to avoid the spreading of negative and destructive feelings of a person in crisis to others present, and to support constructive and positive ones. Adaptation training is carried out with several etiological groups, with patients, their spouses, and families, or even with healthy children of a handicapped parent. The contents can be focused on such physical symptoms as tiredness and fatigue, as well as on cognitive symptoms such as the changes in femininity/masculinity and sexuality within the handicap in question.

What Is the Outcome?

The simplest way of evaluating the results of outpatient rehabilitation is to evaluate changes in the quality of life of the patient and his or her family.

Some results of neuropsychotherapy can be seen in these following examples from our practice.

A patient's going back to work, either to the patient's old job or to a new occupation found together during therapy. The occupation may be totally different, or adjusted, or perhaps only the working hours are changed to better suit the available energy of the patient.

A patient's getting married (after being convinced that it would never be possible), building a house, or having a baby and being able to enjoy time with his or her child.

A patient's gaining the courage to take a trip after years of isolation; acquiring a new hobby or refreshing an old one; being capable of being around others, even strangers, on his or her own.

A patient's maintaining a healthy diet and being able to cook for him or herself.

A patient's keeping him or herself sufficiently clean, washing his or her own clothes, and keeping his or her apartment tidy.

A patient's being able to laugh or smile again after a long period of nothing but anger, worry, or stress.

A patient's being able to cope with chronic pain.

A patient's gaining trust that there is a tomorrow for him, after previous feelings that life has ended after the injury.

A patient's communication with his or her sister, brother, mother, father, or any other relative or friend again, after experiencing an emotional overload and being certain that he or she has been seriously insulted.

A previously suicidal patient's recovery, or, as one patient remarked: "I have to let killing myself be for the time being as I have so many things to do now."

A patient's letting go of murderous thoughts (such as a case in which the start of medical care or diagnosis has been difficult or the feeling of loss very severe, and a patient may plan to kill the one who has caused the accident or the doctor who misdiagnosed him or her in the beginning) and concentrating on living his or her own life instead.

Simply, every step toward normal and more enjoyable life can be seen as a result.

Example of Prior Neurological Problems

Example of Changes in Emotional Reactions and Premorbid Psychiatric or Other Medical Problems

Example 1

KL was a 35-year-old female in a creative profession who had had bipolar disorder since adolescence, with some periods of manic psychosis. On an early winter morning, soon after divorcing her husband, she lost control of her car and spun off the slippery road. The car was crushed, and she had a severe TBI with internal injuries. During the first years with TBI, she had no symptoms of bipolar disorder. She was very cautious in everything and tried to find a new way of living as a different person in new surroundings with almost no connection to her earlier life. After she adapted sufficiently to her TBI and could function on her own without continuous help from others, she had a new and severe manic episode, during which she lost 20 kg of body weight and incurred significant financial losses by traveling to the other side of the world under the delusion that the trip was work related (in reality, the patient had been a medical pensioner for 3 years). The manic episode ended in a bout of deep, suicidal depression. After her recovery, with the help of neuropsychotherapy, the patient was able to regain control of her life by combining her knowledge of both TBI and bipolar disorder. She has learned to control both the quantity and quality of her social contacts, thus gaining the ability to protect herself from excessive stress. After 2 years of neuropsychological rehabilitation and another 2 years of neuropsychotherapy, she has a life with both physical and cognitive activities and a sufficient social network.

The manic period, exceptionally difficult to detect, was one the greatest challenges in the patient's therapy. Just before the manic period, the neuropsychological rehabilitation had ended, as a balance seemed to have been found. Was there a possibility to recognize the difference between activity due to normal recovery after TBI and activity predicting mania? The other great challenge was after the depression—to convince her that all activity does not end in mania. It is possible to be both active and in the control of one's life.

Example 2

TA was a 42-year-old female when she began attending neuropsychotherapy. She had been diagnosed with a very deep and long-lasting depression without psychotic features nearly 10 years prior to her first meeting with the therapist. She had had psychotherapy for nearly the entire time, and she was also in constant contact with a psychiatrist. She had been working as a teacher in kindergarten, but, because of Sjögren's syndrome, she had to quit working 3 years prior to our first meeting. She was on a temporary medical pension at the time. When neuropsychotherapy started, she felt that her life was a disaster. Prior to being diagnosed with Sjögren's, she had a large social network, many good friends, and was involved in different artistic activities. She had had a habit of giving parties at her house for friends, and she enjoyed organizing events. A friend of hers who also has Sjögren's told her of neuropsychotherapy, and she insisted on being able to attend. While having the feeling that there was no life for her anymore, as she got nearly nothing done, TA still wanted to have a chance. From the beginning, she was very cooperative, and working with her has been very intensive and effective. Altogether, TA had 15 different diagnoses, 6 different doctors, and 2 therapists at that time, so the initial instinct as a therapist was not to add yet another therapist to the list. Because of her confidence and the easily formed alliance, therapy was tried and has now continued for 2 years. TA has been granted a permanent medical pension, she has a hold on her life, she recognizes her symptoms, and she has learned how she has to plan her activities so that she gets things done.

The main issue with TA has been recognizing fatigue as a main symptom of Sjögren's and teaching her how to control it. It has also been important to clarify the difference between depression and fatigue. In TA's case, the problem has been fatigue rather than depression. TA has also experienced normal reactive depression due to falling severely ill at a relatively early age. TA had been previously treated as a psychiatric patient due to her chronic fatigue being misdiagnosed as depression. It has been very productive to analyze TA's numerous diagnoses and symptoms together with her. This analysis has shown that she actually has only Sjögren's, whose many different symptoms had been diagnosed as separate conditions. Analyzing her symptoms does not diminish them, but it has given her a certain feeling of well-being, since she is no longer being bombarded with new diagnoses and issues. A better understanding of her disease allows TA to predict possible future symptoms and react more calmly to them if and when they appear. She is also able to tell the difference between the many manifestations of Sjögren's and other, completely unrelated, symptoms (which might indicate some other illness requiring medical attention). In the past, TA had felt that the doctors treating her considered her either a hysterical hypochondriac or a chronic complainer with a somatization disorder. Now that all the threads have been woven together and there is a clear picture of her situation, she no longer feels that the legitimacy of her problems is being questioned.

Example 3

VM was a 51-year-old communal officer when he fell sick. Initially, the nature of his illness was unknown, and he ended up in a coma before the right diagnosis and treatment was found. He had a rare form of vasculitis in small arteries and also in the brain, and with the help of cortisone he recovered to some extent. VM is married to a health professional, and the role of his wife has been very important both in the beginning and later in the course of his treatment and nursing. VM trusts his wife more than anyone else. VM has a large combination of neuropsychological symptoms fulfilling the criteria of dementia. When attending neuropsychotherapy, he was preoccupied with planning how to murder the doctor he held responsible for his ending up in a coma before he got help. He was sure that if that person had admitted that he had no idea what was going on and listened to others, VM could have gotten help much earlier and would now live a totally different and considerably better life. Those initial mistakes may well have been critical, as VM thought they were, but we will never know for sure. Whatever the degree of the doctor's incompetence, he and the anger and bitterness VM felt towards him took up most of VM's time and energy. After 1½ years in neuropsychotherapy, VM finally let go of his plan to murder the doctor, and he allowed himself to enjoy life again.

The combination of extensive brain damage, severe memory problems, poor emotional control, and real or imagined injustices is challenging for a neuropsychotherapist, but the work is worth doing, as we end up with a patient who has the possibility to enjoy his or her life and a spouse whose life is a lot easier when he or she does not have to deal with (sometimes extreme) bitterness in addition to taking care of the spouse, the home, and his or her own life.

Example 4

Five years ago, a 40-year-old mother of three children, RP, had a large stroke in the brain stem and cerebellum. During the first week after the stroke, she had locked-in syndrome. RP started to recover slowly. At first she felt that she was a disembodied tiny person deep in her brain. Gradually, RP began to recognize the existence of the various areas of her body, with her sides being the last parts she "regained." This was 4 years after the stroke. RP has also had a hemorrhage in her left eye, destroying the central visual field and making it impossible for her to handle movement in her visual field. RP's feelings and sensations were also lost after the stroke, and she has had to find and reorganize them. RP has also had to learn to understand the feelings of others. In this sense, she has greatly resembled the android character "Data" from *Star Trek: The Next Generation*, examining the essence of emotions in both herself and in others. RP has an excellent memory, which enables her to function in familiar environments, such as the therapist office. It is impossible for her to go alone to new places, though, because for her there is no depth in visual perception, moving objects do not exist, and objects that cannot be predicted to be there are unrecognizable without intense concentration, logic, and reasoning. Everything RP does must be carefully planned. She has to know in great detail what to expect from unfamiliar environments if she wants to visit them.

A neuropsychotherapeutic approach has been required to understand the imbalance between the many different aspects of emotional reactions and a unique and, in many ways altered, capability to acquire information concerning her environment.

Conclusions

In private practice, there is seldom the possibility to use fancy equipment or expensive training programs. Often the training material is tailored from the patient's everyday life (i.e., functional tasks, social situations, etc.) to serve ecological validity. The period of treatment varies from a single 10- to 20-session rehabilitation period up to longer 3- to 5-year processes. The frequency of appointments varies, depending of course on the goals of therapy and the possibility to attend by the patient. Usually in the beginning of the rehabilitation process, there should be at least one session per week—ideally, even more than one session weekly in the first phase, if possible. Memory problems pose practical challenges for both the content and frequency of the sessions. The need for intensive support usually diminishes gradually after the first 2 years, but repeated intervals of treatment are often needed to fulfill the long-term needs and goals. For some patients, treatment is periodically needed throughout life. In private practice, the intensity of treatment is also dependent on the amount of sessions granted and paid for by insurance or community funding. In singular therapies at postacute stages, it is vitally important for the therapist to keep up networking.

References

Judd, T. (1999). *Neuropsychotherapy and community integration. Brain illness, emotions, and behavior.* New York: Kluwer Academic/Plenum Publishers.

Laaksonen, R. (2007). Introduction to neuropsychotherapy. *Svensk Neuropsykologi 1*(7), 4–6.

Sohlberg, M.M., & Mateer, C.A. (2001). *Cognitive rehabilitation.* New York: Guilford Press.

8

Helping Children with Acquired Brain Injury to Engage in a Neuropsychotherapeutic Process

Hanna Kiiski-Mäki

Introduction

In this chapter, the neuropsychotherapeutic (NPT) approach is reviewed from children's point of view. Although the approach can be used in many neuropsychological rehabilitation settings, this chapter focuses on its utilization in brain-injury rehabilitation. First, I review the core symptoms of children's acquired brain injury (ABI) in order to clarify the need of NPT methods in ABI rehabilitation. I then discuss some central aims and themes repeatedly encountered in children's NPT processes. Next, I describe the challenges neuropsychological deficits bring to the therapeutic process and suggest some clinical solutions. Finally, I give examples on how some methods from "traditional" therapies can be modified to fit in a NPT process with children. Throughout the text, I present examples of discussions and methods included in a NPT process of one of my clients, "Case Anna, 11 years, with ABI of vascular type."

Anna's Background

Anna was born as a healthy baby, except that she had a vascular anomaly in her brain. At 8 years of age, she had a brain haemorrhage, which was treated by embolization. When she was 12 years of age, she had to undergo a brain surgery in order to remove the life-threatening vascular malformation. The procedure was demanding because the malformation was situated deep in her brain. As a consequence, she acquired a severe brain injury. I had worked with Anna already before the surgery in order to prepare and support her for what was coming. Two weeks after the surgery, in the intensive care unit, I met Anna again. She was lying in her bed, unable to walk, having difficulty speaking, unable to recognize people around her, unable to remember anything more than 30 seconds prior, and confused.

ABI in Children: Neuropsychological Core Symptoms and the Need for Psychotherapeutic Support

Acquired brain injury refers to those injuries that are caused by illness, trauma, or other clearly postnatal issues in a neurologically predominantly healthy person. These include injuries induced by, for example, accident or violence (traumatic brain injury), illness (tumours, infections), vascular causes (haemorrhage, brain infarction), seizure-related events, anoxia, and intoxication (Halligan, Kischka, & Marshall, 2003). Acquired brain injuries can be classified according to several criteria, including the mechanics, location, and size of the injury (Halligan, Kischka, & Marshall, 2003). However, these criteria cannot straightforwardly be used to predict the severity or symptoms of a given injury: Similar injuries can induce different sets of symptoms, and, vice versa, persons with identical symptoms can have quite different brain injuries. This applies as well to children, with whom we must also bear in mind the developmental perspective: Injury to an immature brain affects developing neural circuits, thus compromising the whole process of a child's psychological development.

Although every brain injury is individual, there are some core symptoms that seem to emerge, to some degree, in almost every case (Christensen & Uzzell, 1994; King & Tyerman, 2003). These include

- problems with memory (forgetting what was discussed/learned/done a while ago, memory gap related to injury);

- attention/self-regulation (difficulty of focusing, maintaining, and dividing attention sufficiently);
- executive functions (difficulty of planning/monitoring/reviewing own actions);
- control of emotions (unexpectedly strong/extended/inappropriate emotional reactions such as anger, sorrow, cheerfulness, fear); and
- language processes (word finding, understanding complicated sentences, reading comprehension, written expression).

Fatigue (getting extremely tired easily, despite sufficient rest) is also common. These symptoms appear as various problems in children's everyday lives. At school, learning difficulties, restlessness, and behavioural problems are common. At home, these children face difficulties with their homework, fulfilling requested household tasks, age-appropriate level of activities of daily living (e.g., taking care of personal hygiene, dressing, eating) and obeying parents' instruction. Social relations with friends often become compromised. ABI children's behaviour and interests may resemble those of younger children, and they often have problems following quickly progressing conversations in groups.

After brain injury, there is an elevated risk for psychiatric symptoms (Anstey, Butterworth, Jorm, Christensen, Rodgers, & Windsor, McKinlay, Grace, Horwood, Fergusson, & MacFarlane, 2009), which can be primary or secondary. Primary symptoms are caused by ABI itself, affecting brain functions needed for emotional regulation and coherency of thinking. Secondary symptoms refer to psychological reactions to the injuring event, including coping with being a person with ABI, and difficulties in school and close relationships, for example. There are findings suggesting that the risk of developing depression is elevated among persons with ABI (Bay, 2009; Silver, McAllister, & Arciniegas, 2009).

ABI means that something quite upsetting has happened to a previously neurologically healthy child. An accident, violence, or illness has resulted in negative changes in brain functioning. This, in turn, places both the child and her family in an extremely demanding psychological situation. The child usually has to face changes in her skills, body image, level of independent functioning, and capabilities for social relationships. Often these changes require new solutions for daycare, school, playing with peers, hobbies, and everyday family life. Parents, in turn, have to cope with feelings of simultaneous relief (that the child stayed alive) and despair (that the child behaves differently). Some parents even report feeling as if their child is a stranger for some time after injury. Thus, it seems rather obvious that traditional cognitively oriented neuropsychological rehabilitation is not enough in these circumstances.

To meet the psychological needs of ABI children and their families, it is important to apply methods that include psychotherapeutic elements. On the other hand, when we provide psychotherapy for ABI children, we have to bear in mind the demands ABI symptoms bring into the therapeutic process. Often it is not enough to send an ABI child separately to neuropsychological rehabilitation and to psychotherapy. If we do that, we can face two unwanted situations: a neuropsychologist providing cognitive rehearsals for a child who is emotionally too overwhelmed to benefit from them, or a psychotherapist providing therapy for a child whose cognitive deficiencies are too serious for her to benefit from it. The NPT approach, therefore, provides us a way to combine methods of psychotherapy and cognitive rehearsals into a more holistic approach: Children receive cognitive support and psychoeducation in a psychotherapeutically supported rehabilitation setting. Or, from another viewpoint, children receive psychotherapy in a setting where their cognitive deficiencies are well taken into consideration. This provides holistic integrated collaboration with the child.

The First Encounter After Surgery

Anna came to my office for her first session four months after her brain surgery. She was sitting in a wheelchair, her mother pushing her in through the door. Anna was expressing several feelings: There was a mixture of anger, joy of seeing me, and shame.

A (Anna):	[Looking down to the floor with tears in her eyes] Look at me, sitting here as a baby in a carriage.
P (Psychologist):	I see you, sitting like a 12 year old in a wheelchair. Welcome.

Aims and Central Therapeutic Themes of Children's Neuropsychotherapy

Children's NPT processes can be conceptualised as learning processes. Thus, the aims of a NPT intervention can be formulated by considering what kind of knowledge, skills, and insight the child could benefit from learning. Overall, the goal of NPT is to facilitate the development and psychological well-being of the ABI child. The more detailed aims of children's NPT rehabilitation depend on the particulars of the case. Two important factors to be considered when the detailed aims are formulated are the age of ABI child when the injury was acquired and at the beginning of rehabilitation, and her symptoms of psychological distress.

Considering Age at the Time of Injury and at Start of Rehabilitation

The age of an ABI child at the start of rehabilitation gives us a reference of the child's developmental level of cognitive, emotional, and social skills. This, in turn, gives information as to what children at a given age usually can do and cope with, and how they behave on average. However, we need to bear in mind that child development may be affected by ABI. This can happen through primary or secondary routes. By primary routes, I refer to neurological effects due to damaged brain tissue, which can complicate psychological development. Secondary routes refer to psychological distress due to the injury itself, both to the ABI child and her family. A child with long-term severe psychological distress has an elevated risk for developmental delays (Limond, Morris, & McMillan, 2009). Furthermore, there are findings suggesting that parental distress due to child's ABI often affects their resources for parenting (Prigatano & Gray, 2007). This, in turn, can lead to problems in child development.

A therapist should be familiar with both the normative child development and with patterns of possible developmental delays of psychological development. If we want to apply a NPT approach in a child's rehabilitation, the therapist should also have expertise on how brain injury can affect the observed level of child development. Due to brain injury, a child's cognitive, emotional, and social skills often look different from what could normatively be expected in a given age level. For example, an ABI child who has problems with emotional regulation or social skills often behaves, as a result, like a chronologically younger child. There can be difficulties, for example, with delayed need fulfilment, tolerance of frustration, self-soothing, or regulating aggression. Delay in some cognitive skills may also give an impression of a younger child. For example, a 10-year-old child with difficulties in attention regulation can seem to have the attention processes of a 4 year old. Furthermore, most ABI children have learning difficulties: The learning skills of a teenager can represent the learning skills of a third grader.

There has been a common belief that effects of brain injury are milder the younger the child was at time of injury. However, during the past decades, there have been findings suggesting the opposite (Ponsford, 1995). If a child gets injured very early in her life, the injury may have a greater impact on the developing neural circuits. In other words, if a child has already learned a given skill (or, if there is evidence of maturation of a given neuropsychological function), she has better chances of rebuilding it after injury than developing it from the beginning. Thus, the age of injury must also be considered when we evaluate the effects of ABI on child development.

In summary, when building the aims of a NPT intervention, we have to consider both the child's chronological age and her observed level of cognitive, emotional, and social development after the ABI. In practice, the therapist should answer the following questions: (a) What skills should this child master according to the normative developmental level of her age? (b) What kind of developmental delay can I expect to find due to the psychological distress caused by the ABI to the child and her caretakers? and (c) What kind of developmental abnormalities due to the neurological affects of ABI should I expect? Answers to these questions give therapists insight into the formulation of therapeutic aims and selection of therapeutic methods.

Considering Symptoms of Psychological Distress

On top of age-related factors, we have to consider the symptoms of psychological distress when we formulate the aims for NPT intervention. Symptoms of psychological distress or even psychiatric symptoms are common among children with ABI. This is understandable, as these children have faced an accident or an illness that usually abruptly changes their lives quite drastically. Among the most common symptoms are posttraumatic stress disorder, depressive feelings, anxiety and fears, difficulties with self-image and self-esteem, and feelings of loneliness.

Symptoms of posttraumatic stress disorder are common if the injuring event was life threatening, whether in actuality or only experienced as such (Sullivan, Everstine, & Everstine, 2006). Trauma also concerns children's parents and siblings, as well as other close relatives, such as grandparents. Indeed, parents are faced with a dual trauma: On top of their own, they are forced to deal with their child's posttraumatic reactions. Thus, in many cases, NPT intervention has to include elements that consider symptoms of posttraumatic stress disorder. In practice, delayed debriefing work is often needed for some time in the beginning of a rehabilitation process. Dealing with trauma related to psychological symptoms is then one of the basic themes of ABI children's NPT.

Anna's Experiences of Injury

Anna was sitting in my office in her wheelchair. She was looking out the window.

A: [Quietly] Did you know that I could have died? Actually, two times?
P: I know one time, when you had the embolization and something went wrong, a couple of years ago. Did you mean that?
A: Yes. I almost died. And I am sure there was a second time during the last operation. My tummy hurt when they took me, I didn't know if I would see mom and dad ever again. I was thinking how they must roll dead people to the mortuary in such hospital beds. Mom was crying. She also thought I would die. This is horrible, like I am dying here and now. At nights, I see mom crying and the lights in corridor ceiling again and again.
P: It was a frightening situation to all. Sounds like you were afraid of dying.

Anna sat quietly crying, looking away from me. Then she decided the conversation was enough for the day.

A: [Angrily] But now I'll say nothing more about this matter. No. This was enough. Don't you say anything you either.

And I did not. We sat quietly together for a few minutes and let the fear of death fade for the time being.

Depressive feelings are common at some point during recovery and rehabilitation. However, they may not be present immediately after the injury. The child can be too badly injured to be able to conceptualize what has happened to her, and, thus, cannot feel depressed. Furthermore, there is often a time period after injury, when child and her family don't feel depressed, but relieved, because they realize that child stayed alive and "the worst is now behind." Depressive feelings often appear around the time when child comes home from the hospital. The family is then faced with the demands of everyday life, and the discovery that the child cannot cope as she did before. Depressive symptoms of an ABI child can be various: withdrawal, anger, loss of interest in formerly pleasant activities, apathy, sleeping difficulties or excess sleeping, alterations of appetite, sadness, and even attempts at self-injury. We have to bear in mind that some of these symptoms can also be so called primary symptoms of the neurological injury itself. For example, alterations in activation regulation may look like a sleeping disorder, and problems with initiative induce behaviour that may look like withdrawal or apathy. Furthermore, neurologically based difficulties in emotion regulation can induce excessive crying and bursts of anger. Therefore, the therapist and the parents should evaluate the child's symptoms critically and be aware of multiple possible mechanisms behind them.

Anxiety and fears are common after ABI. Children may feel anxiety when they begin to face familiar situations as an injured person. Such situations are, for example, returning to school and hobbies, and meeting with relatives and friends. Often children think important questions, as "Do they still like me?" "What should I say if they ask what has happened to me?" "What should I do if other kids are mean to me?" "What if I cannot cope?" Also, fears related to the injuring event are common. For example, a child can be afraid of going to a place or situation that reminds her of the injury (e.g., getting in a car after a traffic accident, going to a doctor's appointment, having an MRI scan). Children who have ABI due to an illness often fear that the illness will reoccur. This is an extremely difficult situation when this can, indeed, be the case (e.g., tumours, vascular diseases). Thus, helping an ABI child to cope with her anxiety and fears is one important aim of most NPT interventions.

Most ABI children face difficulties with their self-concepts. ABI produces observable changes in how children behave, master age-appropriate skills, control their emotions, and move around in case of injuries to the motor system of brain, spine, and limbs. Injury can sometimes even change a child's physical appearance via scars and lost body parts. The meaning of such changes depends on several factors. First, the child's age at injury tells us something about how we can expect her to react. Small children seem to be quite flexible. After injury, they often start to relearn playing, activities of daily living, and social relations surprisingly decisively—without much sorrow over lost skills compared to how they saw themselves before the injury. This is, of course, due to a still immature self-concept, which is nevertheless going through changes when these children learn new skills and their body grows quite rapidly. Also, toddlers tend to live "here and now" and do not concentrate so much on the past or the future. School-aged children often react to consequences of ABI quite strongly, given that they are aware of their symptoms. These children remember well what kind of skills and activities they already dealt with autonomously before their injury. Thus, the loss, for example, of fluent speech, of maintaining balance in cycling, or of taking care of personal hygiene may be a shock. At the same time, children injured before puberty usually have great difficulties in understanding prospects of rehabilitation and their own role in its success. This understanding tends to come more easily among teenagers, who have more mature thinking skills concerning their own situations. We have to keep in mind, though, what was discussed earlier about the possible effects of ABI to the child's observed level of psychological development: A teenager can sometimes think like a chronologically much younger child.

Many ABI children *feel very lonely* after the acute phase. Often, they have spent a long time in the hospital or inpatient rehabilitation unit, being away from school and hobbies. Although friends are usually given some information about the ABI child's situation, their capability to keep in touch with their hospitalized friend is limited. Teenagers can sometimes visit the hospital by themselves, but younger friends are dependent on their parents for coming to see the ABI child in the hospital. Often, visits are scarce. This kind of separation from friends usually leads to sorrow and uncertainty: Do my friends still remember I exist?

When the ABI child is ready to return to school or daycare, sometimes she is not able to go back to her former learning group. This is because of her neuropsychological symptoms, which can lead to severe learning difficulties and, thus, demand placement in a special education class. In such a case, ABI children might feel completely separated from their former friends until they manage to build new friendships. This, in turn, is often compromised because of ABI children's neuropsychological symptoms. If contact with former friends is reestablished, there are, nevertheless, usually some obstacles. Children and even teenagers often find it difficult to face their injured friend. They do not know what to say or how to react if their friend moves, behaves, speaks, and even looks different. Adults' guidance and support is beneficial during these first encounters.

Sometimes, a child's symptoms after ABI form difficulties for spending time with friends. For example fatigue, linguistic problems, and difficulties in moving around (such as dysfunction of balance or paralysis) call for tolerance and understanding.

Anna's Feelings

Anna wanted to discuss her loneliness.

A: I am bored being at home alone. All my friends can go shopping and to parties, and I cannot. I am like a prisoner.
P: That sounds distressing, indeed. Tell me more about it.
A: Everybody has forgotten me, except Lisa. She comes to visit me after school. But only if I ask her to, and only once a month or so. I wonder if she comes just for courtesy.
P: Imagine—when things with friends are as you wish them to be, how is it?
A: [Smiling] They would suggest themselves that they want to spend time with me. And they would ask me to come out with them. [Thinking] Once Lisa asked if I wanted to come to the mall with her. But I couldn't.
P: Why not?
A: I would have to take my mom with me in case I got too tired or fell down and hurt myself. I will not go anywhere if I cannot go by myself, like all the other girls do! I'd rather be alone.

Anna's mother felt very insecure with letting Anna go out alone with her cane. Anna's balance was not so good, she got easily tired, and she did not understand money and time as other 13 year olds. As a result, Anna had to wait for a long time before she was ready to go out with her friends.

Central Themes in Children's NPT

As we can see, the aims of NPT have to be formulated after considering a wide variety of developmental and symptom-related factors. As a consequence, aims of NPT vary according to the particulars of the case. However, there are some themes that seem to appear in most cases. Next, I go through these themes and provide some examples.

Guiding How to Work in NPT

For most children, coming to a NPT session is their first experience of psychological rehabilitation. They are anxious about who they will be working with and what is going to happen in the therapy room. Therefore, the first sessions are important in building feelings of trust, security, and competency. In other words, the process of NPT should first concentrate on enabling the growth of good alliance between the ABI child and the therapist.

There are some beneficial strategies to follow during the initial sessions, as listed below:

- *Explain clearly who you are.* "My name is Hanna. I am a neuropsychologist. Have you ever heard that word? I know it is a difficult one. [Usually the answer is no.] It's okay; I'll explain it for you. A neuropsychologist is a person who has studied a lot about how children develop, think, and feel. We have also studied what human brain looks like and how it works. We meet children if they have encountered an accident or an illness that has affected their brain. This is what I have heard happened to you, right? You know that doctors examine and treat people if they have an illness or injury somewhere in their body. Well, we psychologists examine and treat people if they have some difficulties with their skills, thinking, or feelings." Of course, the details of explaining who the therapist is must be adapted to child's age, level of linguistic comprehension, and willingness to deal with the particular matter.
- *Depict concretely how many sessions there will be.* This can be done by using a cardboard with a symbol for each session (e.g., a circle). Guide the child to make a mark over a symbol in each session. The remaining symbols (that is, the remaining sessions) can then be easily comprehended.
- *Describe some examples of activities and materials you are going to use.* Sometimes children think NPT sessions resemble seeing a doctor. As a consequence, children may be afraid of having to go through possibly painful or frightening medical examinations. To help in relieving their insecure feelings, it is beneficial to tell them, for example: "Here we discuss important topics together. I can teach you something if needed, and we have activities with pen and paper, computer, and those toys and other things you can see on that shelf."
- *Describe confidentiality.* "You know, there is a rule that all of what you tell me and what you do here in therapy is confidential. That means that I will not talk about them to anybody. You can talk about everything that happens here to whomever you want to, but I cannot and

will not. There is one exception. If something we discuss tells me you are somehow in danger, we together have to talk about it to your parents. I shall, however, first tell you what such matter is, and then we will decide together how we are going to discuss it with your parents."

- *Teach how to discuss matters related to the child's everyday life.* Sometimes, children find it difficult to tell the therapist about events in their daily life. However, it is just those discussions that form the base of therapeutic discussions. Sometimes, children have linguistic difficulties, which explain their problems in talking about their lives. Sometimes, children simply are not used to conversations with an adult, or they might think ordinary daily events are too dull to be told. Children can be helped: "Here our job is to discuss things about your life. Every time you come to see me, I shall ask you to tell me what has happened during the past days. And you know what—I just want to hear very ordinary things, like what has happened at home and in school, and what have you done with your friends. Often when people ask how are you, you perhaps tell them if something extraordinary has happened. But here it is different. Here we can discuss very small and ordinary things." Some children may even need modelling to get the idea of discussing "small and ordinary topics." The therapist can then model: "My days have been quite busy. During the weekend, I cleaned my house, and I did not like it. Then I took a walk in the forest, which was nice. I even saw a rabbit. Yesterday I went to work again. I met five clients. For lunch I had a good salad. In the evening I watched TV; there was news and some movie, which was a bit scary." After repeating this modelling in five or six sessions, most children get the idea of telling the therapist about their ordinary lives. This, in turn, gives the therapist important insight into what is going on in the child's life and what topics could be beneficial to cover in further therapeutic discussions.
- *Clarify the rules of being in therapy.* Most children are curious about what they are allowed to do in the therapy room. The traditional rules in child therapy include: "Here you are allowed to do and speak whatever you want to. There are two exceptions, though. You are not allowed to physically hurt yourself or me, and you are not allowed to deliberately break furniture, destroy the room, or harm our equipment. I take care of you so that you cannot hurt yourself in this room. Here it is safe."
- *Express that you accept the child as she is.* "Sometimes children are worried of what I might think if they have problems knowing and doing things. Here, it is okay to do things slowly, make errors, and say 'I don't know.' I promise you that it is okay. I will not get angry or impatient, and I will not laugh at you in any situation."

Teaching Relevant Facts (Psychoeducation)

Details of ABI are difficult to understand for children and also for their parents. By details, I mean those myriad facts that relate to the initial injuring situation, treatments in hospital, rehabilitation after the acute phase, and anatomy and processes of the brain injury, as represented in the hospital case book and doctors' speech. Often, there is quite a long time period after the injury when children themselves and their parents are so upset that understanding is cognitively compromised. Furthermore, the medical and psychological language related to brain injury is complex and includes strange concepts. As a consequence, injured children can have quite a disintegrated and even erroneous impression of what is going on. Sometimes, there are even assumptions and beliefs that do not represent reality and lead to fears. In these cases, children benefit from psychoeducation.

Psychoeducation means teaching children information they need to create a more accurate and realistic comprehension of such themes as "what has happened to me" and "what kind of an injury there is in my brain." The therapist should carefully choose methods that best ensure understanding, bearing in mind the child's neuropsychological symptoms and her developmental level. Often, it is beneficial to speak in concrete terms, proceed slowly, introduce only one or two themes per session, repeat what was discussed in the previous sessions, and use supporting materials, such as drawings and pictures. My therapeutic equipment includes a plastic model of human brain, which can be held in hand and disassembled into pieces. It is extremely practical and instructive, and most importantly, children usually find it fun! Giving psychoeducation when needed, throughout the NPT process, ensures that children have enough resources to work with other therapeutic themes, after their need for accurate information is fulfilled. This information will be integrated into the metacognitive processing of the child, which further enhances re-education as a whole.

Anna's Self-Knowledge

We had had an energetic session around adaptation strategies for memory difficulties. The theme allowed us to work in an active and quite cheerful atmosphere. Suddenly Anna became upset. She was quiet, looking anxious.

A: I wonder if they left anything inside my skull. I have heard that the anomaly was large … but how large? And they cut it away. Perhaps they took the whole half of my brain. And now there is almost nothing left. Sometimes I shake my head to feel if there is anything inside. I am an empty-headed girl.

P: [I had to think for a while for my answer.] By considering all you know about human brain, do you think it is possible to cut everything away?

A: I guess not, but who knows?

P: I think we could know together. Tell me some examples about what you can do these days.

A: Well, I can stand up from this wheelchair. Not much though. I can watch TV and chat on the Internet. And I go to school, albeit to that stupid special education class. I can read and write. And I remember something. That is about all. I hate myself.

P: Thanks. I'll come back to this self-hating a bit later, but first I'd like to tell you that empty-headed girls could not do those things you can do. You see, a lot of brain is needed to do those things. I have here the text about your surgery. Let's take this brain from the shelf [plastic teaching brain model] and see together what the surgeon says here about what was actually cut away.

And Anna followed calmly my showing her what was actually taken away and what was left inside.

Supporting Realistic Self-Image

In NPT intervention, ABI children's development of realistic self-concepts can be supported by working on the following themes. First, children benefit from finding out on what respect they are still "familiar with themselves." They need to see what they still can cope with and how other people see them. I have found it beneficial to proceed through this theme first, before concentrating on learning about the ABI symptomatology. I have been engaged in several discussions on whether neuropsychologists should help children understand their neuropsychological symptoms at all. The underlying fear is whether we induce depressive reactions or support somehow the development of a negative self-concept. In deciding this dilemma, we have to remember that children nevertheless grow up, and at some point evidently start to notice something "is wrong." Then, it is valuable if they have been offered age-appropriate information about their situation from the very beginning.

Gradually, children tend to become curious about some details of their symptoms after injury. Then it is the time to proceed to discussions about it. According to my experience, at this second stage, children do not benefit from direct psychoeducation, but need sensitive discussions by the so-called Socratic method. There, the therapist helps the child to build understanding by presenting questions, which gradually lead to answers in the child's own mind.

Session Without Wheelchair—Progress and Doubts

Anna came to her session, now without the wheelchair. She had a cane. I was happy for her. Anna had mixed feelings.

A: See, I got rid of that awful wheeling thing! I can walk, I can walk!

She walked indeed, extremely slowly and clumsily. She managed to reach the therapy room, although I was afraid she would fall along the way. Sitting safely, she looked sadly at her cane.

A: Wheelchair gone but this instead. I am like an old person, a hundred-year-old grandmother. I shall not keep this cane for very long, I would rather try without it and fall all the time.

P: I see you have made some important progress. You are walking again. At the same time you seem angry for having to use old people's equipment. Joy and disappointment at the same time.

A: Yes, indeed. I am an old person. My life ends before it's even begun properly.

P: Tell me more about that thought. What do you mean?

A: I have dementia.

P: Dementia?!

A: Yes. They told me in the hospital that I don't remember things properly. If you don't remember, you have dementia. My grandmother had it, and now she is dead. But I think they are wrong. You see, I do remember everything. But if they are right, I have dementia, and that means I am an old person.

P: Yes, if someone has dementia, she or he does not remember things as they should. Have you ever heard of any other condition that could have memory difficulties as symptoms?

A: Other condition? No, I haven't. [Sitting silently for a while] My schoolmate had difficulties in remembering anything she tried to learn. But I don't know if she tried hard enough. [Smiles] And my father! He often forgets things, keys missing and so on.

P: Yes, forgetting things is something that happens sometimes to everybody. Sometimes something just happens that makes a person have memory problems more than usual. You obviously know about dementia as one cause of memory problems. But when you think about your schoolmate, do you think she had dementia?

A: No.

P: Then what could be the case?

A: I don't know. I have heard about learning difficulties. Perhaps she has those. Could they include memory problems?

P: Yes, they could. You found an excellent alternative cause for memory problems. Do you know which organ is needed for remembering things?

A: Yes, we had this at school. The brain! It is inside the skull.

P: Yes, for remembering you need your brain. Now think what could cause memory problems?

A: Something wrong in the brain?

P: Great, you can think very fine about this. Let's move forward. What kind of events could make something go wrong in the brain? [Anna looked at me astonished.]

A: An accident, traffic accident. [Long silence] Brain surgery?

P: Yes, sometimes also brain surgery. And when it is an accident or brain surgery of a young person, it is not the question of dementia. Then, it is called memory deficit.

A: Well, I'll think about it. I don't yet know if memory deficit is at all better that dementia. Nevertheless, I don't have either.

Working with Strong Emotions

Due to the often quite shocking injuring events with which the child has been faced, the therapist should be ready to support working with strong feelings in therapy. Previously, it was normatively thought that talking about feelings after a traumatic event is beneficial and necessary (Sullivan et al., 2006). However, there are also controversial ideas. It has been suggested that concentrating on memories and feelings related to a traumatic event could even be harmful (Sullivan et al., 2006). A safe way to proceed, then, is to provide the child with opportunities and encouragement to express her thoughts and feelings safely, but to respect carefully the child's individual boundaries. Some children may need plenty of time and support, whereas other children are more ready to express their feelings quite early in therapy.

The therapist should be prepared to discuss several themes with the child. Among the most common issues are the questions almost every injured child thinks eventually: Why did this happen to me and whose fault is this? Sometimes answers can be found, but most often they cannot. If someone to blame actually exists, as can be in the case of, for example, violence or a traffic accident, themes of severe anger and revenge usually appear. Most children also experience sadness and shame over, for example, lost skills or physical and neuropsychological symptoms visible to others.

One of the most important but often misleadingly invisible themes to discuss is the child's tendency to protect her close family members. Children often begin to modify their behaviour and communication in the presence of their mother, father, and siblings, in order to protect them from becoming worried or sad. Of course, then children also protect themselves from being forced to deal with their family members' painful feelings.

The therapist's task is to help children understand that painful feelings:

- are normal and not dangerous;
- eventually get less painful;
- can be integrated in daily life along with other, pleasant feelings; and
- don't get worse if they are sometimes discussed with therapist, family members, or safe friends.

Another task is to help children understand that it is not their responsibility to protect their parents from feeling bad—parents are adults who survive and exist to take care of their children, not vice versa. Sometimes this does not seem to be the case, if parents have severe psychiatric symptoms due to their child's injury or other issues. Then, it is important to guide parents to seek psychological support for themselves.

Supporting Psychological Development

One way to conceptualize children's NPT is to see it as a process of supporting the child's psychological development after brain injury. The target would then be age-appropriate development through the necessary developmental phases or steps. However, we must remember that the overall rate of development usually is slower after brain injury. As a result, we should not expect "age appropriateness" of skills too early. Sometimes, compromises over the target of age appropriateness also have to be made. In case of severe injury, there can be such damage in brain tissue that quite broad functional deficiencies will be permanently present. An important guideline in evaluating the child's progress is to compare her skills with her own earlier level of performance. Comparison with the "age average" can sometimes be beneficial, but often does not provide enough information. It can be that the child seems to develop clearly "below average" level all the time, but, compared to her own earlier performance, for example, three months ago, clear development can be seen. This is an important issue related to the motivation of rehabilitation for all the partners: the child, her family, and the therapist.

Themes related to the issue of supporting psychological development in children's NPT are various. In my experience, among the most beneficial are those of autonomy, asking for help, and ideas for the future. Most children with ABI lose some part of their autonomy after injury. They need other peoples' help more than children of their age on average. As mentioned earlier in this chapter, the meaning of this for the child depends on her age. However, many children get confused about the situation. On one hand, they know that growing up means learning to handle things more and more independently. At the same time, however, they need to ask for help in many more situations than they would prefer. The child should be supported to ask for help when needed but, at the same time, keep on practising skills over and over again. Neither of the "poles"—asking for help and performing completely autonomously—should dominate.

What is it, then, that helps us people to struggle forward even in the most painful circumstances? It is the hope for a meaningful, less painful future life. Children under school age often live only here and now and, thus, do not necessarily need support for creating hope for their future. Older children can sometimes be very resourceful and flexible in creating ideas for their future. In some cases, however, hope is lost, and therapeutic support is needed to create it again. Children need to be able to look for a future in which they see themselves as needed and loved by other people, capable of doing beneficial things, and also having fun. Furthermore, most teenagers need to see themselves as young adults who can have a job, create a home for themselves, find a spouse, and, perhaps, have children.

Challenges and Solutions for Neuropsychotherapeutic Work

As described previously, the neuropsychological symptoms of ABI set some special demands for therapeutic work with ABI children. Next, I shall depict these challenges and give some examples of clinical solutions.

Anna's Obstacles in Therapy

When Anna began her sessions with me after her brain surgery and ABI, we faced several serious problems in our therapeutic work. First of all, Anna was always very tired. She began to yawn after just five minutes of sitting and discussion. After a few more minutes, her eyes began to close, and she began to lie on her chair, feeling extremely tired. Anna also had great difficulties in remembering what we discussed 15 minutes ago, let alone during the past week's session. She found it difficult to sustain her attention on one topic or task for more than a few minutes at a time. Her emotions fluctuated vigorously from laughter and joy to sorrow or anger. She had difficulty in remembering words and understanding my speech if I used long sentences or abstract words. On top of all this, she was almost completely unaware of most of her ABI symptoms and how those affected our therapeutic relationship.

Memory Difficulties

Memory difficulties bring two challenges to the NPT process. Successful psychotherapy is a process in which relevant themes are discussed, often repeatedly during several sessions, in order to create a mutual understanding of a particular issue. If the child has memory deficits, this process becomes compromised: The child does not remember clearly what was discussed during the previous sessions, or in the worst case, earlier during the very session at hand.

Although memory deficits often seriously compromise the therapeutic process, there are some methods that can be used to support the child's memory processes. Beneficial equipment includes a white drawing board or large drawing papers. On these, the therapist can represent relevant material by drawing and writing. Simple line

Figure 8.1 Picture of thinking–speaking–acting. *"I will punch you!"

drawings can be used to depict, for example, how people communicate or think (see Figure 8.1). Written lists of key words or sentences can be used as memory aids to what have been understood so far. I have found it beneficial to produce drawings and writing on paper, and to keep those in each patient's own folder. As we look at and read them repeatedly during succeeding sessions, the individually customized memory aids makes them eventually familiar, and this facilitates the remembering of core ideas of therapy. Other methods are following the principles of "only one theme per session" and "go ahead only after you are sure the child understands and also remembers a given therapeutic theme." If we follow these principles, the progress of therapy with ABI children is often quite slow. However, if we take multiple themes per session and progress too fast, most ABI children are not able to build a coherent understanding of what has been discussed overall. As a consequence, important therapeutic aims can be missed, and the child probably ends up being quite confused as to what the therapy sessions are all about. This, in turn, hampers the child's motivation for therapeutic work. Another way of supporting the ABI child's memory is to begin each session by remembering together what was discussed in the previous session. Sometimes this is also needed in the course of one single session: "Let's stop and think what have we discussed so far today."

Language Problems

Successful NPT assumes some means of communication between the child and the therapist. Oral speech; written language; sign language; and language supported by pictures, symbols, or computer programs are all acceptable. Most commonly, oral speech is used, but there are some challenges. Children with ABI most commonly have trouble with finding words while they speak—the speech fluency may not be normal, and they have trouble understanding long or grammatically complex sentences as well as having difficulty with "reading between the lines." Deficits of auditory short-term memory also cause problems in communication situations: ABI children tend to forget rapidly what was just said, and, thus, their listening comprehension is compromised.

The therapist can use several methods to overcome these language obstacles. These include:

- *Make sure the child pays attention to you.* Children with ABI often have attention difficulties. This means they need constant support to notice what is it that they should be doing and thinking at a given moment. Therefore, although the child may have been alert to the therapist's speech a while ago, she might not be alert anymore. Children sometimes need very concrete guidance in order to engage in conversation with the therapist ("Look at me again, please; I'll hold your hand so you remember we are supposed to talk now"; "Listen, now I am going to say something important to you").
- *Speak using a slow speech rate and short sentences.*
- *Follow carefully the child's understanding and repeat your utterance if needed.* Sometimes several repetitions are needed before the child understands what you mean.
- *Be prepared to express what you mean in several alternative ways.* Some of them might be better understood that the others.

Attention Difficulties

Attention processes can be conceptualized from several perspectives. Cohen (1993) describes the processes of focused attention, sustained attention, divided attention, and shifting attention between targets. All of these can be compromised in ABI children. The most important thing for the therapist to remember in every session is not to take the ABI child's attention skills for granted! If the therapist stays alert and doubts in her mind the client's attention, then she usually remembers to give the necessary support. Another important issue to remember is that the processes of attention, memory, and executive functions are closely tied. In many situations, it may even be impossible to separate them. In order to support the ABI child's attention in therapy sessions, the following guidelines may be beneficial:

- *Focusing attention*: Use visual aids on top of mere discussion. Tell the child explicitly when, where, and what she is supposed to do or notice. Use the child's first name when giving her instructions. Seek eye contact before saying important things to the child.
- *Sustaining attention*: Guide the child with spoken words through long-term tasks and situations. Use sound marks (agreed upon together) to help her remember what she was supposed to do (e.g., little bell sound to mean "keep going"). Help her to stay alert with a gentle touch of your hand, for example, on her arm or shoulder.
- *Dividing and shifting attention*: Sound marks can be used here, too (the bell sound meaning "change the task"). Aids for "focusing attention" (see above) can be applied in succession to help the child shift between attention targets. Dividing attention is not recommended for more than two targets at a time—create subprocesses that can be performed in succession, that is, alter a task demanding divided attention into a task that demands shifting attention (for example: write a sentence—first write it down, then read to check spelling—or, first look at me and listen what I say, then look at the picture and think about it).

Fatigue

Most children with ABI have fatigue, and they are often extremely tired during some sessions. Therefore, a neuropsychotherapist's room should include a sofa. I have had patients who literally fall asleep while sitting in a chair. Sitting on a sofa gives children the opportunity to lie down if they feel exhausted. It does not mean they fall asleep, though. Most children have strength to continue conversation if they are allowed to do so lying down. Even drawing, listening to and discussing music, and playing can be managed when the child is lying on a sofa. Some patients need to sleep every now and then for a couple of minutes. Then, it is better to allow them to fall asleep. A few minutes of sleep can produce another half-hour of effective therapeutic work.

If the child has strong fatigue, it is beneficial to try out different schedules for the NPT sessions. Some children can work effectively if the sessions are in the morning hours. Others, on the other hand, work better if they have first got activation during their school day and come for their sessions in the afternoon hours. Coming after school can cause the problem of hunger or thirstiness. If there is no time between school and the NPT session for a snack, it is beneficial to serve some juice for the child in the beginning of the session. Of course, this must be negotiated with parents in order to avoid problems related to allergies or other medical restraints against some foods. The most important thing to remember when working with ABI children with fatigue is to interpret tiredness correctly: It does not mean the child is bored or resists therapeutic work.

Unawareness of Symptoms

One of the most upsetting symptoms of ABI is anosognosia. This refers to child's inability to notice her own neuropsychological symptoms (Prigatano, 2009). In other words, a child with anosognosia is unaware that something is wrong at all. Such a symptom has its pros and cons. Early in the process of getting better, it usually protects child from comprehending the situation: severe deficits in many skills, some skills even lost. In this way, it also protects the child from feelings of despair, depression, and fear. However, severe anosognosia makes it difficult for the ABI child to benefit from rehabilitation. In order to work with the therapist to reach rehabilitation goals, the child needs to understand why all the hard work is necessary. She needs to comprehend that there is a set of symptoms that make coping in everyday life so difficult.

The task of introducing a child to her symptoms is demanding. It must be done both very sensitively and clearly. The method of "debate" should be avoided. By that, I mean depicting some symptoms for a child, who then refuses to believe it. Rather, the therapist should first introduce the symptom of anosognosia itself.

Difficulties with Self-Reflection

Anna was again extremely tired, at 1 p.m. I had tried to verbalise her fatigue several times in previous sessions, but she never seemed to comprehend what I was talking about. Now she was yawning and lying on the sofa.

P: Seems you feel very tired now.

A: I am yawning. It is not because of tiredness, however. I just had a long school day. [two hours altogether on therapy days]

P: I wonder if you remember me asking last week if you were tired. I had that impression. I wonder if it feels bad to almost fall asleep at daytime when everybody expects you to be alert.

A: But I am not. I am just yawning. Let me be! I will not hear anything more about tiredness!

P: Okay. I won't talk about your tiredness. I would like to teach you something about quite a weird symptom some people have after brain injury.

A: There is that word again! Brain injury! I hate it, people with brain injury are delayed, developmentally delayed, and I am not.

P: I know you don't like that word, but I have decided to always say just the realistic words when I do therapy with children. Otherwise, someone could understand wrong, and that would not be good. So, brain injury it is.

A: [Takes a deep breath, smiling] You'll never give up, will you?

P: No, I won't. Let's go back to that weird symptom I told you about. I think it is the most interesting one, too. And, for me as a therapist, one of the most difficult to treat!

A: [Looking excited] Yeah!?

P: You see, some children who have acquired a brain injury don't notice they have any symptoms, even though all other people around them see those. For example, a child may not remember things for more than one minute, and his parents notice that every day, but the child thinks he remembers everything as before.

A: Really? [Thinking silently] You mean like if I didn't notice at all that my left leg does not work properly?

P: A kind of that, yes. Think how it could be and what could happen, if you did not notice there is a paresis in your leg?

A: I would start to walk without any support and then … I would fall down and really hurt myself.

P: Yes, that's probable. I think we need to discuss later about how it could be if you had some other symptoms you are not aware of.

A: [Astonished] Do I?

P: Yes.

Anna became quiet and lay on the sofa, looking at the ceiling. The discussion was over for that session.

Most children are willing to negotiate the possibility of having some symptoms they are not aware of, after first learning there is such symptom as anosognosia. When they get curious about their own status regarding that symptom, they are ready to proceed. The next step is to work together as "private detectives" and gather evidence. It can be found from repetitive daily obstacles or problems with fulfilling demonstrative tasks in therapy room. Sometimes, it is helpful to take video recordings and reflect child's symptoms there. Of course, this must be done sensitively and always include notions of strengths seen on video as well.

Notions on Some Methods Adopted From Traditional Psychotherapy

Doing NPT is not about using exotic methods outside the range of traditional psychotherapies. Rather, it is therapeutic work that combines methods eclectically from other fields of psychotherapy and, at the same time, modifies them according to the ABI child's special needs due to her unique set of neuropsychological symptoms. Therefore, several methods familiar from, for example, cognitive child psychotherapy (e.g., Reinecke, Dattilio, & Freeman, 2003), solution-focused brief therapy (Berg & Steiner, 2003), and expressive therapies (e.g., Malchiodi, 2005) can be applied. Rather than abandoning some method because the child has neuropsychological deficits, the therapist should think: "Okay, how can I modify this method in order to apply it even though this child remembers (speaks/understands/pays attention/regulates her own actions, etc.) vaguely?

For example, let's have a look at play therapy techniques (see, e.g., Landreth, 2002). A set of basic toys, such as a dollhouse, plastic animals, a castle and soldiers, cars, dishes, and a doll create a setting for an unlimited variety of children's play. Choosing the needed toys, building a play scenario, playing, and discussing themes elicited in play provides the child and the therapist with an intensive field of shared experience. The theme of play and the way child does the playing activity both give valuable insight in child's thoughts and feelings. The therapist can either observe the child playing and discuss it afterwards, or he can participate and introduce play themes intentionally in order to bring relevant matters into therapeutic discussion. Play therapy can also be combined with psychoeducation.

For example, events in the hospital or "blood travelling through vessels in the brain" can be demonstrated with toys and other materials. Stories are another beautiful method of play therapy. Either existing stories or stories created by the child, by the therapist, or both child and therapist together can be used for several purposes. I remember creating a story about "poor nerve cells who withered, when blood did not get there in time to bring oxygen and sugar for food." The child wanted to hear the story again and again, and built eventually quite a coherent understanding of what had happened in her brain (infarction at age 7 due to a rare vascular disease). Severe problems with attention or memory can disturb ABI children's playing. In this case, the task of the therapist is to guide the child back to her play, remind her where she was before disruption, or tell her what the theme of the play was.

On top of play therapy techniques, methods of expressive therapies can also be applied (see, e.g., Malchiodi, 2005). Children can draw, paint, and sculpt in order to express their thoughts and feelings. Some children hesitate at, for example, drawing, if they have ataxia of weakness in their hands. Then it is important to ensure child that in therapy room it is not about being a skillful artist. The therapist has to accept all the child's drawing productions and value them by keeping them in a safe place. Gradually, most children find the joy of drawing, painting, and sculpting. They realize that these methods actually help their therapist in understanding them better. If the child's injury makes using hands completely impossible, then existing pictures can be used. For example, postcards, photographs, and pictures from magazines or the internet are suitable. The therapist can ask the child, for example, to choose pictures she thinks say something about the matter at hand (e.g., low self-esteem).

Some children enjoy music. They can bring their own music to the therapy session. A CD-player or computer can be used to listen to the music together. The therapist can then help the child to discuss the meaning of particular music for her. Music can, for example, elicit good or bad memories, or help children to relax or activate themselves. Sometimes, it is the vocals that bring something important to the session. An 8-year-old boy with severe problems in controlling his behaviour at school brought into therapy session a piece of called "Think by Yourself." It elicited deep discussions about who is responsible for that boy's behaviour and whether his own brain can, indeed, be used intentionally in controlling behaviour.

Conclusions

Children with ABI can be helped by NPT intervention, which is an extension of neuropsychological rehabilitation. NPT refers to therapeutic work that combines methods eclectically from several fields of psychotherapy and modifies them according to the ABI child's special needs due to her unique set of neuropsychological symptoms. Aims of NPT intervention should be formulated in cooperation with the ABI child, her parents, and the therapist. Factors to be considered in the formulation process include the child's chronological and developmental age, as well as her symptoms of psychological distress. Throughout the intervention, the therapist must be able to modify the therapeutic methods selected according to the child's unique needs. Neuropsychological symptoms, such as deficits in memory, attention, language, and emotion regulation are not treated as obstacles for therapy, but as challenges for the therapist.

I believe that neuropsychologists often include implicitly therapeutic elements in their work with ABI children. However, the effects of interventions can be strengthened if therapists start to apply psychotherapeutic methods in neuropsychological rehabilitation explicitly and intentionally. This requires professional knowledge and skills from several fields: neuropsychology, developmental psychology, and psychotherapy. Traditionally, these disciplines are not combined explicitly enough in basic or advanced psychology programs. Hopefully in the future, we can see neuropychotherapy as a self-evident branch of neuropsychological rehabilitation, already at the level of basic training in university psychology programs.

References

Anstey, K.J., Butterworth, P., Jorm, A.F., Christensen, H., Rodgers, P., & Windsor, T.D. (2004). A population survey found an association between self-reports of traumatic brain injury and increased psychiatric symptoms. *Journal of Clinical Epidemiology, 57*, 1202–1211.

Bay, E. (2009). Current treatment options for depression after mild traumatic brain injury. *Current Treatment Options in Neurology, 11*, 377–382.

Berg, I.K., & Steiner, T. (2003). *Children's solution work.* New York: Norton.

Christensen, A., & Uzzell, B. (1994). *Brain injury and neuropsychological rehabilitation. International perspectives.* Hillsdale, NJ: Lawrence Erlbaum.

Cohen, R.A. (1993). *The neuropsychology of attention*. New York: Plenum Press.

Halligan, P., Kischka, U., & Marshall, J. (Eds.). (2003). *Handbook of clinical neuropsychology*. Oxford: Oxford University Press.

King, N., & Tyerman, A. (2003). Neuropsychological presentation and treatment of head injury and traumatic brain damage. In P. Halligan, U. Kischka, and J. Marshall (Eds.), *Handbook of clinical neuropsychology* (pp. 487–505). Oxford: Oxford University Press.

Landreth, G.L. (2002). *Play therapy: The art of the relationship*. Hove, East Sussex, UK: Brunner-Routledge.

Limond, J., Morris, L., & McMillan, T.M. (2009). Quality of life in children with acquired brain injury: Parent perspectives 1–5 years after injury. *Journal of Brain Injury, 23*, 617–622.

Malchiodi, C. (Ed.). (2005). *Expressive therapies*. New York: Guilford Press.

McKinlay, A., Grace, R., Horwood, J., Fergusson, D., & MacFarlane, M. (2009). Adolescent psychiatric symptoms following preschool childhood mild traumatic brain injury: Evidence from a birth cohort. *Journal of Head Trauma Rehabilitation, 24*, 221–228.

Ponsford, J. (1995). *Traumatic brain injury. Rehabilitation for everyday adaptive living*. Hove, East Sussex, UK: Lawrence Erlbaum.

Prigatano, G.P. (2009). Anosognosia: Clinical and ethical considerations. *Current Opinion in Neurology, 22*, 606–611.

Prigatano, G., & Gray, J.A. (2007). Parental concerns and distress after paediatric traumatic brain injury: A qualitative study. *Journal of Brain Injury, 21*, 721–729.

Reinecke, M., Dattilio, F., & Freeman, A. (Eds.). (2003). *Cognitive therapy with children and adolescents. A casebook for clinical practice*. New York: Guilford Press.

Silver, J.M., McAllister, T.W., & Arciniegas, D.B. (2009). Depression and cognitive complaints following mild traumatic brain injury. *American Journal of Psychiatry, 166*, 653–661.

Sullivan, Everstine, D., & Everstine, L. (2006). *Strategic interventions for people in crisis, trauma, and disaster*. New York: Routledge.

9

Therapeutic Applications with Different Types of Developmental Disabilities in Young Adults

Sari Haikonen

Introduction

Developmental disabilities associate with educational, occupational, and social functioning in young adults. Cognitive difficulties usually coexist with behavioral and emotional disorders. Adaptive functioning in daily living, from basic skills to more complex independent skills, is usually subaverage. The understanding of overlapping neurological, developmental, neuropsychological and neuropsychiatric symptoms, and reactive emotional problems is essential to achieve therapeutic goals. Communication difficulties associated with developmental problems are challenging for treatment and therapeutic interpersonal processes. Establishing a working alliance is a difficult but not impossible process in cases like mutism and intellectual and developmental disability (IDD). Neuropsychotherapeutic goals are the same as in any other patient group: to build up self-awareness and self-esteem, an inner locus of control, and coping strategies for emotional, behavioral, and cognitive problems. The therapeutic relationship requires individually tailored methods. The challenge is to achieve meaningful adult life despite the continuous need for support in daily living. The experience of meaningful educational, occupational, and social life is possible only if the collaboration with families, other health care providers, and community service providers is successful. Two case reports will be presented to illustrate applied intervention methods and results.

Developmental Disabilities—Definitions and Descriptions

The term *developmental disability* (Goodey, 2001) will be used in a broad sense to include diagnoses of IDD, as well as other types of developmental disabilities, such as cerebral palsy, epilepsy, and mutism, which all share adaptive functioning deficits. Adaptive functioning is the effectiveness with which an individual meets the standards of personal independence and social responsibility expected for his or her age in the areas of self-care, receptive and expressive language, learning, mobility, self-direction, capacity for independent living, and economic self-sufficiency. Developmental disability in this context is not used as a diagnostic medical term with a consistent definition or as an accepted psychiatric term.

Developmental disability co-occurs often with behavioral disorders and mental health problems. Deficiencies in neurotransmitter systems and biologically based overarousal contribute to mental health and challenging behaviors (Heilman, Blonder, Bowers, & Crucian, 2000; Fuster, 2003). Overlapping symptoms and comorbidities of learning difficulties with attention deficit disorder and neuropsychiatric disorders (for example, obsessive-compulsive disorders) have been investigated (Brown, 2005), and various combinations of treatments tailored for particular individuals have been proven successful (Jensen & Abikoff, 2000; Romana, 2003). Due to diminished verbal communication abilities, language cannot be used adequately in the construction of self and adaptive social behavior (Paul, Cohen, Klin, & Volkmar, 1999). For example, if criticized by a superior, the individual may take the critique literally, with the result of highly aroused emotional anger. The quality of life from childhood into adulthood for individuals with a developmental disability (Faulkner, 1999) can be enhanced by timely, appropriate intervention.

Cases of a young man with mutism and a young woman with mild IDD will be presented to illustrate applied neuropsychotherapy methods and results.

Mutism

According to the *DSM-IV*, selective mutism is a persistent failure to speak in specific social situations in which speech is typically expected (American Psychiatric Association, 1994). This is not the result of organic disability to speak but interferes with education or occupational achievement and with social communication. Selective mutism is a multidimensional childhood disorder in which biologically mediated temperament and anxiety components seem to play a major role (Kumpulainen, 2002). Selective mutism has been linked to a number of additional childhood conditions, such as premorbid speech and language problems, developmental disorder or delay, and a variety of childhood psychiatric conditions (Sharp, Sherman, & Gross, 2007). Generalized effective treatment for mutism is possible only after clear diagnostic understanding (Anstendig, 1998). Careful assessment of electively mute behavior and a structured treatment program applied in real communication environments is recommended (Johnson & Wintgens, 2007). Multimodal therapy, including behavior management procedures, has been successful for some persons (Hadley, 1994). At the present moment, pharmacotherapy cannot be recommended as the treatment of first choice, but if other methods of treatment are not helpful, medication can be included (Kumpulainen, 2002).

Mild Intellectual and Developmental Disability

According to the *DSM-IV*, mild IDD (IQ ranging from 50–69) refers to those persons with minimal impairment of daily living skills, academic achievement ranging from grade 2 to grade 4 in basic subjects, and the ability to achieve social and vocational skills sufficient for minimum self-support (American Psychiatric Association, 1994). These persons may need guidance or assistance when under unusual social or economic stress. The problem is that the IQ does not necessarily correlate with overall functioning, so that it is possible to have developmental disability with IQ of 79 or higher and still be unable to manage activities of daily living independently. Behavioral disorders and mental health disorders co-occur often with IDD. The need for psychotherapy has been recognized, but the results (for example, generalization of social skills through self-monitoring) have varied (Misra, 1992). The relationship between working alliance and therapeutic outcomes for individuals with mild IDD has been investigated and proven to be essential to outcomes (Strauser, Lustig, & Donnell, 2004).

Therapeutic Challenges

Developmental disabilities are multidimensional disorders in which different problems seem to play a major role depending, for example, on developmental state, environmental circumstances, personal reactive styles, and earlier experiences. Careful diagnostic assessment (Jakab, 1990) is always necessary for an individual treatment plan. Understanding simultaneous and overlapping neurological, neuropsychological and neuropsychiatric symptoms, and reactive mental health problems and behavioral problems of persons with developmental disabilities is very challenging but necessary for effective intervention.

Individuals with developmental disabilities usually have significant limitations in their ability to think abstractly and communicate verbally. Nonverbal communication, such as eye contact and gestures, is usually limited. The challenge is to adapt communication styles in order to accommodate individual communication needs and to avoid misunderstandings caused by receptive and expressive difficulties. It is necessary to use plain language and short sentences, to speak slowly, and to avoid using leading questions. Between questions and statements, the person must be given time to process the information. A variety of communicative aids, such as pictures and questionnaires with alternatives to choice, may be helpful.

Finding suitable methods for communication is a necessary prerequisite for therapeutic alliance. Working alliance includes a therapeutic bond and agreement about the tasks and goals (Safran & Muran, 2000). The bond (e.g., the extent to which the patient feels understood, respected, and valued), as well as the task and goal dimensions of the alliance, influence one another, and the strength of the working alliance is the major factor in change achieved through therapy (Bordin, 1979). A positive relationship between working alliance and therapeutic outcomes for individuals with mild IDD has been found (Strauser et al., 2004). In addition to communication difficulties, validation needed for therapeutic alliance is difficult, because persons with developmental disabilities are rarely aware of their abilities, disabilities, and challenging behavior. Resistance follows easily from misunderstandings (Leahy, 2001). Working with resistance reports from family members and other support staff are valuable, although not a substitute for direct contact with the individual. It is helpful to have a talk with a family member or support person prior to therapy to get valuable information—for example, the individual's level of functioning, communication strengths, and interests, to avoid needles mistakes, such as asking too many questions of the individual. Collaborative working with family members or other caregivers, health care providers, and community service providers is very important to achieve circumstances in which a person with cognitive disabilities is able to integrate into society and experience meaningful adult life (Sohlberg & Mateer, 2001). The same applies to persons with developmental disabilities.

Therapeutic Goals

Neuropsychotherapy is a problem-oriented approach based on identifying and treating specific psychological (emotional, behavioral, and cognitive) problems resulting from brain illness (Judd, 1999). The same can be applied to developmental disabilities. Establishing and maintaining a working alliance during the whole therapy process is the main target of therapy. The goals are the same as in any other patient group: to build up self-awareness and self-esteem, an inner locus of control, and coping strategies for emotional, behavioral, and cognitive problems. The final goal is to achieve meaningful adult life, despite the continuous need for support in daily living. Agreement of goals and tasks coexists and follows naturally if the bond between patient and therapist is strong. Because of verbal communication problems, high stress can be experienced through emotional and behavioral problems and often through somatic complaints. Understanding and coping with emotional and behavioral problems is essentially important to be able to integrate successfully into society. Because learning difficulties restrict adaptive functioning, cognitive problems must be integrated into emotional and behavioral domains. Communication and adaptive functioning problems need to be worked at in therapy, alongside emotional and behavioral problems.

Methods of Intervention and Results Are Described by Two Case Reports

Case Example One: A 21-year-old Man with Mutism

Background

Matti, a 21-year-old young man with selective mutism, was referred to neuropsychotherapy to improve his independence at home and his ability to integrate into society. Matti still lived at his parents' home with his younger brother. Communication disorders had been obvious from early childhood, and school performance had always been weak. He retook 9th grade but failed to improve his grades. After elementary school, Matti participated in adult high schooling with tailored education for special groups for three years. He had, however, succeeded in passing only one computer course. Studying in a large group was not fruitful. He spent his days playing computer games, watching videos, and listening to music. He had no friends and talked mainly to his younger brother. The parents took care of all household work and supervised his self-care (e.g., washing, dressing, and eating). His parents bought him a dog to get him out of the house at least once a day. He was lonely and frustrated. His earlier therapy was art therapy in small group when he was 12 years old. After about one year, his parents decided to halt the therapy, because he was not motivated and his speech did not get better. The WAIS-III profile of neuropsychological evaluation can be seen in Table 9.1. The profile indicates average or even above-average intelligence in performance tasks that require minimal speech production. It was obvious that Matti was trying to do his best, but every time he became insecure, he interrupted his work and didn't go on.

Treatment

The first contract for neuropsychotherapy was a short-term period (five sessions at 90 minutes, once every two weeks). The reason for this was to find out if the therapy would be of any help. Matti came to first session with his father. He didn't speak a word, and there was no proper eye contact. The father answered every question, and

TABLE 9.1 WAIS-III profile for Matti.

WAIS-III Subtests	Similarities	Arithmetic	Information	Picture Completion	Digit Symbol	Block Design	Picture Arrangement
Raw Scores	16	8	13	23	59	41	15
Standard Scores	9	8	10	14	9	10	10

Matti only nodded if he agreed. He was very stressed. The parents' interview and questionnaires about Matti's earlier development revealed great difficulties with receptive and expressive language, including reading comprehension and writing since early childhood at home, and later, at school. Emotional problems, especially anxiety and depression, and behavioral problems, such as quarrels and aggressive tantrums, were also present since childhood. Relying mainly on the parent–therapist interactions, the therapeutic goals were to be focused on Matti's expressive communication, self-awareness, and self-esteem in learning situations, which had earlier caused him disappointments and prevented him from studying. Coping with emotional and behavioral problems were also central targets since the first sessions. In addition to therapy sessions, it was important to find meaningful activities for daytime. The long-term goals were to find suitable occupational studies and a more independent way of living. It remained unclear to what extent Matti agreed with these targets. Because Matti had very low self-esteem and very high motivation to succeed in cognitive tasks, it was decided to include suitable cognitive tasks in therapy sessions. A computer was highly motivating and engaging for Matti, so tasks were chosen to be computer-based attention, concentration, receptive and expressive language tasks, and memory tasks. Because Matti performed well on attention and concentration and visual tasks, these were included, mainly as a way to increase his awareness of his strengths. Any tasks that included language were difficult for him; they usually caused his anxiety level to increase very quickly, and the ability to perform became blocked. Usually, he gave up as soon as he was insecure about the right answer. In task situations, it became very clear that the reasons for his mutistic behavior were a combination of underlying learning difficulties (mainly language based) and high performance expectations. The difficulties were also strengthened by Matti's shyness and tendency to become stressed easily.

Progress

With computer-based tasks, Matti could finally approve that the best task-performance rate to learn new things was about 80% correct. He could first agree only near 100% performance without getting overly stressed. His motivation to this approach increased when he realized that he could really learn and that it was possible to gradually include more difficult language tasks. Negotiating the therapeutic alliance through cognitive rehabilitation was necessary to strengthen the bond needed for other therapeutic targets. In every session, the self-rating scales (for example, about his strengths and disabilities, personality traits, and feelings) were included and discussed. Language-based pencil and paper exercises were also included, but Matti's motivation for these rehearsals remained low. His task-performance motivation with computer-based tasks remained high, and he started to tolerate uncertainty. Face and gesture expression increased a bit, eye contact was reached once or twice in a session, and he reacted sometimes spontaneously with one or two words and, rarely, with short sentences. Answering questions remained very difficult. Despite his motivation in therapy, we didn't get any closer to finding meaningful daytime activities and integrating him into occupational and more independent social life. He didn't come to therapy sessions by himself, and his father didn't force him to do so, because he was afraid that the motivation for therapy would disappear. For real-life activity, his father proposed some kind of computer course at first, because computer work was very motivating. The suitable course was not found because a full-time course was not acceptable to the family, and studying in large groups had earlier proved to be disastrous. Applied daytime activities for young persons with mutism proved to be very difficult to find. The daytime rehabilitation programs with mental health patients were not the best or accepted choices for the family. The day center activities for young people with autistic spectrum disorders were chosen as the first choice, at first 1 day per week. After an interview, Matti was accepted into the day center and, after a few months, Matti started at the day center for one day per week as planned. His motivation has been high, and more days per week will be included in the future. Neuropscyhotherapy continues once every two weeks, with earlier goals in mind, in collaboration with the family, health care providers, and day center staff.

Conclusion

For successful working in neuropsychotherapy, it was necessary to have a detailed and appropriate description of the cluster of problems, as well as the strengths of the trainee. The goals of the therapeutic procedures must be explicit and clear. Collaboration and constructive interactions with the family and professionals involved in the process are the prerequisite for gainful work. In this case of the mutistic young man, Matti, the working alliance and the emotional bond was built stepwise with the integrating of cognitive remediation and understanding and appreciation of Matti's fragile self-respect. Matti's scope of everyday activities widened, and future prospects seem promising for improvement of the overall quality of his life.

Case Example Two: A 32-Year-Old Woman with Mild Intellectual and Developmental Disability

Background

Anna, a 32-year-old woman with mild IDD, was referred to neuropsychotherapy for one year (90 minutes per week) to improve her independence at home and her ability to sustain gainful employment. Anna still lived with her parents and spent a few hours during the day at a sheltered work program doing small tasks, such as washing dishes and ironing. She had no earlier therapy except rare visits to a community psychologist during the previous year. Neuropsychological evaluation (see Table 9.2 for WAIS-III profile) revealed receptive and expressive language disorders and severe visuospatial disorders. She succeeded at mechanical reading, but her understanding and remembering of the text was poor. Her writing was limited, and she had severe problems with mathematics. She also had executive disorders. Anna met the criteria for attention deficit disorder with hyperactivity (ADHD). She could not concentrate on the demanded activity for more than a few minutes. She was very distractible and impulsive. She also had several obsessive-compulsive (OCD) traits. She got easily stressed, and her anxiety level was high. Her self-esteem was low. Anna's parents reported that she needed constant supervision at home for self-care, could not find anything to do at home by herself, and usually wanted to go into her room, switch off the light, and repeat the same spoken words in the dark for hours. At night she would not sleep at times, and would repeatedly go to the washroom, disturbing her parents. Her social contacts with her few friends were rare, and she sometimes made short visits to her adult siblings' families. She had no hobbies except listening to music. At the sheltered work program, she needed constant supervision, which

TABLE 9.2 WAIS-III profile for Anna.

	Raw Scores	Standard Scores
WAIS-III		
Full Scale IQ	33	53
Verbal IQ	23	61
Performance IQ	10	49
Indices		
Verbal Comprehension	14	70
Perceptual Organization	4	48
Working Memory	9	58
Processing Speed	7	64
Subtests		
Vocabulary	9	1
Similarities	17	6
Arithmetic	2	3
Digit Span	8	4
Information	13	7
Comprehension	11	2
Letter Number Sequencing	4	2
Picture Completion	7	1
Digit Symbol	29	4
Block Design	12	2
Matrix Reasoning	5	1
Picture Arrangement	4	2
Symbol Search	16	3
Object Assembly	13	2

she often experienced as criticism, resulting in her becoming angry. Sometimes she lost her temper and hit a staff member. She constantly wanted to leave the sheltered work program and get a normal job, but she had no idea what she wanted to do.

Procedure and Progress

Anna was highly motivated in therapy. She learned the route to the office and was able to use the bus and train. Her own goal was to get out of the sheltered work program and find a real workplace. At therapy sessions, her agenda at first was to do cognitive rehearsals as much as possible, and she felt that conversation was a waste of time. In task situations, she was very impulsive, quickly trying to do as much as possible without any concern about the quality of her work, or mistakes. She talked all the time, didn't stop for an answer, and demanded constant attention. Gradually, she tolerated more conversation, told about problem situations at home (for example, her self-talk in the dark room) and at the sheltered work program (for example, impulsiveness), and we could negotiate the content of the sessions. After a few months of therapy, she could easily start the sessions by telling about problem situations from the previous week and reporting how she had managed to handle them and was able to stop to think what else she could have done, without obvious hurry to do cognitive rehearsals. Therapeutic focus was gradually shifted into self-awareness by the discussion of strengths and disabilities. This brought up more realistic self-esteem and acceptance of the disabilities. An inner locus of control appeared, and it manifested in the ability to take responsibility of Anna's own decisions, emotions, and behavior.

Notes of strategy Because of communication and abstract thinking problems, it was necessary to use plain language, picture aids, picture diaries, questionnaires (child versions with ready alternatives), and checklists to negotiate therapeutic alliance, including shared goals. Cognitive exercises were included as a part of therapy, but they were selected to serve her daily living needs (for example, mathematical tasks, included money handling, and visuospatial tasks, including time and route handling).

As Anna accepted some changes for her goal to get a real job, it was possible for the author to have shared goals for future activities. She agreed that the first goal would be to get her life more tolerable in the present situation. In collaboration with her, her parents, and the sheltered work program staff (through phone contact and regular meetings at least four times per year), the most important goals were worked toward during therapy sessions, as well as at home and at the sheltered work program. Anna's task was to keep a diary and list practiced tasks between sessions. She also kept a picture diary of therapy sessions, made together with the therapist, at the end of each session, to help her to understand and remember sessions. Because of her executive problems and the need for supervision, it was decided to apply a pictured plan of actions and instructions at home and at the sheltered work program to increase her independence in self-care and work tasks.

Outcome

Anna's parents and the sheltered work program staff reported positive changes, but relapses still occurred under stressful situations (e.g., during a parent's long journey, and after staff changes occurred). Positive changes at home included hobbies and independence (she could go for a walk or see a movie by herself). At the sheltered work program, she behaved more flexibly in changing situations and was able to concentrate on different tasks, such as baking and other kitchen tasks. She was also accepted to a practical training group. The therapy was recommended for a third year with the goal of integrating Anna into society with more independent living and working status. During the third therapy year, Anna has succeeded in obtaining part-time supervised work, which includes assisting an office secretary. She continues in the sheltered work program two days per week. Anna has decided to move out of her parents' home to her own apartment near her parents. During neuropsychotherapy, Anna's quality of life clearly improved, and she could live more independently.

Conclusions

Neuropsychotherapy is a treatment approach that allows us to understand and to treat the combination of developmental, neuropsychological, and neuropsychiatric symptoms, and reactive emotional and behavioral problems. Alliance and engagement are key components in the individual work. Besides professional skills, personal flexibility and coping with uncertainty are also important features in the therapist's metacognitive awareness.

Working with families and/or other caregivers, health care providers, and community services providers is essential to achieving and maintaining therapeutic targets during therapeutic processes, as well as after therapy. The experience of equality and the possibilities of developing personal skills in society despite the continuous need for support are the most effective ways to diminish reactive emotional and behavioral problems.

Neuropsychotherapy applications are effective when included in various combinations of treatments tailored for the particular individual in the specifics of his or her current environment.

References

American Psychiatric Association. (1994). *Diagnosis and statistical manual of mental disorders (DSM-IV)*. (4th ed.). Washington, DC: Author.

Anstendig, K. (1998). Selective mutism: A review of the treatment literature by modality from 1980–1996. *Psychotherapy: Theory/Research/Training, 35*, 381–391.

Bordin, E. S. (1979). The generalizability of the psychoanalytic concept of the working alliance. *Psychotherapy: Theory, Research and Practice, 16*, 252–260.

Brown, T. E. (2005). *Attention deficit disorder: The unfocused mind in children and adults*. New Haven, CT: Yale University Press.

Faulkner, M. S. (1999). Quality of life for persons with developmental disabilities. *Scholarly Inquiry for Nursing Practice: An International Journal, 13*, 239–252.

Fuster, J. M. (2003). *Cortex and mind: Unifying cognition*. Oxford: Oxford University Press.

Goodey, C. F. (2001). What is developmental disability? The origin and nature of our conceptual models. *Journal on Developmental Disabilities, 8*, 1–18.

Hadley, N. H. (1994). *Elective mutism: A handbook for educators, counsellors and health care professionals*. New York: Kluwer Academic Publishers.

Heilman, K. M., Blonder, L.X., Bowers, D. B., & Crucian, G. P. (2000). Neurological disorders and emotional dysfunction. In J. C. Borod (Ed.), *The neuropsychology of emotion* (pp. 367–412). Oxford: Oxford University Press.

Jakab, I. (1990). Neuropsychological evaluation and rehabilitation in mental retardation. *Neuropsychology Review, 1*, 137–164.

Jensen, P.S., & Abikoff, H. (2000). Tailoring treatments for individuals with attention-deficit/hyperactive disorder: Clinical and research perspectives. In T. E. Brown (Ed.), *Attention-deficit disorders and comorbidities in children, adolescents, and adults* (pp. 637–652). Washington, DC: American Psychiatric Press.

Johnson, M., & Wintgens, A. (2007). *The selective mutism: Resource manual*. Milton Keynes, UK: Speechmark Publishing Limited.

Judd, T. (1999). *Neuropsychotherapy and community integration: Brain illness, emotions and behavior*. New York: Kluwer Academic/Plenum Publishers.

Kumpulainen, K. (2002). Phenomenology and treatment of selective mutism. *CNS Drugs, 16*, 175–180.

Leahy, R. L. (2001). *Overcoming resistance in cognitive therapy*. New York: Guilford Press.

Misra, A. (1992). Generalization of social skills through self-monitoring by adults with mild mental retardation. *Exceptional Children, 58,* 495–507.
Paul, R., Cohen, D., Klin, A. & Volkmar, F. (1999). Multiplex developmental disorders: the role of communication in the construction of a self. *Child and Adolescent Psychiatric Clinics of North America, 8,* 189–202.
Romana, M. S. (2003). Cognitive-behavioral therapy: treating individuals with dual diagnoses. *Journal of Psychological Nursing, 41,* 30–35.
Safran, J. D., & Muran, J. C. (2000). *Negotiating the therapeutic alliance: A relational treatment guide.* New York: Guilford Press.
Sharp, W. G., Sherman, C., & Gross, A. M. (2007). Selective mutism and anxiety: A review of the current conceptualization of the disorder. *Journal of Anxiety Disorders, 21,* 568–579.
Sohlberg, M. M., & Mateer, C. A. (2001). *Cognitive rehabilitation: An integrative neuropsychological approach.* New York: Guilford Press.
Strauser, D. R., Lustig, D. C., & Donnell, C. (2004). The relationship between working alliance and therapeutic outcomes for individuals with mild mental retardation. *Rehabilitation Counseling Bulletin, 47,* 215–223.

10

Challenge to Change in the Family Narrative

Tarja Ketola, Liisa Paavola, and Nina Sajaniemi

Introduction

The concept of a "family" is broad. The traditional approach to the family consists of a heterosexual family with *a child*. However, there are couples that remain childless either by choice or due to infertility. An alternative to biological infertility is an adoptive parenthood. There are also single-parent families with biological or adopted children. Remarriage of divorced couples creates new challenges for adults and children in new family constellations. In addition to those situations already mentioned, multicultural families, as well as families with a fundamental religious background often with many kids, set demands to the description of a family concept. It should also be kept in mind that a growing number of children are raised in families with parents representing sexual minority groups. Despite the diversity of family constructions, all of them are somehow living in a shared narrative.

The shared narrative is a combination of each family member's autobiographical episodic memories, which are based on previous experiences of being with others. These memories channel and modify the development of shared narratives. When the relationship is in equilibrium and the family roles are clear, these autobiographical narratives merge together, and they form the new experience of togetherness. *In families suffering post-illness or injury, changes of the same basic conceptualizations can be seen, but the influences of shattered family roles and equilibrium must be worked through in a different way.*

The Essence of Being with Others

The core experiences of being related with others are the base of existence. They are constructed of memories from our primary families and further sculpt our ability to accept and give care and protection in all later relationships. The need for protection is built into our evolutionary nature and it is serves as life insurance. Under an experienced threat, security-seeking behaviour is activated, and an emotional balance has to be found. The balancing strategies, either empowering or devitalizing, depend on the expectations based on previous memories of terminated security-seeking behaviour. Expectations of being worthy of protection are the basis of core assumptions of the self. When these expectations are narrow minded, the balancing strategies are limited as well. Everyday environmental stressors challenge the abilities to adapt and to find a new balance. It can be assumed that the stiffer the emotional regulation system is, the more vulnerable the person is when being exposed to changes. The fragile system increases the risk for cumulating difficulties in adapting to everyday life challenges.

Meeting with Challenges

TBI or other severe neurological injury is always a challenge to both emotional bonding and the tune of the whole family regulation system because of the rapidity of the change. When an external insult disrupts the narrative of one family member's autobiographical narrative, the shared narrative is immediately changed.

The changes in behavioural and cognitive functioning, as well as emotional regulation, set a couple and the whole family in a new and unknown situation, where the old habits and ways to cope may be maladaptive. The former roles between the two adults may change in many ways. In terms of responsibility, caretaking, and communication, the roles that family members take in their shared narratives will be reformulated in more or less constructive ways. When the person who holds the responsibility in the family is injured, the responsibility is in a "free fall" until somebody else accepts it. The consequences may vary from a total disruption of the family to equally shared responsibility when the formerly nonresponsible spouse realizes *existing* hidden capabilities.

In the perspective of caring, the roles of giving and taking care are equally and fundamentally important. If the injured spouse has never learned to receive care, it may be impossible to accept the role of being dependent, even when the need for help is crucial. It may lead to extreme bitterness and anger towards the caregiver. The injury-based incapability of the previous family caregiver to hold the role may lead to a state of "caring vacuum." During this inevitable family turnover, other family members are forced or tuned to reconstruct and take the roles of caring.

The ability to communicate is essential in all relationships. Communication includes the recognition and expression of cognitive and emotional information. Family narratives are created from the shared meanings of these messages. According to structural approach (Minuchin, 1974; Sierla, 1999), the structure of the family is formed from communicative skills, as well as the different family situations in everyday life. The system tries to find the balance between different needs and demands of family members.

While communicating, the emotional tone of messages is interpreted first, and this overlaps cognitive information. In the case of discrepancy, it is extremely demanding to read messages without the bias related to the interpreter's own emotional state. The uncontrolled volume, nuance, or prosody of the expression can fade the true intention of the message. In addition, the lack of emotional variation in expression can jeopardize the communication. Misinterpretations are common in all mutual relationships in the case, everyday conflicts. However, the consequences of these misunderstandings and ruptures have exponentially cumulating effects in the cases of TBI or other severe neurological injuries. The unsolved ruptures and false interpretations in communication may be continuously present. Simultaneously, coping strategies can be poor or even lacking. The process may cause a vicious circle, ending in an emotional disaster. However, the changed situation may channel the family development towards more adaptive and balancing communication.

Reformulating the Past

The above-mentioned changes in shared narrative skills threaten the existence and continuity of family constancy. Thus, the need for a family intervention is evident. The therapist, with a neuropsychotherapeutic insight, sets a goal to combine both psychotherapeutic and neurocognitive knowledge related to brain and mind in the rehabilitation process.

The narrative approach in neuropsychotherapeutic setting means reformulating a new story, narrative, sight, and interpretation to changes, as well as finding new insight and alternatives for understanding mutual relationships. Within narrative perspective, the knowledge of what has happened is conceptualized as a story, and reality can be verbally constructed. The meanings that families give to their difficult experiences regulate their behaviour and interaction.

Total emotional emptiness is a straight consequence of the broken family narrative. The process remains open with a variety of alternatives, either good or bad. When trying to find the optimal, adaptive alternatives, both the therapist and the family need to know the common history of the family. Merging both the old and new narratives is the foundation of a reconstructed presence and a bridge to the future (White & Epston, 1989, 1990; Holma, 1992, 1999).

The need for a new narrative in a family that has met with the crisis of irreversible change is enormous. It is challenging to be sensitive to all the nuances, tones, and voices of the story; the therapist has to decide which stories are worth noticing and valuing. It may happen that both parts of the dyad can only hear and accept some views of the story, and the significant stories may differ greatly from each other. When a family is trying to find ways out of the acute crisis, some decisions have to be made. The common history of a couple gives some guidelines and support, but the heaviness of the present and the future can cause agony and raise difficult questions related to the commitment in the relationship.

When the whole family system is spinning around in a vicious circle, the needs and demands cannot be expressed equally. It is hard to consider the level of devotion to a spouse, who may have lost his or her memories, or parts of his or her identity, or changed into a totally different person. During the state of "narrative vacuum" (Hänninen, 1996), the noninjured spouse is at first hanging in the old shared family narrative. When the situation continues, the spouse eventually realizes that the "overarching theme" has fallen apart. The spouse is forced to rely on his or her past private autobiographical narrative. These narratives are always bridging the past, present, and future. Thus, the risk may be that the emphasis of the narrative script will tune to a dominant narrative path, where all the new experiences are linked with the traumatic consequences of the insult.

The ability to maintain the dialogue between two adults and to be able to express all sorts of feelings gives some tools to approach the changes that are related to getting injured. As far as the couple can see "the significant other" in each other and be able to respect, tolerate, and understand the changes of the spouse, the channels for wiring, tuning, and regulating the emotional interaction remain open. This emotional togetherness has an important meaning for a couple with a history together—no matter whether they will stay together or separate: It gives way to new narratives for both parts of the dyad.

In this article, two cases are presented. The approach in the first case is descriptive: The clue is to reveal the new, shared narrative after the insult. In the second case, the aim is to compare shared narratives before illness with the current narratives in the perspectives of responsibility, care, and communication.

Case 1: Mark & Lise

Nineteen years ago, Mark, a 38-year-old father of a 10-year-old girl and a 7-year-old boy, fell while renovating their home. He hit his head hard and was unconscious when taken to hospital. Tests revealed that Mark suffered from hemiparesis on the left, but the symptoms started to normalize. Mark also had one focal episode and undiagnosed TBI. Seven months after the accident, he returned to work, but in a short while, he had to accept part-time medical pension. This Master of Science in Technology had to start teaching as a regular substitute, as he could not manage his normal work. After 10 years, he had to take a whole medical pension. His wife worked at home, as an artisan.

In the beginning, Mark had a lack of initiative and ability to concentrate; depression; feelings of being worthless, helpless, and hopeless; he was nervous and had difficulties in learning, memory, reading, and understanding. Eight years after TBI, Mark and his wife, Lise, reported difficulties in family life. They had contacted their health care provider, but received no help. At this period of time, Mark started to drink more often and in larger doses, and he started to experience more and more frequent outbursts of rage. Five years after this, Mark abused his wife. This forced them to seek help. Violence was something that just could not happen inside their home. Abusing anyone, let alone his own wife, was unbelievably horrible to Mark. He was then ready to do anything to guarantee that this could never happen again. They first sought family counselling, where the problem was interpreted to be purely psychological. Mark took part in a therapy group for abusing husbands. He felt it was somewhat helpful, but all the time he felt different from the other group members. After this, they contacted a neurological policlinic and a neuropsychologist. In neuropsychological evaluation, TBI was seen as an obvious reason for the problems. Neuropsychological rehabilitation was recommended. At this time, Mark was diagnosed with cancer, and it took four more years before he could attend neuropsychological rehabilitation.

When attending neuropsychotherapy, Mark had no more contact with his daughter, a young adult in her twenties. His wife said: "*I did not even dare to breathe.*"

Lise and the children did not trust Mark. Both children had already left the home. Lise said that she could not leave Mark because it would have been abandonment of a helpless person, but there was nothing left of the marriage.

When neuropsychotherapy ended, Mark had real contact with both children, and the spouses communicated with each other. The method used was written narratives. They started to look into one another's eyes after one year of neuropsychotherapy. The following comments are from both Mark and Lise, given separately in writing between therapy sessions, and then discussed when both were ready to do so.

Marriage Before TBI

In an interview at the time neuropsychotherapy ended, both Mark and Lise said that their marriage had been very good before TBI.

> Mark: Every kind of feeling was allowed, and there was space for them.
>
> Lise: We used to discuss everything that had happened, that was on our minds, and what we wished or planned to do. Both good and bad things were communicated straight. We listened to one another, and we were heard.

Mark: The only difficulties were in the interpretation of nonverbal communication.

Both Mark and Lise: It was allowed to show every feeling there was the way I wanted or needed to.

Lise: We loved to do things together, we were home a lot, there was something going on all the time. I felt that my husband respected me.

Mark: Sometimes work took too much time.

Lise: We were both very spontaneous and creative. He probably even more than I was. Play was an essential part of our life.

Mark: We have always played a lot.

Lise: We had intimacy, tenderness, and sex a lot. Sometimes I would although have wanted even more.

Both Mark and Lise: We shared responsibilities as evenly as it is possible.

Situation After TBI, Before Neuropsychotherapy

Lise: The only feelings that were allowed to me were supporting and considering and taking care of him in the determined frames. I had to observe all the time his reactions, and my own feelings were suppressed. I had to look out for outbursts of rage, and I learned to avoid unnecessary risks.

Mark: I expressed mainly bad feelings.

Lise: We could not communicate. He took nearly everything I said as an insult. It is easier to communicate with the children in puberty than a man with TBI.

Mark: Then I did not understand even clear language. If one does not understand, it is impossible to believe anything the other one says. Because I did not understand myself, I had no chance to understand others.

Lise: Humour did not exist in our lives.

Both Mark and Lise: We both were fighting alone with our feelings.

Lise: Life was totally different than before. I had to use all my creativity to get some hold of the everyday life. I had to take all responsibility. I even shared responsibility rather with children than their father. Everything was done by me and the children while he was resting. Doing anything was always more fun when he was totally away.

Mark: I had all the time in the world, and I used it holding pipes in a bag for 15 years. I took responsibility of nothing; it was like I was a third child.

Lise: The only way to play was my work, my art.

Mark: I think playing would have been allowed, but I dared not; there was nothing we would share.

Lise: There was no intimacy, tenderness, or sex. I brought it up on several occasions, but it made the situation even worse.
Mark: There was nothing.

After two years of neuropsychotherapy, they described their situation as follows:

Lise: Even now I watch my husbands' moods, and expressing my own feelings is yet far from what it has initially been. I don't need to be afraid anymore, and there is space for some feelings. I do not expect so much anymore.
Mark: Now I think again and again how to express myself to avoid hurting my wife anymore. I have insulted and wounded her enough already. The threshold to confidence is rather high yet.
Lise: There are still problems in communicating. When it is so difficult, I tend to be silent a lot more than before. I communicate the necessary, and when I have energy then something "just for fun." It is not fun to speak alone while the other is in his own world.
Mark: It is good that we have agreed to tell everything as frankly as possible.
Both Mark and Lise: There is not much humour in our relationship, but some anyhow.
Lise: I can show my feelings, but they are partially faded and wasted away. I try now to be more sincere, to be myself, to show my feelings, though there is a well-developed and alert controlling unit in the back of my head.
Mark: My actions seem nowadays to speak for themselves and whatever they want to say.
Lise: Playing is far from this life. I even tried to forget my art for a while, but now it is slowly coming back.
Lise: There is hardly any intimacy, tenderness, or sex; some tenderness is anyhow on its way back to our lives.
Mark: Not nearly enough.
Lise: I am used to this situation, and I even have given some responsibility back to him. But at the end, I feel I have the responsibility of our family. I take no responsibility or credit of his personal affairs.
Mark: I still have the feeling that she has to take care of everything.

Remarks Related to Case 1

This marriage fulfilled both Mark's and Lise's emotional, cognitive, and social needs when the family narrative was unbroken. After

Mark's TBI, the narrative was totally broken. Responsibility was undivided; Lise had it all. She also had to give care to all who needed it, but was not able to get any care herself. Communication was minimal, and the emotional tone was mostly frightening. Lise missed her partner, whom she formally could have trusted in everything, and with whom it was fun to be. Mark was disappointed with himself all the time and could not understand his actions. The most frightening act was the incident of abuse, which was completely against everything Mark had always believed. The total difference of these two situations meant that these spouses had a long bridge to build from the first narrative to a new and possible present one. The deep trust that Mark and Lise had had, and the rewarding life they lived before TBI changed their relationship, was the basis from which they could find faith and strength to work towards a new narrative.

Mark and Lise could have avoided most troubles if they had received proper information and support early enough after Mark had got his TBI. They both could have avoided the despair they were experiencing when neuropsychotherapy started. Lise was able to choose to stay in the relationship, as she could see both the possibility of leaving and the possibility for change in their relationship. Most importantly, she become again a partner instead of the assistant and caretaker she had been for years. The most important moment in the course of the therapy was when Mark and Lise for the first time in many years looked each other in the eye. After that, they started communicating with each other, often, if not always, without a mediator. A lot of time and trouble would have been saved if Mark and Lise would have begun therapy with the knowledge of both the neuropsychological effects of TBI and the understanding of relationships and emotions within a year or two after Mark's TBI.

Case 2: Henry & Irene

Henry is a 51-year-old male. Eleven years ago, he had a sudden, major epileptic seizure at home. At the hospital, a massive AV malformation was found, and he immediately underwent surgery. The extremely demanding operations caused severe complications: the loss of vision in the right eye and narrowness of vision in the left eye. In addition, the epileptic seizures remained and turned out to be partly resistant to medication. Mild memory impairment and cognitive slowness were the only neuropsychological deficits that were recognized. One year after the insult, Henry returned to his demanding work as an organization welfare consultant.

Nine years after the first insult, he had a right hemispheric infarction in the areas of the brain operation. After the acute phase, Henry tried to continue his work. However, the cumulative neuropsychological deficits made it impossible.

The following narratives are from the interview with Henry and his wife. The thematic division is based on our ideas of the emotional regulation in the situation where the old narratives are not usable anymore.

Responsibility—sharing and taking:

Irene: It seems that our way to share everyday duties has changed enormously. I feel that the responsibilities related to money belong to me, even though I am not at all interested in economical issues. Before Henry's illness, money topics have been his territory, and he is still very keen in these issues.

Henry: Previously, I took more responsibility of family matters, but now my wife has been forced to take that role. It is a very difficult change for me, also in emotional level.

Within the changes of the equilibrium in the area of responsibilities, the interview revealed a new emotional tone of being related.

Irene: Togetherness feel much more serious and routine based. Part of my experiences might be related to our long history together, I am not sure.

Irene: Playfulness has always been allowed for both of us. The internal child has always been around in our everyday life, and it still is.

Caring—emotional bonding and expression:

Irene: The expression of feelings has certainly been allowed in our long marital relationship, both in the past as well as in the present. The other issue is whether they are shown in the same way or not. I may regulate the expressions of anger or irritation. In one way, this is an issue related to protection and care, but on the other hand, I am not happy with it. The negative feelings, they are the ones that I show less than before.

Henry: The feelings have been shown earlier, and also nowadays, when the time has moved on from the acute times of falling ill. I feel more safe, and also sense that I am accepted with my weaknesses and the diminished abilities.

When the expression of feelings has changed, it inevitably creates challenges in interpreting intimate information as well. Shaded body messages are difficult to code, and thus, the ability to accept physical contact might be compromised.

Irene: Physical closeness may not have narrowed, but the sexual intimacy has diminished indeed. I often wonder whether this is related to aging or what, both me and Henry being not so interested in sex.

Henry: Tenderness and closeness has increased. Considering sex, I feel myself unsecure, quite contrary than before.

Irene: We have always spent much time together, however, the ways of commonness have changed. Nowadays, we are forced to make more plans, and doing things together is much more time consuming than it used to be. Cooperation is often difficult, while I get easily irritated because of Henry's slowness. I react and adapt easily to new events, exactly as Henry did before.

Henry: Previously, I did not have enough time to focus on the wife and me. Now I am overwhelmed with time. On the contrary, my wife has a lack of time and, therefore, she is sensing the unnecessary feeling of guilt.

Communication—receiving and interpreting messages:

Irene: I think that communication between us has always been pretty good. On the other hand, we both tend to interpret nonverbal messages too sensitively. Our mutual language is not as well functioning as it used to be. I feel that my temper is very quick, and sometimes I have difficulties in waiting for a sign that my messages have been received, and answered as well.

Henry: We do communicate, but we cannot always get ourselves expressed as we wished. The nonverbal communication is not always heard as it was meant. The common language both exists and yet has no existence.

Irene: I feel that both of us are hiding negative feelings and irritation. That leads to emotional overload and exaggeration of angry expressions, or the need to cry weeks after the struggle. On the other hand, we are also able to talk very openly about all our feelings related to us.

Henry: I was able, and I still am, to be exactly who I am and how I feel.

While communicating, the shared sense of humour is of fundamental importance. During a long relationship, humourous nuances and tones of all expressions are merged to form a shared, mutual understanding for both hidden and unhidden contextual meanings.

Irene: The sense of shared humour has weakened; especially all comments related to personal space are experienced more or less as an insult instead of a joke. Joking about everyday matters is rare. Black humour has totally disappeared.

Henry: We have always been able to understand our mutual humour, and still are.

Concluding Remarks

From the clinical point of view, the neuropsychotherapeutic approach is a way to combine the past, present, and future in both psychotherapeutic and neurocognitive perspectives in challenging family narratives. If either approach is left out, the core of the human mind, with its connections to the brain, would be missed.

Neuropsychotherapeutic insight deepens the understanding that even the slightest change in the integrated areas of the neural network in the brain cause variable outbursts in the level of behaviour. Within these changes, the family system, as well as shared narratives, must be reconfigured. In addition, the neuropsychotherapeutic setting creates a safe and protective surrounding for bridging the old narratives and new experiences.

References

Hänninen, V. (1996). Tarinallisuus ja terveystutkimus. *Sosiaalilääketieteellinen aikakauslehti* 33/96, 109–118.

Holma, J. (1992). Modernista perheterapiasta kohti postmodernia? *Perheterapia, 4*, 4–11.

Holma, J. (1999). The search for a narrative—Investigating acute psychosis and the need-adapted treatment model from the narrative viewpoint. *Jyväskylä Studies in Education, Psychology and Social Research*, 150[1].

Minuchin, S. (1974). *Families and family therapy*. London: Tavistock.

Sierla, J. (1999). Salvador Minuchin ja strukturaalinen perheterapia. In J. Aaltonen and R. Rinne (Toim.), *Perhe terapiassa—vuoropuhelua vuosituhannen vaihtuessa* (pp. 246–256). Jyväskylä: Gummerus.

White, M., & Epston, D. (1989). *Literate means to therapeutic ends*. Adelaide, South Australia: Dulwich Centre Publications.

White, M., & Epston, D. (1990). *Narrative means to therapeutic ends*. New York: W. W. Norton & Co.

11

Neuropsychotherapeutic Elements as an Integrative Part of Holistic Rehabilitation Programs

Sanna Koskinen and Jaana Sarajuuri

Introduction

Traumatic brain injury (TBI) is a disorder of major public health concern because of its high incidence, prevalence, and economic consequences. Patients and their family members are faced with long-lasting changes and suffering while attempting to manage with the consequences of the injury. TBI affects people of all ages and is the leading cause of long-term disability in young adults (NIH Consensus Conference, 1999). TBI is more common than breast cancer, HIV/AIDS, spinal cord injuries, and multiple sclerosis combined (Brain Injury Association of America, 2004). Estimates of the prevalence of TBI are only frequently reported in the world's TBI literature, and the number of people living with TBI-related disability is not known. According to the available estimates, the prevalence of TBI is 7.8 million in Europe and 5.3 million in the United States (Langlois, Rutland-Brown, & Wald, 2006; Tagliaferri, Compagnone, Korsic, Servadei, & Kraus, 2006).

TBI is defined as an insult to the brain due to an external mechanical force. The main external causes are falls, traffic accidents, and violence (Langlois et al., 2006; Tagliaferri et al., 2006). TBI leads to physical problems (e.g., fatigue; problems with sleep and arousal; paresis; and impairments in balance, vision, smell, and taste; as well as headache and epilepsy), cognitive problems (e.g., impairments in executive functions, problem solving, speed of cognitive processing, memory, and attention), and emotional and behavioural changes (e.g., emotional lability, depression, anxiety, irritability, impulsiveness, decreased initiation, apathy, loss of emotional drive, and problems in communicative abilities). Moreover, TBI affects the person's image of self and coping strategies, and leads to restrictions in establishing interpersonal relationships and returning to productive life. The problem of unawareness is crucial. Unawareness related to TBI has implications for participation in rehabilitation, outcome, and the emotional, as well as psychosocial, well-being of patients (Fleming & Ownsworth, 1991, Prigatano & Schachter, 2005, Prigatano, 2006).

TBI is a heterogeneous disorder, and different forms of rehabilitation are needed for different subgroups of patients and at different phases over the course of recovery to optimize outcomes (Cope, 1995; Cicerone et al., 2005). According to the modern approaches, patients need to learn to become aware of their difficulties to learn to compensate for them when necessary and to make realistic commitments and healthy choices in their lives (Prigatano, 1999).

Psychotherapy is now an approach used within several models of neurorehabilitation (Coetzer, 2007). However, this therapeutic intervention has not always received universal support. From the historical perspective, psychotherapy for TBI patients has been neglected, due to problems of unawareness and other cognitive disorders (Ownsworth & Clare, 2006; Coetzer, 2007). Due to the significant and disabling emotional and behavioural changes after TBI, patients cannot be adequately treated with conventional psychotherapy. Therefore, a specific form of psychotherapy, neuropsychotherapy, is needed (Judd, 1999).

During the last decades, neurorehabilitation has developed tremendously, resulting in many different treatment programs. In general, these models encompass behavioural, cognitive, compensatory, and holistic approaches to rehabilitation. The need for emotional reintegration and adjustment are central to some models of neurorehabilitation, most notably the holistic model (Coetzer, 2007).

Holistic Rehabilitation Programs

According to the evidence-based studies (Cicerone et al., 2000), persons with TBI are best served by a holistic, multidisciplinary, and neuropsychologically oriented rehabilitation in which psychotherapy is the core element of the intervention. Addressing awareness is an integral element of holistic rehabilitation programs. According to Prigatano (1999), the main challenges in the rehabilitation of TBI patients are as follows: (a) understanding the nature of the neuropsychological disturbances, (b) remediating, compensating, or helping the patient to cope with those disturbances, (c) alleviating personal suffering, and (d) helping the patient to make choices that improve the quality of life.

Historical Perspective

Kurt Goldstein, an eminent pioneer in the development of holistic rehabilitation, stated that brain-injured patients need environments that help them to avoid catastrophic reactions. In this environment, the individual can engage optimally in various remedial activities, which will gradually culminate in the individual finding new meaning in life after rehabilitation (Goldstein, 1942, 1959). Yehuda Ben-Yishay incorporated many of Goldstein's ideas and developed a milieu, or holistic, rehabilitation program in 1978 in New York (Ben-Yishay et al., 1985; Ben-Yishay 1996; Ben-Yishay & Daniels-Zide, 2000). The emerging role of psychotherapy for patients and their family members was characteristic of the Neuropsychological Rehabilitation Program that George P. Prigatano established in 1980 in Oklahoma (Prigatano, Fordyce, Zeiner, Roueche, Pepping, & Wood, 1986; Prigatano, 1999). In Europe, Anne-Lise Christensen, who was influenced by the work of A. R. Luria, started a holistic program at Copenhagen University in 1985 (Christensen, 2000). Based on these pioneering programs, several programs were established in Europe. A Finnish program, INSURE, was established in 1993 in Helsinki

(Kaipio, Sarajuuri, & Koskinen 2000; Sarajuuri, Kaipio, Koskinen, Niemelä, Servo, & Vilkki, 2005; Sarajuuri & Koskinen, 2006).

Elements of Holistic Programs

The main elements of holistic programs include the promotion of a therapeutic milieu, psychotherapy and cognitive retraining carried out in individual and group settings, supported work trials, family education and guidance, and follow-up procedures. It has been pointed out that the conventional way of viewing outcomes of rehabilitation methods of brain-injured persons in terms of return to competitive work or to the ability of the patient to perform work-related tasks misses the bigger picture of rehabilitation (Ben-Yishay & Daniels-Zide, 2000). That is why we should begin to develop a quality of life (QoL) target in the field of neuropsychological rehabilitation, as well as valid tools capable of measuring progress towards those targets.

Neuropsychotherapy in Holistic Programs

During past decades, there have been considerable improvements in TBI rehabilitation services. Today, psychotherapy—or more specifically, neuropsychotherapy—is a vital component of any form of neuropsychologically oriented rehabilitation. According to Laaksonen (2007), neuropsychotherapy today can be viewed as an alliance between recent advances in the domains of neuroscience, neuropsychological rehabilitation, and psychotherapy. Psychological balance and well-being depend greatly on the availability of information and therapeutic support. Only if the patient is sufficiently knowledgeable about the injury, personal reactions, and prognostics, can he or she understand what is happening and distinguish between self-related, injury-related, and reactive phenomena. An ability to see oneself apart from the injury relieves uncertainty, confusion, shame, fear, and feelings of lack of control arising from altered and partly unpredictable functioning of the brain and mind (Kaipio et al., 2000).

Several authors state that most models of psychotherapy are effective not because of the differences between them but because of the common factors they share: therapeutic contract, operations, and bonds, as well as self-relatedness, in-session impacts, and the phases of treatment made up of sequential events (Coetzer, 2007). The process of psychotherapy begins by establishing a therapeutic alliance between the therapist and the patient. According to Prigatano et al. (1986), the main components of psychotherapy with brain-injured patients include the following: The therapist must start by providing an explanation, a model for understanding what has gone wrong that the brain-injured patient can handle; the patient must be taught new ways of behaving in order to maximize social competence (the insight component); the psychotherapist and the rehabilitation team must instill a sense of hope in both the patient and the family, while also striving to be realistic and face the truth. Besides individual format, psychotherapy can be carried out also in group settings. The aim of group psychotherapy is to help patients break down their sense of social isolation and to identify their present emotional and motivational difficulties. A group format also provides approval, support, and a sense of belonging.

The Finnish Application of the Holistic Approach: The INSURE Program

The Finnish application of the holistic program, the INSURE program (the Individualized Neuropsychological Subgroup Rehabilitation Program), is a postacute, interdisciplinary, six-week rehabilitation program for selected groups of TBI patients. The core of the program is neuropsychological rehabilitation and psychotherapy with vocational interventions, as well as follow-up support. The neuropsychotherapy group is the heart of the program. The INSURE program has been under development since 1991, and has been used in its present form since 1993. About 300 patients have been treated in this program during the last 15 years. The program has been described in detail elsewhere (Kaipio et al., 2000; Sarajuuri & Koskinen, 2006).

The INSURE program is recommended for TBI patients who have the potential to resume productive lives and to achieve stable psychological adjustment. Referrals for the program come from hospitals, insurance companies, the public health care system, and private clinics throughout Finland. For other TBI patients not selected for the INSURE program, various kinds of rehabilitation services are available, and patients receive information and recommendations regarding appropriate rehabilitation.

The INSURE program is a postacute treatment program, which means that, in general, patients start the rehabilitation program at least one year after their injury. However, patients with injuries from as far as 20–30 years have been treated successfully. Four separate INSURE subgroups are formed each year for the six-week rehabilitation program. The subgroups are small, normally consisting of five to six patients, which ensures intense working conditions. Special care is taken in the selection process of the patients to ensure that the groups are as homogenous as possible in terms of age, education, severity of the injury, and socioeconomic status. Homogeneity facilitates peer solidarity and support. Also emphasized in the selection of group members are social appropriateness and motivation to learn healthy ways of communal adaptation. The critical nature of personal commitment is emphasized during the recruitment interview, which is conducted by one or two senior neuropsychologists from the program. Patients are independent in their daily life activities, and their physical disabilities are only slightly incapacitating. Applicants average from 20 to 55 years of age. The time between the selection interview to starting the program ranges from a few months to 1 year, depending on the final formation of the homogenous subgroups. It is noteworthy that the very knowledge of being selected as a participant in the program has salutary effects on the behaviour and attitudes of candidates who are waiting to commence treatments. Members of the interdisciplinary rehabilitation team consist of two neuropsychologists, two neurologists, a rehabilitation nurse, two social workers, two speech and language pathologists, and a physical therapist. Consistency of treatments and uniformity of adherence to the realization of clinical objectives is ensured when the staff membership is comprised of professionals who realize the need for and are committed to the development of a common way of formulating, assessing, and implementing treatments. Medical consultations are arranged, usually with specialists in neuropsychiatry, neuroradiology, and psychiatry. The staff works closely together to foster consistency among the various rehabilitation activities. The importance of therapeutic alliance, which refers to the patient and therapist working together to achieve certain goals, is also emphasized. The program is directed by a clinical neuropsychologist. Each patient is assigned a primary therapist—a neuropsychologist—whose task is to coordinate and monitor the implementation of the treatment plan.

The program simulates the stress of working days and the challenges of social interaction required in everyday life. The days start at 8:30 am and end at 4:00 pm on weekdays. Patients are treated in group and individual rehabilitation formats. Many typical symptoms reveal themselves only in group settings, during interaction with others. Every morning begins with an Orientation group, led by a neuropsychologist, in which the members determine individual goals for the day, for the program, and for the future. It aims also to promote both psychological and physiological arousal, and to foster personal orientation.

The Neuropsychotherapy group is the heart of the program. It meets four days a week. The guided group sessions focus on such themes as understanding the nature of the typical TBI sequelae and their impact on the lives of the patients; understanding how and why these deficits affect their personal emotions and social lives; and learning to cope with these deficits and stress. The participants also have individual neuropsychotherapy sessions three or four times per week. The patients are taught to assess their goals for work and education realistically, bearing in mind the postinjury changes in their resources.

The Cognitive group-remedial sessions are held twice a week. The aim is to help the patients to: (a) understand the rationale for cognitive remedial training procedures that are capable of ameliorating the interferences of attentional disorders, poor information processing abilities, and memory problems with higher-level reasoning functions; (b) practise compensatory skills capable of enhancing cognitive skills; and (c) transfer lessons learned from the rehabilitation setting to real life.

Group activities of various kinds are used to reinforce and enrich the program. Enjoyment of life, motivation, and the pleasures of friendship and society are emphasized in planning activities and in forming relationships. In the Pragmatic group-communication sessions, patients are guided by speech and language pathologists to communicate their thoughts more effectively. The "Pictures-of-Self" workshop enables patients to express their emotions and feelings about the changes in their lives that were caused by the brain injury. These sessions aim to help them in the process of self-examination by means of collages made up of different materials, such as photos, fabrics, and mosaics. The patients are able to focus on meaningful childhood memories, express feelings about their families, point to personally meaningful achievements, and examine their progress in their rehabilitation. As they review their presentations to each other, they may gain better insights into and control over their lives, which may in turn help them to further diminish their confusion and the psychological stress related to the injury and its consequences. The Quality-of-Life group sessions deal with practical issues concerning everyday life and well-being. The Sport, Relaxation, and Jogging groups aim to encourage the members to start or restart sport activities. Particular attention is also paid to possible TBI-associated injuries or symptoms, such as cervical injuries, pain, sleep disturbances, and posttraumatic stress disorders.

Participation of the significant others is a crucial part of the program. A two-day INSURE seminar is held during the latter part of the program. Patients, their significant others and employers, as well as professionals from the public health care system, are called together to share information and to learn about experiences following TBI. During the seminar, plans for the next step in the rehabilitation process are reviewed and operationalized. It is also during these seminars that former participants in the INSURE program are invited to present their experiences postdischarge. Such presentations offer the current participants concrete examples of adjustment after rehabilitation. The most successful previous patients are viewed by the other participants as positive role models.

Supported and individually tailored vocational interventions are also essential elements in the INSURE program. They help the patients to find productive activities that fit their interests and abilities. When it is considered to be an adapted and practical goal, patients are encouraged to have supported work trials in the general market, where they could possibly continue after the program. These interventions are coordinated with the local social and health care units and the system liable for the care in each case. Once a suitable work trial placement is found, the patient receives tailor-made neuropsychological support to ensure his or her success and stable emotional adjustment. The follow-up support is arranged through the public or private health care services. Most patients continue with individual outpatient neuropsychological rehabilitation for different periods of time following completion of the program. On completion of an INSURE program, patients should have substantial knowledge about TBI, a sound basis for understanding and coping with TBI-related changes and for participating in productive living according to their own best self interests. On the whole, the INSURE program is designed to be reasonable in cost and length to make it appealing and possible to patients with different sources of reimbursement.

The effectiveness of the INSURE program has been evaluated by a two-year outcome study with a matched group of control patients who received conventional clinical care and rehabilitation (Sarajuuri et al., 2005). The results showed that the productivity of the treatment group was significantly better than that of the control group. These results are consistent with those reported in previous studies on the efficacy of holistic rehabilitation programs.

Case Study

A case study will be presented to illustrate how neuropsychotherapy in a holistic setting may potentiate the rehabilitation process.

Background

Twenty years ago, at the age of 19, MM was attending his military service, when, during a weekend leave, he and his girlfriend got into a car accident. His consciousness was altered for two weeks and the post-traumatic amnesia (PTA) lasted for over one month, both indicating a very severe TBI. In computerized tomography (CT) scans, injuries were found in the left temporal horn, left lateral ventricle, and in the white matter. At that stage, left hemiparesis, double vision, and a broken leg were diagnosed. After hospitalization for two months, his father took a photo of him standing in front of the hospital. He wrote at the back of the photo, "A new beginning." He thought that his life had returned to its previous state. This thought was to be in his mind for the next 15 years.

In the two neuropsychological assessments two and four months after the injury, deficits were found in his cognitive processing and memory, as well as in his emotional control. Nine months after the injury, the neuropsychological assessment did not show any more problems in his cognitive functioning at the operational level. However, the young man himself reported changes in his behaviour and emotional reactions. He received no therapy except physiotherapy for the leg. The reasons that this young man did not get any neuropsychological intervention at the acute stage could be that the neurological deficits recovered soon, and because of his good intellectual capacity. The findings of the three neuropsychological assessments during the first year did not seem to predict future problems.

Life-Course with the Supportive Elements of the Environment

The cognitive capacity of the young man had been very high before the injury; he had a stable social background and close social contacts with his family, relatives, and friends. In his attitudes he was very demanding and cultivated the idea that, "As a son of two teachers, he had to get along in life." Ten months after the injury, he started his studies at the university, as had been his plan before attending his military service and before his injury.

Throughout his studies, he had problems with fatigue, memory, and learning. He managed by taking obsessively excessive amounts of notes and studying them instead of his books, and with the help of the other students. He completed his educational practices in a foreign country, made mistakes, but managed because his employer was very supportive and a great fan of his home country. He got tired easily and had to take long naps during the afternoons. During his vacations from the university, he worked in a bank. He made continuous mistakes and was criticized by his supervisor. He felt humiliated and cried repeatedly. He had problems in controlling his behaviour and emotional reactions. There were also problems in his social contacts with the other students, for which he tried to compensate with alcohol abuse. Later, when looking back on his studies, he recalled that the other students had given him a nickname, "Dummy," and questioned whether he was "a bird or a fish." However, at that time, he did not realize the degree of the difficulties he encountered and went on without hesitation.

In spite of the problems in his studies, he graduated within normal time limits. He did not get a permanent job but managed to get periodic employments, one after the other. He did not wonder about the reason for not getting a permanent job and did not realize how much supervision, support, and help he needed from his employer. He got married and had three children. His wife took care of all the responsibilities of the household and the children. He started to build a house by himself and ran his first marathon. Shortly after the house was ready, his wife went back to work after staying at home for five years. At the same time, his employer changed, and two big plumbing accidents occurred in their new house. The new boss was not as supportive as the previous one and questioned his working ability. He got depressed and, for the first time, looked for help, first from mental health services, and then from his employee's health care. Finally he was referred to neurological consultations and was further referred to the INSURE program 20 years after his TBI.

The Treatment Procedure in the INSURE Program

The neuropsychological assessment in the beginning of the INSURE program revealed problems in vigilance and sleep, executive functions, emotional functions, behaviour regulation, as well as problems with interpersonal interaction and communication. Problems were evident also in his memory, attention, speed of cognitive processing, and psychomotor functions. He got easily irritated; his behaviour was impulsive; he was overly talkative and depressive. His awareness of the injury-related problems was poor, but he understood the need for professional help.

He was very motivated for the therapy, and the therapeutic alliance between him and his neuropsychologist was good. The main goals for the therapy, made in agreement between the therapist and MM, were increasing awareness of the injury of both the patient and the family; increasing the patient's self-esteem; treating the emotional and behavioural changes; increasing the control over the whole life-situation; assessing the ability to work; creating alternative possibilities to support the working ability; ensuring the economical situation in the future; and arranging for future therapy near his home.

The neuropsychotherapy in the INSURE program was carried out in the individual and group formats as described above. In MM's own words, one of the main targets of the neuropsychoterapy was dealing with "the theme of secret" (i.e., telling the significant persons in his life about the TBI). One important task was "walking within memories" (wandering around in the same environment where MM had been studying and meeting his future wife 1 year after his injury). Psychoeducation and peer group support were the starting points for the treatment. Different creative techniques (music, pictures, writing), and using metaphors and analogies were the central elements. The discussions between the therapist and MM's wife, and between the therapist and MM's employer, were the starting points in making realistic plans and choices for the future. After the 6-week intervention, a supported work trial in cooperation with his supervisor was arranged in the patient's previous working place.

Figure 11.1 Pictures-of-self group: 2.5 weeks after starting the INSURE program

At the end of his time in the INSURE program, MM wrote: "… It's much easier to live now, when I know what this is all about, and how to prevent the problems. I don't have to perform all the time and to prove myself and to my loved ones that I am a good person."

MM's verbal expression of a picture at the end of the rehabilitation program (see Figure 11.1):

> This blue one is a ship's bridge for navigating. You can see three routes of where to go (brown, green, and dark blue lines). The colors are neutral. After the INSURE program, I'll have many routes. The grey color indicates fog. It's difficult to see what is ahead. The yellow color on the top indicates light. There is radar on the roof of the bridge, which helps in choosing the right route and keeping on it. Through the radio antennas, it's possible to get external messages about where to go. On the sides of the bridge there are rear-view mirrors—although I don't know whether they exist on ships. A golden border can be seen on them, just like on the dark clouds, as well. Also a very black, sad, color can be seen. However, out of the yellow line I can see that the future is bright and sunny.

MM's verbal expression of another picture at the end of the rehabilitation program (see Figure 11.2):

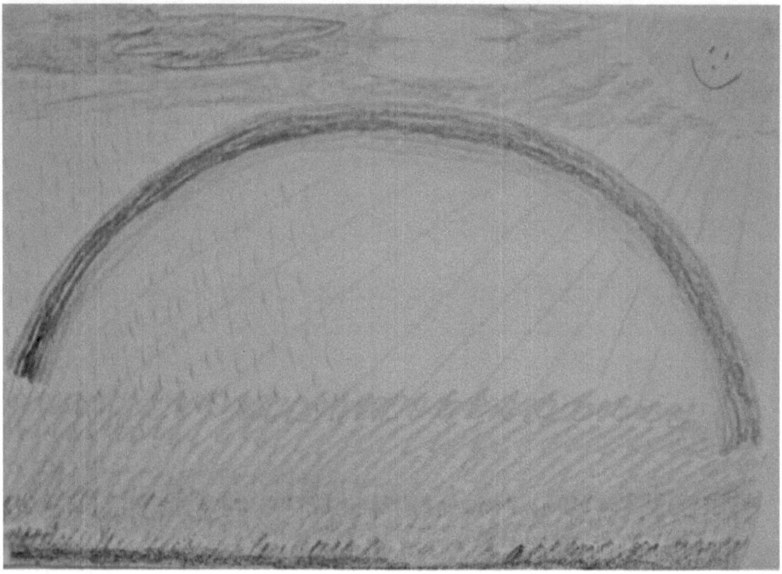

Figure 11.2 Pictures-of-self group: 3.5 weeks after starting the INSURE program

> The sun is found also in this picture. I first started to draw this rainbow. Without the sun it is not possible to see the rainbow, but it also rains then. After the rain, it will always be fair weather. My previous life is presented on the left side. There are black clouds. The clouds become paler, and then follows a light summer cloud, and finally the sun. The sun is always shining, as we who have flown in a plane know. There also must be rain falling. The water, warmth, and light maintain the life on the grassroots level. The green color represents the new growth. The brown ground is the fertile layer. The black layer is the basement on which everything is built. There is a treasure at the end of the rainbow. I didn't think of the treasure when I made the picture. One can never catch up to the treasure, because the end of the rainbow does not really exist. It's a continuous search.

After the INSURE program, outpatient neuropsychotherapy started once a week and is still going on two years later. The work trial started at his previous working place, although his employer had earlier refused to renew his temporary employment contract. After a while, he moved over to another place for work trial. This new place had been a dream of his previously, and new administrative arrangements made it possible for him to get a part-time work trial. In the follow-up, the most important point has been, that he now realises his restrictions and strengths. He has returned to his previous activities, such as running, but his goals are now less demanding. He even has restarted his voluntary work in a volunteer fire brigade. He still makes notes and writes down important things to remember, but not in a compulsive way. He is finally finding his own form of life in his present life-situation.

Concluding Remarks of the Case

The neuropsychotherapeutic interventions in the frame of reference of holistic neurorehabilitation showed a significant effect on the well-being of the patient, even though it started 20 years after the injury. Both the patient and his family found the information and psycho-education important in increasing the awareness of both the patient and the family members. The patient's self-esteem increased as he got names for the problems he had faced throughout his adulthood. The therapeutic alliance between MM and his therapist was vital in the efforts to overcome the problems. The interpersonal bond between the therapist and MM was sound, although from time to time it had to be negotiated from the point of view of too much dependency. Creating the tasks and goals for a period of 6 weeks was challenging and had to be reflected both to the history of 20 years with the disability, and to the future plans for the individual therapy after the INSURE program. The clear structure and the therapeutic milieu of the INSURE program helped to set certain goals and tasks, which were common to all the participants in this intervention.

References

Ben-Yishay, Y. (1996). Reflections on the evolution of the therapeutic milieu concept. *Neuropsychological Rehabilitation, 6*, 327–343.

Ben-Yishay, Y., & Daniels-Zide, E. (2000). Examined lives: Outcomes after holistic rehabilitation. *Rehabilitation Psychology, 45*, 112–129.

Ben-Yishay, Y., Rattok, J., Lakin, P., Piasetsky, E.B., Ross, B., Silver, S., Zide, E., & Ezrachi, O. (1985). Neuropsychologic rehabilitation: Quest for a holistic approach. *Seminars in Neurology, 5*, 252–259.

Brain Injury Association of America. (2004). Retrieved January 15, 2009 from http://www.biausa.org/ellements/aboutbi/factsheets/TBIincidence.pdf

Christensen, A-L. (2000). Neuropsychological postacute rehabilitation. In A-L. Christensen and B. Uzzell (Eds.), *International handbook of neuropsychological rehabilitation* (pp. 151–163). New York: Kluwer Academic/Plenum.

Cicerone, K.D., Dahlberg, C., Kalmar, K., Langenbahn, D.M., Malec, J.F., Bergquist, T.F., Felicetti, T., … Morse, P.A. (2000). Evidence-based cognitive rehabilitation: Recommendations for clinical practice. *Archives of Physical Medicine and Rehabilitation, 81*, 1596–1615.

Cicerone, K.D., Dahlberg, C., Malec, J.F., Langenbahn, D.M., Felicetti, T., Kneipp, S., Ellmo, W., … Catanese, J. (2005). Evidence-based cognitive rehabilitation: Updated review of the literature from 1998 through 2002. *Archives of Physical Medicine and Rehabilitation, 86*, 1681–1692.

Coetzer, R. (2007). Psychotherapy following traumatic brain injury: Integrating theory and practice. *Journal of Head Trauma Rehabilitation, 22*, 39–47.

Cope, D.N. (1995). The effectiveness of traumatic brain injury rehabilitation: A review. *Brain Injury, 9*, 649–670.

Fleming, J.M., & Ownsworth, T. (2006). A review of awareness interventions in brain injury rehabilitation. *Neuropsychological Rehabilitation, 16*, 474–500.

Goldstein, K. (1942). *After-effects of brain injuries in war: Their evaluation and treatment.* New York: Grune & Stratton.

Goldstein, K. (1959). Notes on the development of my concepts. *Journal of Individual Psychology, 15*, 5–14.

Judd, T. (1999). *Neuropsychotherapy and community integration. Brain illness, emotions, and behavior.* New York: Kluwer Academic/Plenum publishers.

Kaipio, M-L., Sarajuuri, J., & Koskinen, S. (2000). INSURE program and modifications in Finland. In A-L. Christensen & B. Uzzell (Eds.), *International handbook of neuropsychological rehabilitation* (pp. 247–258). New York: Kluwer Academic/Plenum.

Laaksonen, R. (2007). Introduction to neuropsychotherapy. *Svensk Neuropsykologi 1*(7), 4–6.

Langlois, J.A., Rutland-Brown, W., & Wald, M.M. (2006). The epidemiology and impact of traumatic brain injury. *Journal of Head Trauma Rehabilitation, 21*, 375–378.

NIH Consensus Conference. (1999). Rehabilitation of persons with traumatic brain injury. NIH Consensus Development Panel on Rehabilitation of Persons with Traumatic Brain Injury. *Journal of American Medical Association, 282*, 974–983.

Ownsworth, T., & Clare, L. (2006). The association between awareness deficits and rehabilitation outcome following acquired brain injury. *Clinical Psychology Review, 26*, 783–795.

Prigatano, G.P. (1999). *Principles of neuropsychological rehabilitation.* New York: Oxford University Press.

Prigatano, G.P. (2005). Disturbances of self-awareness and rehabilitation of patients with traumatic brain injury. A 20-year perspective. *Journal of Head Trauma Rehabilitation, 20*, 19–29.

Prigatano, G.P., Fordyce, D.J., Zeiner, H.K., Roueche, J.R., Pepping, M., & Wood, B.C. (1986). *Neuropsychological rehabilitation after brain injury.* Baltimore: The Johns Hopkins University Press.

Prigatano, G.P., & Schacter, D.L. (1991). *Awareness of deficit after brain injury. Clinical and theoretical issues.* New York: Oxford University Press.

Sarajuuri, J.M., Kaipio, M-L., Koskinen, S.K., Niemelä, M.R., Servo, A.R., & Vilkki, J.S. (2005). Outcome of a comprehensive neurorehabilitation program for patients with traumatic brain injury. *Archives of Physical Medicine and Rehabilitation, 86,* 2296–2302.

Sarajuuri, J.M., & Koskinen, S.K. (2006). Holistic neuropsychological rehabilitation in Finland: The INSURE program—A transcultural outgrowth of perspectives from Israel to Europe via the USA. *International Journal of Psychology, 41,* 362–370.

Tagliaferri, F., Compagnone, C., Korsic, M., Servadei, F., & Kraus, J. (2006). A systematic review of brain injury epidemiology in Europe. *Acta Neurochirurgica, 148,* 255–268.

12

Summary of Applications of Psychotherapeutic Methods in Neuropsychotherapy

Ritva Laaksonen and Mervi Ranta

Introduction

The aim of this chapter is to give an overview and summary of the psychotherapeutic approach and methods usable in neuropsychotherapy (i.e., treatment of neurological and neuropsychiatric patients, or clients in clinical practice). Our aim is also to give an idea as to how this can be possible by combining neuropsychological and psychotherapeutic knowledge with additional psychotherapeutic training for neuropsychologists. The first part of this chapter is concerned with aspects and elements of the interpersonal process and proceeding in the intervention. Working methods will also be summarised, and, finally, case illustrations will be presented to give life to pragmatic conceptions of what can be done in real life interventions.

A psychotherapeutic approach is required in all applications of neuropsychological rehabilitation, but there are also special demands for certain types of problematic behaviours, due to emotional disorders, changes in self-awareness, poor collaboration in the intervention process, or recognised psychiatric disorders needing treatment.

In most of the chapters of this book, the authors have demonstrated what can be done even in cases of very severe problems after TBI, ABI, and neuropsychiatric syndromes due to other causes. Here we summarize further the psychotherapeutic methods for the interventions in neuropsychotherapy.

Planning of Treatment: "What Works for Whom"

The initial phase is that of studying and assessing the patient's background carefully and the planning of intervention procedures. For case conceptualization, information is needed from several domains of knowledge. It is important to understand the possible complicating factors, as well as the strengths of the sufferer of brain dysfunction. The initial evaluation should reveal facts about:

- Etiology and lesion data (type of injury, time of onset, localization, extent of damage, and the neuropsychological sequelae)
- Premorbid status: personal and social
- Complicating factors: PTSD, phases of crises, emotional and behavioural problems
- Strengths to facilitate recovery
- Immediate family and other social connections, or networks
- Economic support (insurance; county, state, or private funding)
- Time allowed for treatment, as well as available professional services

Jenny Ponsford and collaborators (Ponsford, Sloan, & Snow, 1999) have described working with adjustment, as well as PTSD problems, after TBI. The writings introduce pragmatic guidelines for implementing treatment plans, goals, and procedures after head trauma.

Special demands and strategies for children and adolescents after TBI have been described by Margaret Semrud-Clikeman (2001). Her suggestions cover a vast amount of domains to be supported and dealt with in addition to the cognitive dysfunction. Emotional and behavioural problems may be difficult to deal with, and the adjustment process and reentry to school is dependent on a holistic approach by parents, teachers, and peer groups, as well as the individualized therapy illustrated with cases in the earlier chapters of this book.

After it has been possible to make the treatment plans, as well as timing, for the procedure, the targets for intervention can be set. If it is a ten-session postacute plan, it has to be very well focused. If the time is not restricted, plans can be made for more intensive and process-oriented type of intervention, rather than simply first aid. However, in all cases, negotiating a good working alliance is important.

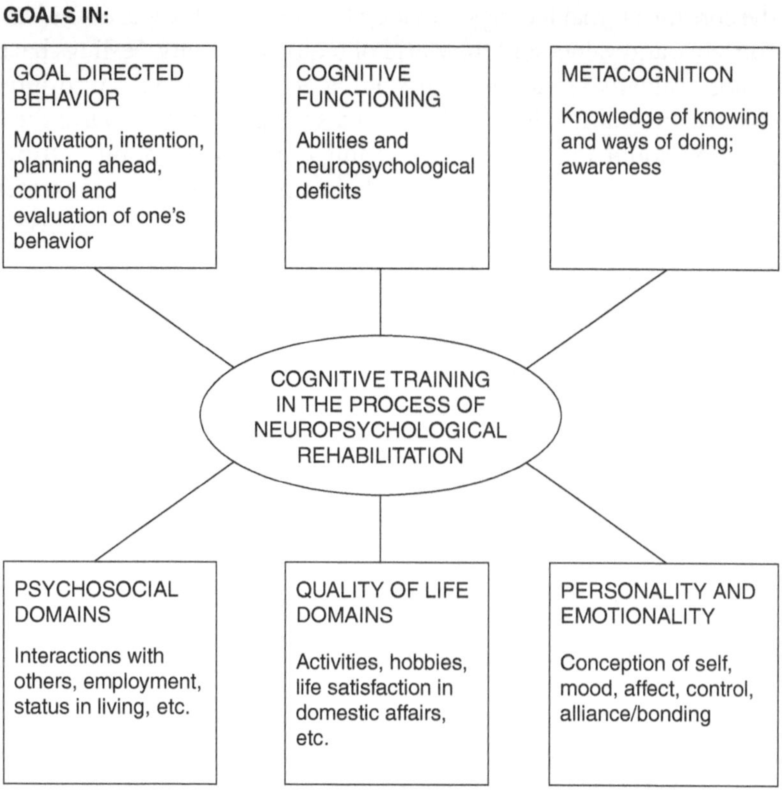

Figure 12.1 The target domains for a holistic neuropsychotherapeutic approach

The target domains for a holistic neuropsychotherapeutic approach are featured in Figure 12.1.

Interpersonal Prerequisites for Efficient Collaboration and Working Alliance

The goals of neuropsychological rehabilitation vary according to the patient's needs. Compensatory strategies have been emphasized, as well as adjustment and emotional reintegration. However, whatever the goal may be, the interpersonal collaboration and therapeutic working relationship should be an explicit element in the treatment process.

Today, we can find contextual guidelines from various sources and psychotherapeutic approaches. In the cognitive constructive model, the core idea is that feelings provide a link between the world of ideas, concepts, and values and the world of biological reality. Feelings have major evaluative functions (Greenberg & Safran, 1987). According to Greenberg and Paivio (1997), feelings tell people how to live their lives. We could add to this the meaning of emotional bond in treatment collaboration, which can tell therapists how they construct the working alliance and manage their treatment—their practice—toward the most optimal result.

The elements of a good working alliance are *tasks*, *goals*, and *bonding* in dynamic interaction (Safran & Muran, 2000).

The quality and adequacy of the alliance can be measured by a working alliance inventory (WAI), a term coined by Hovarth & Greenberg (1989). When constructing a good working relationship, certain interactional and reciprocal elements are recommended in the role of the therapist as organizing principles:

- Warmth, appreciation, and trust
- The same wavelength, communication symmetry, reciprocal feedback, and validation of expression
- Empathy as a process (identification, incorporation, reverberation, and detachment)
- Sensitivity and flexibility
- Support of self-worth in the context of new insight
- Identification of ruptures and resistance
- Professional attitude and genuine and humane behaviour

Empathy as process has been described by Sundeen, Stuart, Rankin, & Cohen, (1998). All the process elements, from identification with the sufferer's problems and state of mind to detachment from the situation, are important for understanding and also for freeing oneself of too much worry and loss of objectivity. The creation of ruptures can enhance the process, or break the bond. Resistance has been described earlier in this book in Chapter 6. Robert Leahy (2001) has differentiated between different sources creating resistance, either interpersonal or intrapersonal. Creation of ruptures cited in the following list have been well presented by Safran & Muran (2000).

Typical Elements in Collaboration Leading to Creation of Ruptures Can Be:

- Different goals
- Misunderstanding the meaning of tasks

- Resistance
- Moral attitude
- Misunderstanding hope and hopelessness
- Provoked effects
- Transference
- Dependence—attachment distortions
- Overcontrol
- Guilt feelings
- Experiences of invalidation
- Contradicting hopes and responsibilities
- Overcompliance

In negotiating the working alliance, ruptures need to be corrected. Safran & Muran (2000) suggest the following contextual strategies:

Correcting Ruptures in the Interpersonal Process:

- Correcting misunderstandings
- Collaborative examination of core themes
- Understanding resistance
- Validating constructively the ongoing experience
- Creating new experiences in the working relationship

Validating the other person's feelings, wants, difficulties, and opinions in a nonjudgemental way is one of the key aspects of therapeutic communication, even when confrontation will also have to be used particularly in syndromes of unawareness, neglect, or denial.

Bonding in Negotiating the Working Alliance

Negotiating the alliance can proceed in the following stages, according to Greenberg & Paivio (1997).

Phase I: Bonding

1. Attend to, empathize, and validate feelings. Convey understanding of the client's bad feelings or painful experiences and validate how painful and difficult the struggle is.
2. Establish and develop a collaborative focus. Identify the underlying cognitive–affective process or generating conditions. Identify as foci

of therapeutic work such generating conditions as self-criticism or dependence an interpersonal loss.

Phase II: Bonding—Evoking and Exploring

3. Evoke and arouse. The bad feeling or painful experience is brought alive in the session or regulated.
4. Explore/unpack cognitive–affective sequences in the painful experience, or that generate the bad feelings.

Phase III: Bonding—Emotion Restructuring

5. Access the core maladaptive emotion scheme and/or primary emotional experience.
6. Restructure. Facilitate restructuring of core schemes by challenging maladaptive beliefs with newly accessed primary adaptive needs/goals and resources.
7. Support and validate emergence of more self-affirming stance. Support mobilization of resources, self-soothing capacities, improved affect regulation, and self-empathy.
8. Create new meaning. Promote reflection. Construct a new narrative and new metaphors to capture new meanings (Greenberg & Paivio, 1997). (Note: In the constructivistic therapy approach, the term *scheme* is used instead of *schema*.)

Bonding in these various phases is interwoven into the interpersonal relationship in a certain order that can build up a secure base for the process-oriented intervention.

Complicating Factors in Negotiating a Good Working Alliance

There are several factors that can complicate the construction of alliance. Neuropsychological dysfunctions may create impasses for working procedures. Poor self-awareness due to frontal, subcortical, or right hemisphere lesions will have to be worked with as the first goal when resistance in the recovery process occurs. Fleming, Strong, and Ashton (1996) have described this type of obstacle after TBI, and they also introduced a questionnaire for measuring awareness. Onsworth and collaborators (Onsworth, Turpin, Brook, &

Fleming, 2008) describe an ABI case, CP, with poor self-awareness after thalamic stroke. They present a qualitative analysis of CP's rehabilitation designed to tackle metacognitive skills in a structured manner. The authors conclude that construction of self-knowledge may occur in rehabilitation through a bidirectional feedback process between the client and the therapist, rather than one-way feedback to the client about the deficits from the clinician.

This emphasis of a collaborative approach includes a specific focus on identity by linking meaning, goals, and tasks. Premorbid personality traits, core beliefs, and schemas, as well as basic assumptions about life, can also cause impasses, if not recognized. Interindividual differences form a challenge to individually tailored programs, as well as group interventions. Some of the traits in emotional and behavioural reactions that may cause process problems can be seen in the following conceptual domains:

- Conceptions about self and others: imbalance with shame; self-evaluation with guilt, fear, etc.;
- Behaviour toward self and others (rudeness instead of empathy, mistrust instead of trust, assertion problems or overcompliance);
- Attitudes (good–bad, right–wrong dichotomy);
- Values (achievement, perfection, effort, or indifference);
- Poor metacognition.

These traits may be of premorbid origin or acquired after brain damage.

Metacognition—A Link to Awareness

How to create awareness after brain injury is not an easy task, even though necessary for treatment efficacy. Metacognition can serve as a metatheoretical guideline to work with unawareness.

Components of metacognitive reflection have been described and defined by Cornoldi (1998). The different components include:

1. Metacognitive reflection (people's beliefs and interpretation of cognitive activity);
2. Metacognitive knowledge (people's beliefs concerning all possible aspects of cognitive activity);

3. Metacognitive conceptualization of a task (metacognitive reflection present at the moment of starting a task and during execution);
4. Metacognitive attitude (overall metacognitive knowledge, with cognitive, emotional–motivational, and behavioural implications);
5. Specific metacognitive knowledge (knowledge concerning specific aspects or cognitive functioning).

When understood this way, metacognitive processing can be a link to awareness. It may be partly conscious with good initial metaknowledge. It may be also tacit and covert, when the patient is periodically unaware of the changes due to injury. However, it can be worked with in the intervention procedure using a strategic method. Structured but relaxed discussions of the nature of cognitive functions, disturbances, and the meaning of intentional collaboration, as well as therapeutic exercises for recovery, can create new insights and motivation.

The psychotherapeutic approach and methods are dependent on the theoretical framework of the therapist and the methods he or she is able to master. They are explicit systematic tools for reaching mutual goals with the patients.

Most of the psychotherapy techniques introduced in this chapter have been adopted from cognitive psychotherapies. However, the creative and experimental strategies also originate from other sources.

Answers for the meaning of creative writings, particularly metaphors and poems, have been studied and described by Teasdale and Barnard (1993). They state that metaphors and poems are more closely integrated with emotions than is common dialogue. This implicational speech also captures emotional change better than fact-based knowledge alone.

All experiential strategies are useful tools for emotional changes and recovery. Music, both with or without lyrics, is emotionally charged and has the effect of intensifying the patient's or client's contact with the self and the world. People tend to remember things that have an emotional component. Elements of music can evoke sensations and experiences that enhance recovery. Preference of music chosen is influenced by previous experiences the person has had. This can create trust and change the mood (Levitin, 2007).

Mindfulness-based therapeutic methodologies provide potentially useful theoretical and therapeutic windows into a range of affective disorders (Segal, Williams, & Teasdale, 2002). Mindfulness methodology has united Eastern meditative practices and Western epistemologies and practices, according to the aforementioned authors. This provides a potential use for sufferers of brain injury in individual cases needing experiential contact with themselves: awareness of thoughts, feelings, and bodily sensations. Scientific studies on the effects of brain function are beginning to appear, so this could prove to be a useful tool in the future.

Examples of Methods

- Psychoeducation (neurological/psychological);
- Methods of dialogue;
- Creative methods (for experiential schematic and reflection of meaning);
- Narratives (for coping and understanding);
- Poems and music (for coping and emotional experiencing);
- Drawing/painting (for emotional expression);
- Role playing (for social "clumsiness" and interpersonal problems);
- Empty chair (for insight and empathy); and
- Imagery (for feelings of security and relaxation).

All of these methods have been used by neuropsychotherapists in the finish training tradition.

Psychoeducation

In neuropsychological intervention, psychoeducation is necessarily multidisciplinary—drawing from neuroscientific, psychosocial, and psychotherapeutic knowledge. We therapists communicate to our clients something that they most likely never knew about themselves. The author's experiences carry memories of hospital patients saying, "Now I understand. I saw the black spot in my CT-scan the neurologist showed me, and you explained to me the mechanisms of my memory disturbance," and "I don't have to feel guilty. I can also understand my family members now. They did not have this information, and that is why they told me that I don't try enough." Shame and guilt can be diminished by psychoeducation, together with new insights.

By utilizing psychoeducation in combination with motivational process in rehabilitation procedures, the patient's awareness can be increased. This may require time and effort, but it can be a concrete way of working towards awareness through the neuropsychotherapy process. This can also be said of neuropsychological rehabilitation with psychotherapeutic orientation. With psychoeducation, we can show appreciation and professionalism, and we can convey new knowledge to the patient.

Dialogue

Forms of dialogue discussed in this context have been adopted from cognitive therapy. Freeman, Pretzer, Fleming, and Simon (1990) have listed ways of carrying dialogue that can also be useful with neurological and neuropsychiatric patents or clients.

These techniques are overviewed in the following:

1. Understanding the idiosyncratic meaning.

   This is particularly relevant when the therapist finds it difficult to understand and follow the basic meanings in the dialogue. In this way of working, one should be alert to clarify the client's terminology. (Therapist: "I would like to understand this in more detail. Can you rephrase it?")
2. Guided association/guided discovery.

   Through a simple sequence of questions ("Then what? What would that mean?"), the therapist can help the client to explain the significance he or she sees in events.
3. Examining the evidence.

   The effective way to challenge a dysfunctional thinking process is to examine the supporting existence for the ideas. Together with validation, this could be used for sufferers of poor self-awareness.
4. Challenging absolutes.

   Client: "No one will care or understand me."
   Therapist: "No one really? Does it include me, or everyone in your family?"
   Client: "Not everyone; my wife will understand."
   Therapist: "So it is not really no one."
5. Reattribution and turning adversity to advantage.

   Therapist: "Can you see anything good, or positive in this experience?"
   Client: "It is strange, but without this trauma, I would never have found my strength."

This way of conversing may be difficult when a lot of negative events and bad things have happened. However, if the client is blaming himself or others, and feelings of guilt and anger are overwhelming, it is helpful to try to proceed towards change in thinking to find a broader view, and even something positive in "disaster."

Creative Methods

The choice of methods is based on the knowledge of the patient's dysfunctional behaviour, conceptions about self, and interests. Particularly the more creative methods using poetry, music, or art depend mostly on the patient's premorbid talents and interests. They may have been spontaneous ways of coping with ideation of altered self, as in case of Maria below. Systematic art therapy programs, such as the Sarie Mai method, will be described later in this chapter.

Cognitive rehearsal is integrated into the treatment process according to the necessity of treating cognition. It is not within the scope of this chapter to deal with cognitive exercises or treatment programs, but of course it is to be borne in mind that they form part of the procedure (see Chapter 1).

Case Study: Maria

Creativeness in the form of poetic writing can be a helpful coping strategy for experiencing strangeness when compared with peers. The feeling that something is missing in the inner world and self, of not being a whole integrated personality, is well described by Maria.

Maria was 12 years old when she was hit by a motorcycle while crossing the street. No TBI was diagnosed after the incident, nor was Maria examined for TBI at all. The diagnoses came much later. At the acute phase, Maria had fractures in the left leg, which also remained shorter than the right. She experienced amnesia of the accident for at least a few hours, but no loss of consciousness was reported.

Now Maria is a 45-year-old music teacher, who had continued school and higher education at the university with utmost effort, not knowing what was wrong with her till the age of 38, when she finally had the diagnosis: an MRI indicated TBI signal changes in the left frontal area. Maria's poems tell about her emotional experiences towards herself and the world when she was 18 and not knowing that she had a brain contusion. The poems are authentic experiences and were translated into English from Finnish for this book by Maria herself.

To Be an Individual, Is It a Sin?

Maybe I am all the way
a false layout natural whim or space button
misprint or misspoke
whatever
Well, maybe I am not anyway
the sunshine of the family
rose-apple-lingonberryboy
or a girl
I really am not
an individual, individualist
or an cone of a spruce—tree
in the shade of the woods, in the night of the blessed
not knowing what is the name of this day
space is there
but yet it is something
when the little seed of an apple is concerned
a seed who has a home in a red apple
A figure which moves in the night of the poor
means a lot
sometimes too much
but you can't help it
if you have been born with violets in your eyes
well, it is just a moment

A Thought

This morning at home
today at school
tonight at home
without nothing
Tomorrow morning at home
tomorrow day at school
tomorrow night at home
without nothing
And future shows—oh my—so shiny
that one must cover the eyes with a sheet and
be blind

The Sarie Mai Method of Using Art

Creative or expressive methods have been used in psychotherapeutical settings abundantly. However, in neuropsychological treatment procedures, the use has not been as common.

In neuropsychotherapy, there are many kinds of neuropsychological symptoms that can be difficult in the perspective of traditional psychotherapy—problems in verbal expression, memory, executive functions, behavioural problems, difficulties in recognizing feelings—either one's own or others'. In neuropsychological rehabilitation, the neuropsychologist can use many methods to cope with these symptoms. Neuropsychotherapy often continues after the active phase of neuropsychological rehabilitation. Art therapy offers the opportunity to activate the neural integration and ultimately higher cortical functions that come from mentalizing personal idiosyncratic epistemologies (how we know who we are; Hass-Cohen & Carr, 2008). In neuropsychotherapy, there are also many possibilities to use methods from art therapy in dealing with still-existing neuropsychological problems. The production of art works recruits activity from several brain regions and their functions: planning, motor control, hand–eye coordination, memory, long-term memory, concepts, semantic knowledge of the world, emotional circuitry, the hippocampal formation of the parietal lobes, the control of meaning and space, global and detailed perception, disembedding strategies, sustained attention, and other widespread neuronal networks, to name a few (Zaidel, 2005). Brain structures provide alternative paths for accessing and processing visual and motor information and memories, and art therapy is uniquely equipped to take advantage of these alternative paths and activate them through the use of various art media in therapy (Lusebrink, 2004).

An example of an art therapy method that is very suitable to neuropsychotherapy is the Mai Color Glossary, developed in the 1970s by Sarie Mai, a Canadian art therapist and nurse (Mai, 1987). In the Mai Color Glossary (MCG), the patient uses colors and symbols to express feelings and relationships. The MCG was originally developed to provide a comprehensive tool for art therapy assessment that was easily administered, would facilitate therapeutic interventions, and would effectively tap into individual differences and feelings. The aims of the MCG are to assess immediately existing coping skills and the patient's ability to express and verbalize feelings, to assist the patient to communicate these feelings using a nonthreatening technique, and to lay the groundwork for supportive therapeutic relationship. The MCG can be also used as an assessment tool in the first interview and as a therapeutic technique in subsequent sessions. This technique is suitable for children and for adults. It has been used with psychiatric patients, oncology patients, victims of sexual abuse, and also with student supervision (Mai, 1987; Trent, 1992).

The basic premise is that each individual has his or her own color and symbol preferences; during strong emotional experiences, these colors and symbols can change. The therapist must remain with the patient throughout the entire session to provide and promote therapeutic support. Equipment needed are papers sized A4, a pencil and ruler, a color box with eight colors, felt-tip markers (blue, red, yellow, green, black, purple, orange, and brown). The first sheet of paper consists of columns titled at the top of each column as "word," "color," and "symbol," and the remaining space titled as "written response," and horizontal lines with words for the word column one in each line ("happy," "sad," "love," "angry," "fear," "pain," and "separation"); the words may be adapted according to the specific needs of the patient. The patient chooses his or her color for each specific word. Each word will be completed horizontally, (e.g., "happy"—color, symbol, and written response) before proceeding to the next word. At the end of the assessment, the therapist will have a complete color glossary that includes colors, symbols, and a series of incidents that describe each feeling for that moment.

In the second phase, the patient is asked to draw with pencil, on a second piece of paper, a full length picture of him or herself and show where and how in the body, he or she experiences each of the seven stimulus words already used in the glossary; the same color choice is given as before.

In the third task, the patient is given a choice of different art media and asked to create a picture using one of the stimulus words each session; again he or she is asked to put him or herself into each picture.

When this is complete, it is possible to analyze the information given from the colors, symbols, incidents, and placements with different feelings for the patient. The MCG technique provides a framework to stimulate discussion and exploration of a wide variety of feelings and experiences. It can also lead to the discovery of new information. This discussion is done in an unstructured and nondirective manner; the patient frequently expresses other important related experiences at these times, and further feelings that are aroused can be worked through at this time.

There are a couple of neuropsychological case examples with this method using the first task.

The first case is a young girl, J, age 16, who suffered brain damage in a car accident. One family member lost her life in the same accident. J's neuropsychological symptoms were unexpectedly mild, visible in her verbal expression and memory; with emotional expressions, she was quite passive, but understandably grieving. She got intensive neuropsychological rehabilitation and returned to high school after a couple of months, and she was able to continue her studies well. We continued neuropsychological rehabilitation with verbal rehearsals, and she started to speak more about the accident and what had happened to her. She had to work very hard to find words for her thoughts, and so I suggested MCG, which she willingly accepted.

Figure 12.2 shows her colors and symbols.

Figure 12.3 shows her picture of herself.

MCG opened up a new way to talk about different feelings and allowed the process of grieving to begin—grieving both her own injury and the death of her family member in a healthy way at the developmental stage of her personality.

The second case is a male, age 40. He suffered brain damage in a sports accident, was paralyzed, and lost his speech ability at the beginning, but recovered slowly. When we first met for neuropsychological rehabilitation, he was already walking without any equipment, but suffered difficulties in bodily balance; his speech was dysarthric, and he could use only simple words; his behaviour was quite impulsive. In his neuropsychological rehabilitation, there was need for verbal exercises but also need for impulse control exercises, which brought up his present feelings and feelings before the accident, and the need for coping with them. He had always been very keen on different sports, but after his accident, returning to his lifestyle was not easy. He felt quite hopeless at the time of making the MCG (see Figure 12.4). His picture of himself (see Figure 12.5) gave us a start to further process his feelings of loss resulting from the accident.

The third case is a young man who sustained severe brain damage in a motorbike accident when he was 15 years old; he had also many other traumas in his back and legs. He came to neuropsychological rehabilitation to prepare himself for possible professional education

Do your own color glossary assessment using the following seven feeling words-*happy, sad, love, angry, pain* and *separation.*

Word	Color	Symbol	Written Response
Happy	yellow		Well, at least it's good to be, when you are glad. I don't like yellow, but it is somehow a glad color.
Sad	black		I think black is in a way a sad color. You cry when you are sad—maybe I don't need to explain more.
Love	purple		Red is supposed to be the color of love, but I think it is more. The heart is, of course, conventional, although I think, the heart of a human being has not a big part in the love.
Angry	black		When you are angry, everything seems to be quite dark and there may be some flashes of lightning in the sky.
Fear	yellow		The yellow reminds me of a classmate. She frightens me, she is like a psychopath—when you are with fear, you feel yourself small and insignificant.
Pain	red		From the pain I remember the blood. Blood is red and it is bleeding.
Separation	black		Almost everything dealing with separation is dark. You are quite alone then.

Figure 12.2 Self-analysis exercise

many years after the accident. He was very ambivalent to the plans made for him. He wanted very much to cope with his condition, but he was always very tired, felt pain, and couldn't settle to talk or to do anything else.

His MCG is shown in Figure 12.6.

The verbal responses to the colors and symbols he declined to do, because he could not decide what all would belong to that category.

Figure 12.3 Draw a full-length picture of yourself. Show where and how in your body you experienced each of the seven *feeling* words.

Do your own color glossary assessment using the following seven feeling words-*happy, sad, love, angry, pain* and *separation*.

Word	Color	Symbol	Written Response
Happy	yellow		I am satisfied now. A pleasant meeting, something I suggested or something like that.
Sad	brown		My failure. Or the sickness or the death of my nearest.
Love	blue		Life is beautiful, beautiful. Everything is tasting so good and nothing harms you, when you are in love.
Angry	red		To someone, who is doing something wrong on purpose. I try to avoid this feeling.
Fear	brown		Fear, that something bad will happen. The fear of high places.
Pain	black	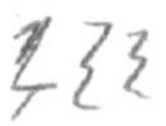	The physical pain, for example the tooth pain, you cannot think of anything else but the pain.
Separation	blue and red		The longing.

Figure 12.4 Self-analysis exercise

By viewing his picture of himself (see Figure 12.7) with the symbols of fear everywhere, we were able to begin speaking about his pain, which was almost unbearable every day and took all his strength away from him, although he did not complain about it aloud.

The fourth case is a nearly 30-year-old woman with brain damage from bicycle accident about five years prior. She had undergone neuropsychological rehabilitation elsewhere in the acute phase and recovered well, but still suffered strong fatigue, which had made it

Figure 12.5 Draw a full-length picture of yourself. Show where and how in your body you experienced each of the seven *feeling* words.

Do your own color glossary assessment using the following seven feeling words-*happy, sad, love, angry, pain* and *separation.*

Word	Color	Symbol	Written Response
Happy	white		
Sad	black		
Love	grey		
Angry	black		
Fear	grey		
Pain	black		
Separation	black		

Figure 12.6 Self-analysis exercise

impossible to do her work in the field of art craft. She was referred to me for advice for to coping with her brain damage. She kept asking if there really was something wrong with her. She looks normal; she acts and speaks normally; she is clever and does well socially when she wants, but she cannot earn money sufficiently—because of this, she is dependent on other people. Her MCG (see Figures 12.8 and

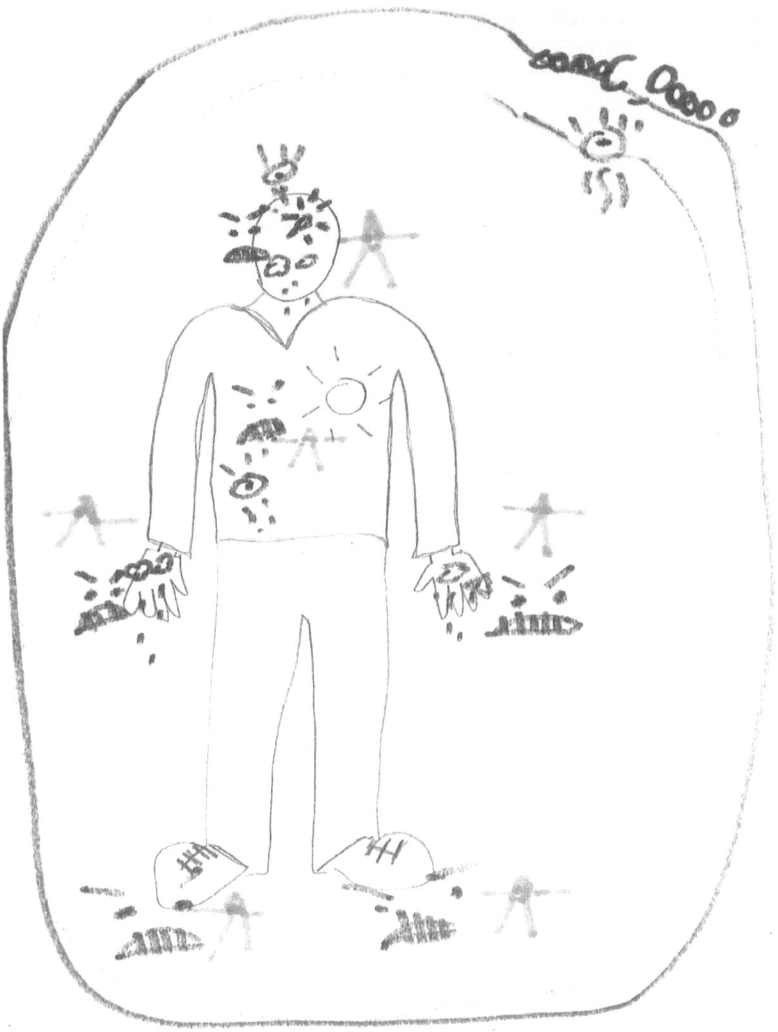

Figure 12.7 Draw a full-length picture of yourself. Show where and how in your body you experienced each of the seven *feeling* words.

12.9) reveals very widely her emotional disappointments due to the accident, and that became the focus in her neuropsychoterapy. She was a talented picture-maker, and she continued to process her emotions with new less-structured pictures.

Do your own color glossary assessment using the following seven feeling words-*happy, sad, love, angry, pain* and *separation.*

Word	Color	Symbol	Written Response
Happy	yellow		Nice people. Money. Good exercise and food.
Sad	grey		Running out of money. Fighting. Giving up.
Love	red		Right human, in a right time.
Angry	brown		Disagreements with people. Bills not paid.
Fear	purple		Power
Pain	red		If you hurt yourself
Separation	red		The solution.

Figure 12.8 Self-analysis exercise

Examples of Neuropsychiatric Syndromes and the Neuropsychotherapeutic Approach

Neuropsychotherapeutic procedures have been used with neuropsychiatric problems as described earlier in this book. The terms ADHD and ADD are differentiated depending on existing hyperactivity or rather mainly attention deficit. Children and adults with ADHD pose a particular challenge, with both neuropsychological deficits

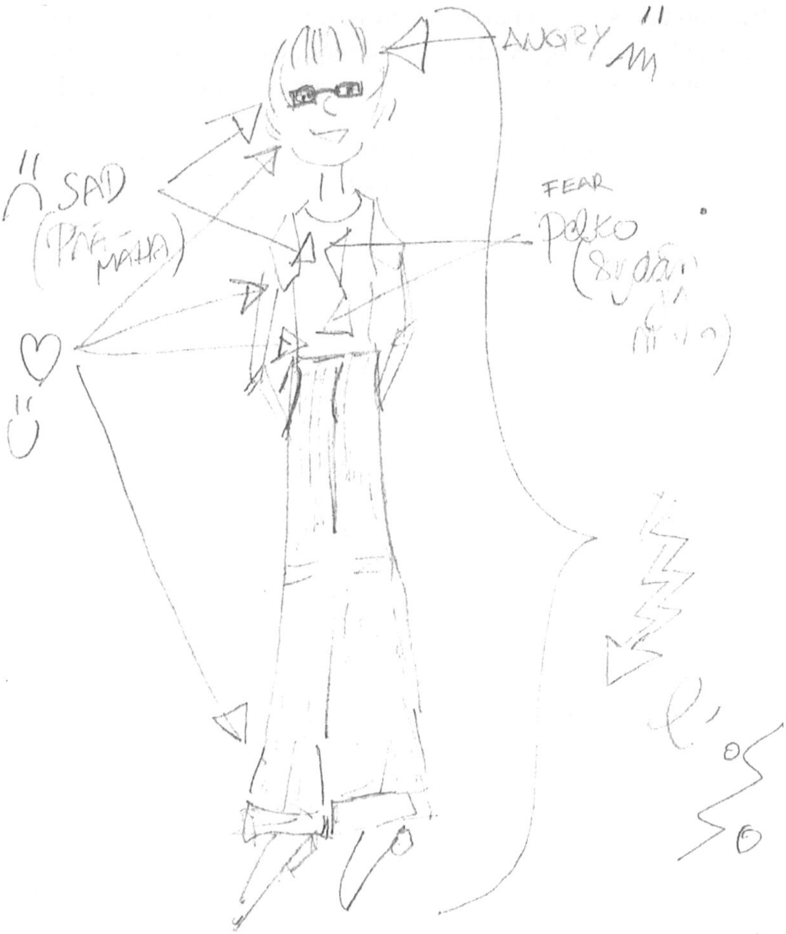

Figure 12.9 Draw a full-length picture of yourself. Show where and how in your body you experienced each of the seven *feeling* words.

and psychiatric syndromes varying from emotional and behavioural problems to specific psychiatric symptoms, such as agoraphobia, or other types of anxiety or depressive disorders. By definition, ADHD is a developmental neurobiological disability characterized by deficits in attention and executive functions and/or hyperactivity and impulsivity.

Adult ADHD typically causes deficits in organizing, prioritizing, and activating oneself to work; focusing, sustaining, and shifting attention to tasks; regulating alertness, sustaining effort and processing speed; managing frustration and modulating emotions; utilizing working memory and accessing recall; and/or monitoring and self-regulating action (Brown, 2005). Some, but not all, adults also have hyperactivity, which may be limited to feelings of restlessness. These deficits generally cause marked impairment in educational, occupational, and social functioning of adults with ADHD.

Amen (2001) has described specific types of the disorder, which affect everyday behaviour. He gives an estimate of the prevalence of ADD as 6% of the population, of which less than 2% receive treatment. Many ADD sufferers are never hyperactive. This group can be easily overlooked because they don't draw attention to themselves.

The approach of Amen is based on SPECT imaging and the clinical correlates of behaviour. Amen classifies six different types of ADD on the basis of his research.

- Type 1: Classic ADD sufferers are inattentive, distractible, disorganized, hyperactive, restless, and impulsive.
- Type 2: Inattentive ADD suffers are inattentive, sluggish, slow moving, have low motivation, and are often described daydreamers or couch potatoes.
- Type 3: Over focused ADD sufferers have trouble shifting attention, frequently get stuck in loops of negative thoughts or behaviours, and exhibit obsessive worrying and inflexible behaviour.
- Type 4: Temporal lobe ADD sufferers are inattentive, irritable, aggressive, have dark thoughts and mood instability, are severely impulsive persons, and experience chronic low-grade depression, including negative thoughts and feeling hopelessness and worthlessness.
- Type 5: Limbic ADD sufferers are inattentive persons, and experience chronic low-grade depression, including negative thoughts and feeling hopelessness and worthlessness.
- Type 6: Ring of fire ADD sufferers are inattentive, extremely distractible, angry, irritable, overly sensitive to the environment, hyperverbal, extremely oppositional, and experience cyclic moodiness.

Amen suggests specifically tailored interventions. However, his general guidelines are as follows: education, emotional and social support, medication, school and work strategies, thinking skills, and coaching and self-regulation experiences (Amen, 2001). Amen also introduces The Amen Clinic ADD Type questionnaire for profiling.

The handicaps of these various ADD/ADHD symptoms are often seen by most of the people in interpersonal contact, whether in private life or at work, but the real sufferer is the person experiencing the problems.

Neuropsychotherapeutic procedures and methods can be, as has been shown, cognitive–behavioral and/or neuropsychological, and knowledge of the therapeutic elements of the interpersonal process as well as proper tools with which to work make intervention most fruitful.

Case Study: Gabriella

Gabriella is an example of a young woman who came to therapy at the age of 26, when her world was falling apart. She had been diagnosed an ADHD sufferer, with a psychiatric diagnosis of agoraphobia, among other things. She had used different ADHD medications, but none had really helped her. Her history revealed teasing already from the age of 4. She had been easily provoked already as a child. All the years of her life had been very difficult, but she had graduated from high school and wanted to make a career after that, with no success thus far. She had unfinished training as a school assistant behind her, and when coming to therapy, she felt inferior in all fields of life. She had a compensatory goal of being a schoolteacher, but that was far beyond the possibilities when therapy began. The main problem was that of how she would get to therapy. Every session was an effort. She was afraid of walking in the street. When she first started to come to therapy, there was an agreement made with her, that she would call if she could not walk a block from her home. At times, she could; at other times, she could not. When she was able to reach the therapy sessions, the sessions were very fruitful. It appeared that she was a very intelligent young woman with a traumatic past. She had several somatic problems—an eating disorder, often upset stomach, and difficulties in getting activated in general for any kind of daily work.

The memories of her school years had made her afraid of schoolmates, whom she did not want to meet in the street. No bus trip was possible, and often she took her dog out during the night, when the streets were empty. Her home was a mess, and her ability to organize it was impaired.

We worked together for a total of approximately eight years, including breaks for a few months.

Over time, improvement and progress was observed. Gabriella gained a more confident attitude toward herself and strengthened her self-esteem. She went back to school to finish her training. She made new friends and an independent home for herself. Eventually, she was able to take her dog to a dog park during the day, and to get to know other dog owners.

Therapeutic Methods

In her therapeutic work, in addition to dialogue, the Albert Ellis ABC-paradigma RET (Ellis & Bernard, 1985) was used for difficult situations and anxiety. With the ABC method the activating event (A) is recorded for cause of distress; immediate thoughts and beliefs; (B) are written down as well as consequences; (C) emotions and behavior. These are further analyzed for less dysfunctional thoughts and emotions. Assertiveness training in real life situations was also encouraged. The therapeutic alliance was strong throughout the many years of therapy. No cognitive exercises were needed, but psychoeducation was an element in the interactive process to build up a realistic image of self for the patient.

Outcome towards the end of the therapeutic procedure showed that Gabriella could live a life with quality: After finishing her training, she obtained a permanent job with her local school district. She could take the bus to work and other places. She had friends and a social life.

The final thing that was problematic was to keep her home tidy. A coach was suggested for that.

In the follow-up, there appeared to be some problems at school because of Gabriella's straightforward communication. She hoped for some help in interacting with others, because she did not want to have ruptures in interactions at work. Her metacognition was very good in understanding how she might provoke misunderstanding with others. In her work with students, she was doing well. She even felt that aspects of the attention disorder were helpful in the classroom.

Asperger Syndrome

Asperger syndrome is usually congenital, and rarely contracted after brain injury in the first few years of life (Gillberg, 2002). The phenomenological manifestations of the syndrome cover a variety of psychological, behavioural, emotional, and cognitive characteristics that have a biological basis. First descriptions of this syndrome date back to the 1920s through 1944. Hans Asperger published his paper on the condition referred to as "autistic psychopathy" (Gillberg, 2002). Diagnostic criteria for the syndrome have been classified by several authors. The official diagnostic criteria are described in *ICD-10* (WHO, 1993)[1]

For the purpose of this book, the authors have chosen to describe the most striking and clinically perplexing traits, as far as therapeutic interaction is concerned, rather than diagnostic criteria that we see often:

- social isolation (no close friends and avoiding others);
- impaired social interaction, clumsy social approach, difficulty in seeing and understanding feelings of others;
- impaired nonverbal communication (limited facial expression resulting in difficulty for peers to read emotions, inability to convey messages with eyes, avoiding looking at others, not using hands to aid adequate expression);
- speech and language peculiarities (overtalkative or noncommunicative, concrete and dichotomous way of understanding and speaking, repetitive patterns of speech, voice deviations);
- preoccupation with unusual and circumscribed interests;
- oversensitivity to sensory stimuli;
- repetitive behaviours resembling OCD problems;
- motor clumsiness; and
- various cognitive profiles, normally executive problems, never at the highest levels of intellectual ability.

The first step in neuropsychotherapy is to find the most adequate way of communication and to understand the basic problems: what causes the most suffering.

Case Study: Peter

Background

Peter, now 47 years of age, had been a good student and popular among his peers at school. He graduated with excellent grades, performed military service, and was accepted to university for engineering studies. At the age of 25, he was in a car accident and suffered several injuries in the neck, lungs, right leg, and knees, as well as left hemisphere frontal contusion. He was neuropsychologically assessed, but no rehabilitation was arranged. A year after the traumatic event, he was depressed, even suicidal. After psychiatric therapy, he received the diagnoses of OCD personality and bipolar mood disorder, for which he was treated for about 10 years. During this time, he was also diagnosed with Asperger syndrome, which complicated further insurance services and funding. Ten years after the psychiatric diagnosis and 13 years after the trauma, Peter was again assessed neuropsychologically. Executive and memory functions were clearly dysfunctional, but he had managed to graduate from the university. When the neuropsychotherapy process began, Peter was working on his doctoral thesis. Before that, he had had a short work history. He was married and had two children, but his attitude towards himself was very insecure, and he needed a lot of support and guidance to be able to work according to his potential capacity.

Neuropsychological rehabilitation with a psychotherapeutic approach finally began 13 years after the accident. Peter completed his doctoral thesis and indicated ability as a scientist and researcher, even though he was unable to get a job anywhere in his industry. In the laboratory where the professor was very understanding and helpful, he was able to work under special mentoring and supervision.

The methods and procedure in Peter's neuropsychotherapeutic intervention were:

- bonding and forming the therapeutic relationship;
- psychoeducation;
- coping strategies for executive problems (calendar recording and instruction notes, feedback and guidance);
- emotional strength and endurance for overworrying, and understanding the metaworry;
- family and network meetings.

Outcome After Neuropsychotherapeutic Collaboration

Peter is working with high-standard scientific projects. He is able to live with the insecurity and fear of discontinuation of work and income. No episodes or relapses of depression have emerged. Peter will have to endure continuous challenges with his behaviour and social interactions, but he has gained many metacognitive skills to help him in everyday life. He has a sense of humour and indicates rewarding empathy towards others. Therapeutic encounters continue regularly, but infrequently. The first three years were the most intensive weekly sessions. The entire intervention period has been nine years, with summer breaks.

Conclusions

We have tried to shed light from theoretical, as well as practical perspectives, on the domains of knowledge and procedures that can be used in varied types of neuropsychotherapeutic interventions for different etiological groups suffering from central nervous system disorders, either acquired or developmental. The experience of the authors has confirmed that our approach has been worthwhile to engage in and develop further. Updating current knowledge with new research data should be a continuous endeavour, as well as further expanding of working possibilities with children and elderly patient groups.

References

Amen, D.G. (2001). *Healing ADD. The Breakthrough Program That Allows You to See and Heal the 6 Types of ADD.* New York: The Berkley Publishing Group.

Brown, T.E. (2005). *Attention deficit disorder. The unfocused mind in children and adults.* New Haven, CT: Yale University Press.

Cornoldi, C. (1998). The impact of metacognitive reflection on cognitive control. In G. Mazzoni and O. Nelson (Eds.), *Metacognition and cognitive neuropsychology. Monitoring and control processes.* London: Lawrence Erlbaum Associates, Publishers.

Ellis, A., & Bernhard, M.E. (1985). What is Rational-Emotive Therapy (RET)? In A. Ellis and M.E. Bernard (Eds.), *Clinical applications of Rational-Emotive Therapy* (pp. 1–30). New York: Plenum Press.

Fleming, J.M., Strong, R., & Ashton, R. (1996). Self-awareness of deficits in adults with traumatic brain injury: How to best measure the brain injury. *Brain Injury 10,* 1, 1–15.

Freeman, A., Pretzer, B., Fleming, K., & Simon, M. (1990). *Clinical applications of cognitive therapy.* New York: Plenum Press.

Gilberg, C. (2002). *A guide to Asperger syndrome.* Cambridge, UK: Cambridge University Press.

Greenberg, L.S., & Paivio, S.C. (1997). *Working with emotions in psychotherapy*. New York: Guilford Press.

Greenberg, L.S., & Safran, J.D. (1987). *Emotion in psychotherapy*. New York: Guilford Press.

Hass-Cohen, N., & Carr, R. (2008). *Art therapy and clinical neuroscience*. London: Jessica Kingsley Publishers.

Hovarth, A.O., & Greenberg, L.S. (1989). Development and validation of the working alliance inventory. *Journal of Counseling Psychology, 36*(2), 223–233.

ICD-10 Classification of Mental and Behavioural Disorders. Diagnostic Criteria for Research. World Health Organization, Geneva: 1993.

Leahy, R.L. (2001). *Overcoming resistance in cognitive therapy*. New York: Guilford Press.

Levitin, D.J. (2007). *This is your brain on music: The science of a human obsession*. New York: Penguin Inc./The Plume Book.

Lusebrink, V.B. (2004). Art therapy and the brain: An attempt to understand the underlying processes of art expression in therapy. *Art Therapy: Journal of the American Art Therapy Association, 21*(3), 125–135.

Mai, S.E. (1987). *The Mai Color Glossary. Instructional manual for an art therapy assessment technique*. London: The University of Western Ontario.

Onsworth, T.L., Turpin, M., Brook, A., & Fleming, J. (2008). Participant perspectives on an individualized self-awareness intervention following stroke: A qualitative case study. *Neuropsychological Rehabilitation, 18*(5/6), 692–712.

Ponsford, J., Sloan, S., & Snow, P. (1999). *Traumatic brain injury. Rehabilitation for everyday adaptive living*. New York: Psychology Press Ltd.

Safran, J. D., & Muran, J.C. (2000). *Negotiating the therapeutic alliance. A relational treatment guide*. New York: Guilford Press.

Segal, Z.V., Williams, J.M.G., & Teasdale, J.D. (2002). *Mindfulness based cognitive therapy for depression. A new approach to preventing relapse*. New York: Guilford Press.

Semrud-Clikeman, M. (2001). *Traumatic brain injury in children and adolescents. Assessment and intervention*. New York: Guilford Press.

Sundeen, S.J., Stuart, G.W., Rankin, E.A.D., & Cohen, S.A. (1998). *Nurse-client interaction. Implementing the nursing process*. St. Louis, MO: Mosby.

Teasdale, J.D., & Barnard, P.J. (1993). *Cognition and change. Essays in cognitive psychology*. Mahwah, NJ: Lawrence Erlbaum Associate Publishers.

Trent, B. (1992). Art therapy can shine a light into the dark history of a child's sexual abuse. *Canadian Medical Association Journal, 146*(8), 1412–1422.

Zaidel, D.W. (2005). *Neuropsychology of art*. East Sussex, UK: Psychology Press.

Epilogue

The authors of this book had their first gathering on January 21, 2005. Most of us already knew each other. The gathering was based on the beginning of a three-year training program for specialized clinical neuropsychologists, who had already completed, or where completing their post-graduate university studies in clinical neuropsychology. All the members of the group were working in rehabilitation services and carried out assessments of neurological, and/or neuropsychiatric patients. The training program was initiated by Ritva Laaksonen, who had the inspiration at a post-congress workshop organized by Barbara Wilson and Robin Tate in Uluru, Australia. There, Tom Teasdale from Denmark had presented Michael Schönberger's study on the significance of therapeutic alliance in a holistic neuropsychological treatment program, originally created in Denmark by Anne-Lise Christensen.

The Finnish training program had a supervision group nominated by the Finnish Neuropsychological Society. It included two colleagues: Mervi Ranta and Helena Jahnukainen. Soon, Mervi Ranta was involved in close collaboration in the creation of the training process. Mervi Ranta's psychotherapist training in addition to training in clinical neuropsychology and vast experience in clinical work made the collaboration a fruitful one.

The program contents covered 30 full days of theory: seminars and tutoring on selected books on psychotherapy and neuropsychology. Supervision of 68 hours and 80 sessions of personal psychotherapy for the participants were also included in the 3-year program. This book reflects on the initial professional skills of the participants as well as the influences of the tailored training program. The ultimate aim is to have the training lead to a subspecialty within neuropsychological rehabilitation. The Finnish Neuropsychotherapy Association was established in 2009 and now, in 2012, the second training program is on the way. So the future seems promising. The first international workshop organized by the new association took place in Coiano, Tuscany in September 2012.

Acknowledgments

In this context, we want to express our gratitude and sincere thanks to Professor Barbara Uzzel for her encouragement in initiating the book and help in contacting the publisher. Professor George Prigatano has been our icon, teacher, model, and support for years. In proceeding with the realization of this book, we want to thank architect Seppo Laaksonen for his support, enthusiastic collaboration and technical as well as practical expertise all along the process.

We also want to give our warmest thanks to our family members for their patience and kindness in everyday life while we were every now and then more absent than present.

We owe the deepest gratitude to our clients in neuropsychological rehabilitation, who have given us the challenge to develop our methods in neuropsychotherapy. We also want to express our special thanks to the clients who have given permission for us to use their personal stories as case examples in this book.

Ritva Laaksonen and Mervi Ranta
Helsinki, October 18, 2012

Index